Praise for *When Should Law Forgive?*

"In a world of noise and confusion, animated by vengeance, Martha Minow is a voice of moral clarity: a lawyer arguing for forgiveness, a scholar arguing for evidence, a person arguing for compassion."

—Jill Lepore, best-selling author of *These Truths*

"No one but Martha Minow could have written this brilliant, and brilliantly readable, meditation on the role of forgiveness in the law and of the law in forgiveness . . . [showing how] to move forward and rebuild while both remembering the past and getting past it."

—Laurence Tribe, author of *To End a Presidency*

"In a book at once compassionate, nuanced, and tough-minded, Martha Minow brings together in an illuminating conjunction a set of issues that at first glance seem to have nothing whatever in common: horrific crimes committed by child soldiers, corporate and student debt, and presidential pardons for unrepentant criminals. All of these, as Minow brilliantly shows, raise the same pressing and contentious question: For what offenses and under what conditions should a just legal system offer forgiveness? This is a legal minefield through which *When Should Law Forgive?* provides an indispensable guide."

—Stephen Greenblatt, Pulitzer Prize winner

"In this time, so shaped by reactionary and 'call-out' cultures that foster harsh, virtue-signaling condemnation of others, this brilliant book carries a profound reminder: for a diverse society to cohere as a humane society, it has to have the capacity—rooted in law—to forgive and reconcile. This book's inspiring discussion of how the law can do this is a beacon to that more humane society."

—Claude Steele, author of *Whistling Vivaldi*

"Martha Minow's work on how societies can recover from large-scale tragedies and human-rights violations has been transformational. . . . Her insights are smart, thoughtful, and rooted in a deep, nuanced understanding of what justice sometimes demands."

—Bryan Stevenson, founder of the Equal Justice Initiative

"Minow's new book thoroughly explores one enduring means of conflict resolution that is far too often overlooked: forgiveness."

—Judge Ketanji Brown Jackson, *Law360*

"Minow's compassionate, knowledgeable, and nuanced examination of the gains that may follow policies that substitute forgiveness for rigid legal remedies is groundbreaking."

—*Publishers Weekly*

WHEN SHOULD LAW FORGIVE?

WHEN SHOULD LAW FORGIVE?

MARTHA MINOW

W. W. NORTON & COMPANY

Independent Publishers Since 1923

For information about permission to reproduce selections from this book, write to
Permissions, W. W. Norton & Company, Inc., 500 Fifth Avenue, New York, NY 10110

For information about special discounts for bulk purchases, please contact W. W. Norton
Special Sales at specialsales@wwnorton.com or 800-233-4830

Manufacturing by LSC Communications, Harrisonburg
Book design by Patrize Sheridan
Production manager: Julia Druskin

Library of Congress Cataloging-in-Publication Data

Names: Minow, Martha, 1954– author.
Title: When should law forgive? / Martha Minow.
Description: New York : W. W. Norton & Company, [2019] |
Includes bibliographical references and index.
Identifiers: LCCN 2019014868 | ISBN 9780393081763 (hardcover)
Subjects: LCSH: Clemency. | Forgiveness. | Pardon.
Classification: LCC K5135 .M56 2019 | DDC 345/.077—dc23
LC record available at https://lccn.loc.gov/2019014868

ISBN 978-0-393-53174-9 pbk.

W. W. Norton & Company, Inc., 500 Fifth Avenue, New York, N.Y. 10110
www.wwnorton.com

W. W. Norton & Company Ltd., 15 Carlisle Street, London W1D 3BS

1 2 3 4 5 6 7 8 9 0

To my students

Contents

WHEN SHOULD LAW FORGIVE?

INTRODUCTION

—

Legal decisions may contribute to rebuilding broken worlds.
—Jill Stauffer[1]

Ours is an unforgiving age, an age of resentment. The supply of forgiveness is deficient. Hateful expression erupts online wherever social media platforms allow the general public to make anonymous comments. Perhaps fueled by economic dislocations and by leaders unscrupulously engaging in blame games, ungenerous public policies and bitter political fights foster suspicion between people of different nationalities, races, and backgrounds. The United States is particularly punitive in defining, prosecuting, and punishing crimes, especially if the accused is a member of a racial minority. As of 2018, the United States is the most incarcerating nation in the history of humanity.

In contrast, the United States has a generally forgiving policy toward debt, especially business debt, with bankruptcy procedures allowing companies a fresh start. This notion of a fresh start is in fact at the core of forgiveness in any setting.[2] But individual Americans in debt face more barriers, and U.S.

bankruptcy law since 1998 expressly excludes student loans, even though the companies issuing those loans and the for-profit schools that fail to deliver meaningful education can obtain bankruptcy relief. Internationally, sovereign debt in European, South American, and African countries generates dramas of stringency, followed by failures to pay and scrambles for practical solutions. Forgiveness—letting go of justified grievances—is a human capacity cultivated across societies and is even built into legal systems.

WHEN DOES AND WHEN SHOULD LAW FORGIVE?

Forgiveness enacted by law alters legal consequences. As a system of rules and institutions that govern human conduct, law expresses grounds and consequences for justified grievances, but it also offers methods to forgive wrongdoing. Expungement of criminal convictions, discharge of debt through bankruptcy proceedings, and executive pardons are examples of forgiveness through law. Law may itself enact forgiveness by forgoing otherwise applicable legal accountability and refraining from blame. Law can be a tool to convert suffering into opportunity.

By *forgiveness*, I mean a conscious, deliberate decision to forgo rightful grounds for grievance against those who have committed a wrong or harm.[3] Forgiveness in this sense is expansive; it includes but is not confined to instances where wrongdoers acknowledge and seek to repair the harms they caused, as well as situations where victims and others consciously decide to set aside otherwise warranted grievances for their own benefit and for the broader good. A man who served in the armed forces may decide to forgive his brother who evaded a draft—who in turn may forgive their arguments about it, allowing both to move on to a better relationship. Forgiveness does not come into play without acknowledgment of wrong; for individuals, it is also not incompatible with expecting legal consequences for those who committed harms. The mother of a murder victim may decide to forgive the perpetrator but still expect criminal prosecution and punishment. Legal rules may penalize those who apologize and, in so doing, make both apology and forgiveness less likely. Legal institutions and public officials refrain from proceeding against or even erasing findings of wrongdoing.[4]

This book asks: When can and should legal officials and institutions promote forgiveness between individuals? When can law itself be forgiving? What can we learn by comparing legal treatments of criminal offenses and debt—two fundamental areas of wrongdoing where forgiveness has been a legal option across civilizations and for centuries? And do comparisons between law in the United States and aspects of international law offer useful insights?

To ask these questions is to invite and test a comparison between legal systems and how people treat one another more informally. We say "Forgive me?" when we arrive late to a date, when we need someone to repeat a phrase we missed, or when we do something much more egregious. Forgiveness, tolerance, mercy, and kindness figure prominently in philosophical and religious traditions, including humanism, Christianity, Judaism, Islam, Buddhism, Baha'i, Hinduism, and Confucianism, and in ancient practices of native peoples in Hawai'i, Canada, New Zealand, Sierra Leone, and elsewhere.[5]

So many traditions have words and rituals that cultivate the human capacity to forgive. Forgiving involves ceasing to let the wrongdoing count in one's feelings toward the wrongdoer, even while maintaining recognition of the wrong.[6] One may forgive a person without forgiving the wrongful act itself. "Forgiveness is the act of admitting we are like other people."[7] In contrast, some urge forgiveness precisely because of limitations in comprehension of others' behavior and motivations.[8] Forgiveness encourages people to take the perspectives of others, to understand the larger pressures and structures affecting others' actions, and to prioritize creating a shared future over holding on to resentments from the past.

The capacity to forgive, in turn, serves as a resource that enables individuals to overcome resentment and conflict. Nelson Mandela, who led the movement against South Africa's apartheid system and then orchestrated the peaceful transition to a democratic government embracing human rights, modeled generosity focused on the future rather than rancor centered on the past. "Resentment is like drinking a poison and hoping it will kill your enemies," he once observed.[9] Requesting forgiveness marks a step toward repentance and redemption in relation to divine authority and in relation to family members, neighbors, co-workers, and even strangers; offers of forgiveness are human efforts to follow divine example.

While some traditions treat forgiveness as a response to apology, repentance, acts of reparation, or acceptance of sanctions, others support forgiveness without any preconditions.[10]

Forgiveness can benefit an offender—relieving a sense of isolation or offering solace and acceptance. "Forgiveness offers something that punishing cannot give: in forgiving, we allow the wrongdoer to make a genuinely fresh start; the slate is wiped clean," explains the philosopher Lucy Allais.[11] A survivor may hope that the act of forgiving a wrongdoer will transform the wrongdoer in a way that impersonal punishment cannot. By reinviting offenders into the moral community of humanity, by demonstrating care and connection, some aspire to change them.[12] When an identifiable victim wants to forgive and seeks an apology, the focus is on the wrongdoer who has changed or has the potential to change.

Some, though, forgive unilaterally, with no expectation of change by the wrongdoer. The act of forgiving can afford the forgiver not only the prospect of psychological release but also a chance for moral betterment.[13] Forgiving, in this view, means breaking the cycle of vengeance and resisting the desire to see the wrongdoer suffer. A spouse may think, "I won't forgive until my spouse apologizes," but she could instead forgive without a prior apology. The forgiver can stretch herself to deal with what she cannot comprehend or control and, in so doing, elevate herself, avoid bitterness, prevent a cycle of revenge, and free herself from the kind of preoccupation with a felt wrong that can distort her own life and sensibilities. Forgiving thus creates the opportunity for moral self-improvement.

Research on human health, depression, and family counseling suggests that forgiving others, after being hurt by their actions or words, can enhance physical, emotional, and spiritual well-being.[14] Letting go of a grievance may offer more to the one who forgives than to the one who receives forgiveness.[15] By forgiving the wrongdoer, the victim of a crime or broken promise can let go of resentment, regain a connection, or feel empowered simply by making the choice to forgive. Someone who worked for Coretta Scott King, the widow of Dr. Martin Luther King, Jr., explained that "after her husband's death, I felt that some people tried to take advantage of her generosity and tried to use her for their political agenda. I was amazed at her poise in handling those situations. She told me that if you don't forgive people, it will kill you."[16] Rabbi Harold Kushner argues that victims should forgive not because the other deserves it but because the victim does not want to turn into a bitter, resentful person.[17] Author Jodi Picoult puts the point vividly: "Forgiving isn't something you do for someone else. It's something you do for yourself. It's saying, 'You're not important enough to have a stranglehold on me.' It's saying, 'You don't get to trap me in the past. I am worthy of a future.'"[18]

The choice not to forgive can also be empowering. Scholars of medicine and psychology increasingly value forgiveness, as do scholars of political science, conflict resolution, and philosophy.[19] The affected individual can be encouraged but not forced to forgive. An adult who suffered abuse as a child at the hands of a parent has rightful grounds for grievance and by declining to forgive may experience authority and self-worth—even maturity in overcoming a taught tendency to try to please. Forgiveness is and must remain the exclusive prerogative of the individual; forcing or even pressuring a victim to forgive causes them to experience a new harm, loss of autonomy, and subordination arising from the prior harm. Privately or publicly pressuring a victim to forgive can be a new victimization, denying the victim her own choice.[20] It may painfully cancel the victim's own decision to forgive—or not to forgive. Indeed, pressure to forgive may itself cause psychological distress.[21]

Forgiveness is pivotal in many literary works. In Tolstoy's 1887 novella *The Kreutzer Sonata,* the main character is acquitted for murdering his adulterous wife, then begs his fellow train passengers to forgive him. In Khaled Hossein's 2003 novel *The Kite Runner,* the main character tries to forgive himself for not helping a friend who was assaulted. In George Eliot's *Middlemarch* (1871–72), Dorothea struggles to resist forgiving too readily even as her capacity for sympathy is rendered sympathetically. Toni Morrison's 1987 novel *Beloved* asks whether a mother's deliberate killing of her child can be forgiven, given the context of their capture after escaping from slavery.[22] Requests for forgiveness also fill the lyrics of much pop music, detailing mistakes and apologies between lovers, parents and children, individuals and their gods, and citizens and governments.[23]

Forgiveness can happen on a collective scale. Strangers as well as people who know one another can and do grant forgiveness, such as when a group of mothers of gun-violence victims and mothers of shooters—strangers to one another—came together in Washington, D.C., in 2008 for reconciliation and comfort in a "Forgiving Mother's Tea."[24]

Forgiveness need not bar prosecution or other legal consequences for the wrongdoer. When the one wronged lets go of resentment and a claim for punishment, this does not compel others to do so; nor does this act of private forgiveness divest the public of responsibility and power to enforce social norms through customs and rules. Indeed, one who forgives can also advocate punishment for the wrongdoer as a public act, upholding public norms. This demonstrates the potentially different domains of law and forgiveness. Forgiveness operates in the interpersonal realm; the legal system depends upon impersonal processes. Through forgiveness, I may forgo my anger and hatred toward someone who has harmed me, but I do not and cannot alter the requirements of just deserts or the policy seeking to deter similar wrongdoers in the future.[25]

A private act of forgiveness thus could be consistent with public criminal prosecution, or it could lead the forgiver to request to forgo prosecution or refrain from participating in it. Forgiveness and legal punishment both partake in the view that offenders should be treated as full members of a community that demands responsibility by all members for their actions.[26] A robust view of forgiveness, though, may call for changes in the legal process and legal rules themselves.

RESTORATIVE JUSTICE

Following a civil war or mass violence, a nation seeking to address crimes against humanity or the crime of aggression may pursue alternatives to trials. In 1995, inspired in part by Argentina's 1983 National Commission on the Disappearance of Persons, South Africa launched its Truth and Reconciliation Commission (TRC), a prime example of a "transitional justice" mechanism.[27] Over the three years of its operation, the TRC invited victims to tell their stories. It also invited perpetrators to apply for amnesty, conditioned on their showing that their actions had been limited to a political rather than a personal goal, and that the means they used were proportional to that political goal.[28] And the TRC held hearings on potential reparations, although little came from that part of the process.

Archbishop Desmond Tutu, reflecting on his work as chairman of the TRC, observed, "Forgiveness means abandoning your right to pay back that perpetrator in his own coin, but it is a loss that liberates the victim."[29] During the hearings, he hoped that victims would forgive. Some criticized him for expecting forgiveness from victims, but he acknowledged that their forgiveness should not be taken for granted and indeed reflected magnanimity.[30] Alex Boraine, a minister who had argued for the TRC's formation, served as its vice-chair and later also described the general lack of vengeance expressed by people testifying at the hearings.[31] He imagined reconciliation as nonviolent coexistence, while Tutu conceived a more robust process in which perpetrators made public confessions and repented, then victims forgave.[32] Although the TRC did not require survivors to confront those responsible for torturing or injuring them, in some instances testifying before the commission could be painful. Experts at South Africa's Trauma Centre for Victims of Violence and Torture estimated that half or more of the hundreds of people it served had experienced serious psychological problems after testifying or reported regret at having done so.[33]

The TRC drew criticism from opposing sides. Challenged in court by the African National Congress (ANC) and by the family of Steven Biko,[34] the commission's proceedings and report also drew fire from former government officials, police, and political leaders.[35] One study indicates that of 429 participants in the TRC process, only 72 discussed forgiveness, only 10 percent were willing to forgive wrongdoers who took responsibility for their deeds, and only seven reported willingness to forgive without conditions.[36] One study found that 30 percent of participants reported feeling pressure to forgive.[37] Little has come of the TRC's consideration of reparations, and the ongoing violence and distrust in South Africa will affect ultimate assessments of the TRC. The political cartoonist Zapiro vividly captured problems in a drawing showing Archbishop Tutu standing on ground labeled "Truth" on one side of a chasm, and the ground on the other side labeled "Reconciliation."[38]

Even with its flaws, the TRC offered a forum for discovering and revealing past wrongdoing both by the government and

TRC Cliff © 1997 Zapiro. Originally published in *Sowetan*. Republished with permission—For more Zapiro cartoons visit www.zapiro.com.

by its opponents. It coincided with a peaceful political transition despite fears of mass violence. It inspired similar efforts in Rwanda, Sierra Leone, Cambodia, Liberia, and nearly forty more countries.[39] One commission in Northern Ireland placed priority on recovering the truth about violence during the Troubles for the sake of accountability and moving forward.[40] It identified five possible methods: drawing a line under the past; internal investigations by organizations that participated in the conflict; community-based projects; a commission for truth recovery; and a commission for historical clarification.[41]

Analyses of what did and did not work with the TRC are moving beyond the anecdotal to more rigorous research. Public perceptions across different groups largely credit the TRC with bringing out the truth.[42] Its process did coincide with the relatively peaceful political transition to democracy and with high levels of reported willingness to engage with politics and to respect the legal system.[43] A United Nations initiative has articulated principles for reparations that in turn have informed work by the International Criminal Court and the International Convention for the Protection of All Persons from Enforced Disappearances, adopted by the UN General Assembly in December 2006.[44]

Truth commissions and reparations are restorative justice initiatives that involve victims, offenders, and other community members in alternative, forward-looking discussions and actions. Restorative justice aspires to integrate forgiveness within the judicial process, rather than simply correct its excesses, and it seeks to engage victims, offenders, and community members in efforts to make matters right in the present and in the future. Building upon traditions among Native Americans and First Nations in North America, Maori in New Zealand, and other cultures, restorative justice processes tend to focus on the future more than the past and on the community as well as on the immediate victim and offender.[45]

Archbishop Tutu advanced the idea of restorative justice in his speeches and writings about the TRC. His 2000 book *No Future Without Forgiveness* inspired retired Chicago judge Sheila Murphy to create restorative justice circles deployed in schools to involve victims, offenders, and others in discussions of incidents that otherwise would trigger disciplinary proceedings.[46] In the circles, students, teachers, administrators, and other affected parties discuss what happened, who is affected and how, what responsibilities each person has, and what steps should be taken to repair the harm.[47] Some schools use the circles proactively to prevent bullying and conflicts by building community awareness and trust.[48]

Similar practices underway in local communities both respond to conflict and try to prevent it. Working through mediation, community-based conferences, neighborhood reparative boards, or peacemaking circles, restorative justice programs ask victims to let go of their justifiable grievances at least enough to engage with the offenders to help them rejoin the community.[49] That is a lot to ask of people who have been victimized, even when the identities of the victims and the relevant community are clearly defined.[50] In empirical studies in Great Britain, victims expressed more satisfaction with restorative than adversarial processes and expressed eagerness to help offenders turn their lives around, but they seldom used the word or concept of forgiveness.[51] Perhaps for this reason, restorative justice has been used largely for minor crimes such as vandalism,[52] though some also urge restorative justice efforts to deal with hate crimes and other serious offenses.[53]

Based on this premise, many juvenile courts in the United States use restorative justice initiatives. After a finding of guilt or a guilty plea, they may involve the offender, the victims, and other community members in a sentencing agreement that reflects the offender's understanding of how the victims have been hurt, the victims' understandings of the offender's circumstances and needs, and the community members' willingness to help.[54] Such restorative efforts often broaden awareness of social and cultural factors influencing individuals' wrongdoing. Restorative justice efforts, in Archbishop Tutu's words, try "to understand the perpetrators and so have empathy, to try to stand in their shoes and appreciate the sort of pressures and influences that might have conditioned them."[55]

In restorative justice initiatives for juveniles, one common element is restitution: the wrongdoer provides services or works to repair the damage he or she has caused. Repainting houses, landscaping properties, and washing cars and dogs are examples of restitution in sentences given by juvenile justice courts.[56] Restorative efforts in juvenile justice try to make youthful offenders' accountability to the victim primary while also developing their competencies.[57] One city in Great Britain offers restorative justice meetings in a supervised, controlled, and safe environment where the victims can tell the offender about the effects of the crime and suggest possible ways of repairing the harm.[58] The participants nominate local community projects that involve young people in charitable or mul-tiagency efforts and pursue work that is of personal interest or practical benefit to the victim.

The language and examples of leadership offered by Nel-son Mandela and Archbishop Tutu offer inspiring narratives and images to communities thirsty for hope. Between 2014 and 2016, Colombia negotiated a peace agreement with the FARC, a revolutionary armed forces group. The agreement provided a process for granting amnesty for political crimes both to former FARC members and to members of state troops. Here, as with individual instances of forgiveness, a focus on the past shifted to focus on the future without eras-ing the past. Liliany Obando, a human rights activist charged by the Colombian government with "rebellion," received amnesty, permitting her both freedom and an opportunity to apply for employment. Colombia's effort, like South Africa's TRC, reflects hope that a forward-looking and forgiving pro-cess will prevent cycles of revenge by publicly acknowledging past wrongs and by investigating violations of human dignity on the part of the prior government and by those who fought against it. Legal rules and procedures can encourage or at least not punish expressions of apology or forgiveness, and they can support specific victims and societies in general to adopt more forgiving attitudes.

Forgiveness by law, though, raises further questions: How can law forgive? How does forgiveness by law differ from for-giveness by individuals? What are the arguments for and against forgiveness through law? What are and what should be the lim-its of forgiveness within law?

How Can Law Forgive?

Jumping from discussion of personal to political forgiveness is problematic. How can public officials such as police, judges, and presidents speak for individual victims of severe crimes and violations of human rights? Groups, jurisdictions, and nations operate very differently from individuals. One woman whose husband had been imprisoned and tortured under apartheid testified to South Africa's TRC, "A commission or a government cannot forgive. Perhaps only I could do it. But I am not ready to forgive."[59] Yet if forgiveness is about letting go of particular attitudes and emotions, such as anger, perhaps only individuals, not legal institutions, can forgive.[60] Individuals often feel resentment and desire vengeance; legal systems do not have feelings, and people who hold official positions in the law are supposed to cabin their feelings when they administer the law.

If forgiveness means letting go of justified resentment, then law and legal institutions involve forgiveness by letting go of justified grievances. Legal officials may exercise lawful discretion and decline to pursue legal consequences of wrongdoing, or they may use their lawful powers, such as commutations or pardons, to relieve consequences. Debt forgiveness—excusing wrongful nonpayment of loans—is another common practice, one that can be achieved through a creditor's private action or through legal procedures for bankruptcy or amnesty.

When a government takes steps in the direction of forgiveness, it is not working to reconcile the individuals directly involved in the wrong. Rather, it exercises its authority over the legal consequences of obligations and wrongdoing.[61] Individuals' letting go of their justified feelings of grievance is another matter, and so is the use of law to nudge or press individuals to forgive.

Accordingly, government officials cannot behave like victims who know in their hearts whether they want to forgive. Legal institutions face choices about whether to proceed with imposing consequences for wrongdoing. In some circumstances, governments may be the only entities with standing to forgo pursuit of accountability for crimes against humanity, precisely because such crimes transcend any individual, and government officials in that sense represent the dignity of every individual in the world, but they cannot take over the prerogatives of survivor victims when it comes to matters of individual forgiveness.

Mindful that individual victims must retain their prerogative over their own decision about whether to forgive, consider these examples of roles that law has played in enacting or promoting forgiveness:

- Hammurabi's Code (Mesopotamia, approximately 1745 BCE) freed farmers in debt from the obligation to pay creditors when their crops failed or were destroyed. It also limited the period of forced labor for debtors who sold themselves or their family members into servitude to pay off debts.[62]
- Starting in eleventh-century England, petitions to the king allowed people to seek relief from the ordinary common law process. By the fourteenth century, greater use of the king's "equity" powers emerged in response to growing rigidities in the common law practices.[63]

- In the United States and in modern international settings, law is deployed to express grievances through criminal law and through civil actions. Legal institutions can determine when to forgo imposing legal consequences for particular acts; they can lift burdens from obligations and permit pardons and other methods to lighten criminal punishments. Bankruptcy proceedings allow people drowning in debt to coordinate responses to creditors and to have a fresh start. When a community or society decides to direct issues of criminal or financial wrongdoing to a process that promotes restitution and restoration of relationships, it embraces an approach that is more forgiving than retribution.

- When police, prosecutors, judges, presidents, and governors forgo otherwise authorized legal action for a crime in order to encourage interpersonal forgiveness, legal forgiveness is at work. Judicial discretion could also be used for alternative sentences for individuals prosecuted after acting in self-defense against an abuser or for taking part in a crime under the pressure of their abusers.[64]

- Executive power to pardon individuals charged with or convicted of a crime, judicial processes to seal or expunge a criminal record, and amnesties created by statute or treaty can avoid or reduce the negative effects of criminal charges or convictions.[65] Governments can also restrict consideration of conviction in conjunction with employment or licensing, and they can ban inquiry into prior critical records during the process of hiring.[66]

- Legislatures can enact amnesty laws to eliminate any record of crimes by barring prosecutions or civil suits, although sometimes they do so conditioned on testimony, surrendering arms, providing reparations, or showing remorse.[67] Some amnesties involve hearings that give victims a chance to ask questions and "heal their memories."[68]

- Amnesties may be enacted in ordinary times. In the United States, President Ronald Reagan signed a 1986 immigration law, dubbed the "Reagan Amnesty," that permitted about three million people who were in the country unlawfully to gain legal status.[69]

Illustrated by these examples, forgiveness within law takes three distinct routes. First, judges and legislatures can enact categorical treatments of wrongdoing that alter or otherwise reduce consequences. They may offer amnesties to groups. They may undertake debt forgiveness initiatives, like the U.S. Internal Revenue Service's "offer in compromise," which allows individuals who are close to insolvency to reduce taxes they owe, upon demonstrating, through full disclosure of their resources, their inability to pay.[70] They may let go of otherwise applicable legal sanctions because of the wrongdoer's identity (for example, age or mental capacity) or the time period of the events. Some may see categorical defenses, excuses, and justifications as kinds of legal forgiveness.

Second, legal systems can enable and support the exercise of discretion by legal officials toward leniency rather than punitiveness. Some written and unwritten norms work in the other direction, such as compelling parking meter officers to issue quotas of parking tickets, or promoting prosecutors who achieve a quota of convictions for serious offenses.[71] Instead, discretionary authority is granted to police, prosecutors, and judges, presidents and governors, and other officials within legal systems, who can use it to forgive legal consequences of wrongdoing.[72] Yet in the United States, contemporary criminal justice practices suppress the merciful options once afforded by official discretion.[73] Absent guidelines or training, exercises of discretion can fail to garner public support or respect.[74]

Third, law—formal rules, legal institutions, and the people who implement them—influences whether individuals are likely to express forgiveness. Courts and other legal institutions can make room for voluntary expressions of apology and forgiveness, shielding those who make such interpersonal expressions from legal liability or even rewarding them. Such opportunities can be at the margins of the formal legal system, taking place in corridors or meetings before or after the law does its work. Or the legal system can itself facilitate mediation sessions where individuals can express regrets or apologies and those dealing with injuries can voice their feelings, including decisions to forgive. Such efforts carry the risk that state-backed pressure could make such expressions insincere and feigned; this danger is explored further below. Legal mechanisms may embrace even more fully the goals of reconciliation and forgiveness, the route taken by restorative justice initiatives in the criminal law setting.

Law Can Affect Forgiveness by Individuals

Simply providing space away from the courtroom for disputing parties to meet—and setting rules that exclude their conversations from the trial process—might occasion expressions of apology and forgiveness that the physical and emotional separations created through legal process would otherwise impede. Forgiveness between people often requires that they at least have sufficient proximity to encounter each other; spending time to consider the possibility of forgiveness and seeing the other person in reality rather than in memory or imagination may make forgiveness more conceivable.[75] I asked the commissioners of South Africa's TRC whether they made amnesty conditional on apologies. They told me they decided not to do so, because then no offer of apology could be viewed as genuine. One TRC staff member, however, brought together mothers of the young men known as the Gugulethu Seven, who were killed by the apartheid-era South African Police, with the government informant, another black South African, who had tipped off the police. The informant was applying for amnesty; the mothers were separately involved in giving testimony to the victims committee. Pumla Gobodo-Madikizela, a psychologist working with the TRC, brought them together for an informal meeting, captured in the 2000 film *Long Night's Journey into Day*. Most of the mothers initially said they could not forgive the informant and chastised him. He hung his head and apologized. Then, one by one, each of the mothers said she forgave him. These acts of forgiveness took place in an informal setting and were not compelled by or even formally organized by law. Rather, they were prompted by the existence and proximity of the TRC.

Like religious and psychological resources, legal institutions have the potential power to affect individuals who hold legitimate resentments. They inevitably influence human relationships. They lack the primary relationship of victims to perpetrators, but they can influence whether forgiveness between people is more or less likely. Courts are meant to hear and resolve disputes. Law can give people chances to meet together in spaces where they may apologize and forgive. It may require spouses on the brink of divorce to try to mediate their disagreements. A good mediator will call upon each spouse to express the other's grievances and desires. They might even find common ground in resenting the mandatory mediation exercise. Legal rules and procedures can create incentives for apologies, enable amnesties and pardons, and create opportunities for reconciliation in such diverse contexts as divorce, criminal law, and intergroup violence. These forms of forgiveness emphasize forward thinking and invite people to draw upon or develop personal ties and social norms. Thirty-six U.S. states have "apology laws" prohibiting admissibility at trial of certain expressions related to sympathy or apology.[76] The law can exclude apologies from consideration in any proceeding. It may also force statements of apology and forgiveness, though it cannot compel the feelings they are meant to express. That encourages apology and may prompt forgiveness.

Legal officials often have discretion in enforcement, even when there are actual grounds for concluding that someone violated a law or an enforceable promise. When officials enforce the law rigidly, they deny the flexibility they often have. Victor Hugo's classic 1862 novel *Les Misérables*, and its 1980 musical adaptation, illuminate the human costs that an unforgiving law imposes not only on the criminal defendant but also on the law enforcer. In the story's climax, the escaped convict Jean Valjean mercifully spares the life of Javert, the police inspector who has spent years pursuing him, shocking the man of the law with the power of forgiveness. So removed is Javert—the "consummate legalist"—from the human rituals of forgiveness that he drowns himself, unable to reconcile human generosity with the label of criminal in the one he chased for so long.[77]

Police officers, prosecutors, and judges have duties to enforce the law. Consider this story: A minister in a large city was short of time and couldn't find an available parking space, so he parked in a no-parking zone. He put a note under his car's windshield wiper that read, "I have circled the block ten times. If I don't park here, I'll miss my appointment. *Forgive us our trespasses.*" When he returned, he found a citation from a police officer, along with this note: "I've circled this block for ten years. If I don't give you a ticket, I'll lose my job. *Lead us not into temptation.*" The humor works, if it does, because the Christian Lord's Prayer includes both an admonition to forgive and a caution against temptation.[78]

I came to the subject of forgiveness due to the intensely serious issues of law's limits in the face of mass murders, rapes, abduction of children, and genocide. Such acts defy conception, let alone the generosity of spirit involved in forgiveness. In these circumstances, private or public pressure on a victim to forgive looks like a new victimization, denying the victim her own choice.[79] Pressure to forgive may reflect racial and gender hierarchies, as powerful political and social traditions may suppress or discipline the anger of people of color and women.

Yet it is hard not to be in awe of the extraordinary and memorable public demonstration of forgiveness made by some family members of the nine people killed during a 2015 prayer session at the Mother Emanuel AME Church in Charleston, South Carolina: they offered their forgiveness to shooter Dylann Roof. Others expressed condemnation, one saying she hoped he would go to hell.[80] As Roof remained unrepentant about both firing seventy-seven shots and his stated intention to start a race war, some family members of the victims said they were still working on forgiving him; others said their forgiveness did not mean he should avoid punishment.[81] The daughter of murdered Ethel Lance said, "I will never talk to her ever again. I will never hold her ever again. You hurt me. You hurt a lot of people. But God forgives you. I forgive you."[82] Reflecting disciplined religious practice, another surviving relative explained, "We have no room for hating, so we have to forgive."[83]

Some concerned observers have argued that this story shows how white people set the terms for acceptable grieving by blacks, deflecting justified anger and treating systemic violations as occasional.[84] The philosopher Myisha Cherry specifically criticizes public calls by journalists for blacks victimized by white or state violence to forgive, because the requests disrespect the victims, normalize oppression, and underscore racialized roles. White victims are not publicly asked to forgive in the same way.[85] The journalism professor Stacey Patton observes, "Black families are expected to grieve as a public spectacle, to offer comfort, redemption, and a pathway to a new day," in a way that no one expects of others.[86]

Others warn that gendered dimensions of forgiveness raise cautions about using law to encourage or induce it. From studies suggesting that women are better at forgiving than men, to historical and literary analyses of supplication and apology, Western culture often connects women and forgiveness.[87] Expectations that women will perform emotional labor, assertions of innate biological differences between men and women, and societal grants of authority to men all contribute to pressure women both to forgive and to ask for forgiveness.[88] In this light, any increased use of law to promote forgiveness risks reinforcing gendered expectations or placing unfair pressure on people's emotions.

On the other hand, some individuals, due to their religious tradition or personal beliefs, find forgiveness to be a worthy aspiration. By forgiving, individuals may express their faith and reclaim their dignity and power over the burdens of grief and victimhood. Public pressure to forgive may strip the process of these possibilities, but legal institutions may create space for wronged individuals to consider whether and when to forgive.

What Are the Arguments in Favor of and Against Forgiveness Through Law?

Law may not always be capable of facilitating forgiveness, and, in some circumstances, seeking to do so could seem insulting or offensive. Yet a call for forgiveness can be a way to tame otherwise vengeful sentiments. Arguments for lessening legal sanctions have ancient roots. The famous retributive punishment notion of matching the loss of an eye by taking the eye of the offender was in fact an effort to confine punishment that otherwise could escalate into a blood feud.[89] Punishment can never make a victim whole, so the desire for ever more punishment can spiral without limit. Hence the notion of proportionality captured in "an eye for an eye" has a forgiving theme against the alternative of escalating responses. In some legal systems, proportionality considerations can be sufficient to guard against extreme punishments, but in the United States, they have failed to restrain excessive responses to crimes, at least in the eyes of some observers.[90]

Law itself can be more or less forgiving, and when it is unforgiving, it can clash with the views of the victims it is meant to protect. Family members of murder victims have organized in the United States against the death penalty.[91] Advocates for battered women have argued for recognition of the reasons why a victim of domestic violence may kill her abuser even when she is not immediately at risk of a physical assault. Such arguments may assist in persuading a judge or a jury that the battered individual's response was reasonable, or that she subjectively believed she was in imminent danger—aspects of a defense against the charge of intentional homicide.[92] Legal systems devise defenses and excuses to reflect ideas about when an otherwise blameworthy act should trigger less than the prescribed consequences. A more general argument presses for forgiveness rather than blame to guide criminal justice in liberal societies.[93]

Impulses toward forgiveness are strengthened by frustration with laws that seem unfairly punitive. Stringent legalism in the hands of individuals enforcing the law is compounded by the dynamics of politics and economics that shape legal rules and sanctions. In the United States, prosecutors seeking election victories have incentives to call for the expansion of criminal laws and escalating punishments, which in turn give prosecutors greater leverage in bargaining for guilty pleas.[94] When law is administered in ways that seem unfair or needlessly cruel, it can give rise to new resentments. Many individuals and families affected by mass incarceration carry grievances about the legal system, its biases, and its effects. Police officers, judges, and juries can exercise their discretion toward leniency, but they may do so in ways that seem or actually are inequitable, discriminating, intentionally or unintentionally, on the basis of race, class, familiarity, or other factors that should not matter before the law. The problem is that discretion can lead to unfairness, treating similar violations differently, but rules applied without individualized treatment can also produce overly harsh responses.[95]

Official acts of forgiveness, such as pardons or grants of amnesties, can produce practical and symbolic good. For instance, debt forgiveness alters otherwise oppressive relationships and reduces devastating or even impossible burdens. In disputes between neighbors—over a property line, foliage trimming, or the brightness of outdoor lights—mediation can help the parties become more forgiving and more cooperative, giving them the chance to see the issue from the other's perspective and to remember that on other occasions they will need to get along.

Steered by the high moral ambitions of reconciliation, compassion, and peace, the law may fall short of these tall goals. When a government takes steps in the direction of forgiveness, it is not working on reconciling the actual individuals directly involved in a wrong. When an official offers a pardon, the act itself does not repair the relationship between victims and wrongdoers. Strict law enforcement versus merciful relief: the contrast is not simply one of sentiment or case-by-case judgment. In South Africa, some have wondered if efforts at forgiveness simply covered up wounds the TRC was intended to heal.[96]

Legal forgiveness may stoke resentment in victims. Legal institutions that forgo imposing prescribed legal consequences in particular instances may prompt new resentments for their perceived unfairness. Perceptions of unequal treatment, even those that are not founded in facts, particularly stoke resentment.[97] Restorative justice asks much of victims who may understandably see working with offenders and the community as a new burden they did not seek. Studies of the TRC report ambivalence and disappointment, with negative and mixed views about its work.[98] The liberalization of bankruptcy laws can engender a sense of unfairness, especially if the benefits seem to favor those who are well off more than others, or if resulting increases in risk-taking cause new societal dangers.[99] Individuals may develop new resentments of the legal system, but resentment of an unforgiving legal system—and doubts about its legitimacy—poses risks just as severe.[100]

PARTICULAR RISKS IF LAW PROMOTES INTERPERSONAL FORGIVENESS

If courts direct people to consider forgiveness or pressure them to do so, the result may well reduce compliance with rights and duties. There is no guarantee that those who respond to legal incentives to forgive in fact become more compassionate or forgiving. Victims who seem to forgive may actually be reflecting fear or a lack of self-esteem. A victim of domestic violence may decline to prosecute not out of forgiveness but out of fear of reprisal. This may be especially the case for victims of spousal and elder abuse. Legal actors should treat an assault as a violation of public norms, not of the victim's desires.

Some may object that legal institutions should not create openings for interpersonal forgiveness, because law should avoid influencing people's emotions. Caution should be taken to ensure that victims are not pushed to forgive. Forcing someone to forgive can be counterproductive as well as wrong. A victim's choice not to forgive can be empowering, expressing a fair expectation of accountability and responsibility. Resentments arising from someone's wrongdoing are crucial wellsprings for a sense of justice.[101] A wrong should be made right; an intentional harm should be met with a consequence.[102] This idea is central to law: pursuing rights and correcting wrongs are law's heartland.

A precondition of forgiveness is taking the perspective of another, but it should not involve abandoning one's own perspective and experience.[103] Similarly, care should be taken that legal actors do not coerce offenders to give apologies or make restitution, and that offenders' own past victimization does not recede from view with the focus on victims' needs.[104] Because law has powers to incarcerate, fine, and stigmatize, even conversations by legal officials carry significant influence on the emotions of affected individuals, and that power can be abused.

At the same time, there is no neutral position for the law when it comes to people's emotions. Legal frameworks inevitably affect emotions; pushing toward forgiveness is not worse than pushing toward revenge, adversariness, or bitterness. Individuals may feel pressured to relinquish their own justified resentments. Law does affect its participants and their feelings and relationships.

Law may construct adversarial processes that render forgiveness less likely. Participating in a lawsuit affects everyone involved. It can be emotionally draining; it can push the parties even farther apart; it can magnify negative emotions that exist because of the underlying conflict. In divorce and child custody matters, the adversarial process often increases bitterness and blame, as each side tries to win the all-or-nothing contest.[105] Someone asked to forgive a former spouse may be offended. Similarly, criminal justice systems that deploy victim impact statements also direct and amplify emotions, pressuring judges and juries to impose more severe punishment, especially when the victim has high social standing or the survivors are educated and eloquent.[106] The victim impact statement process may cause victims to dwell in and amplify their negative feelings.[107] Litigation can enlarge the distance and tension between disputing parties. For this very reason, commercial actors in long-term relationships of mutual benefit often agree to forgo litigation and even formal legalities.[108]

Adversarial litigation emphasizes opposing arguments and sharpens conflict. The support for forgiveness by people backed by religions, cultures, and varied experts can collide with legal procedures. In the absence of laws shielding apologies from use as evidence, an adversary may use the very offer of an apology from the other side as evidence to support his or her claims of having been wronged. The specter of litigation chills expressions of regret. Lawyers, like doctors, suffer psychologically from legal constraints limiting their ability to apologize and seek forgiveness.[109] A victim's offer of forgiveness can undermine, in fact or in appearance, the process of seeking legal consequences through a criminal or civil trial. It is wise to be cautious and humble about using law to shape—or manipulate—the feelings of individuals. But it is no less important to acknowledge that legal institutions one way or another affect people's emotions.

Enabling individuals to forgive does not require them to forgo legal action. Forgiveness actually requires *not* halting blame, because only where there is blame is there something to forgive.[110] The decision to prosecute for a crime remains with the government, not with the victim. Legal officials may ask a victim of a physical assault whether to prosecute, but crime harms the whole community, not the immediate victim alone.[111] After a conviction, the court can turn to the victims of the crime and introduce the possibility of their forgiving the offender to reduce the punishment. At the same time, courts can offer victims the chance to speak, confront those charged with abusing or terrifying them, and perhaps let go of their burdens. In the sentencing phase of the trial of Dr. Larry Nasser, who was found guilty of raping and abusing young gymnasts in his care, Judge Rosemarie Aquilina permitted victims to speak, telling them directly: "Leave your pain here. . . . Go out and do your magnificent things."[112] Rachael Denhollander, a survivor of Dr. Nasser's abuse, drew on her own religious background in concluding, "Forgiveness is giving up personal bitterness and personal desire to retaliate, but the standard of rightness does not go away if I release my resentment." In her reflections, she suggested, "Forgiveness is my personal, internal response to my abuser," but "Justice is not in opposition to forgiveness. Rather, justice is the foundation for forgiveness."[113]

WHAT ARE THE LIMITS OF FORGIVENESS WITHIN LAW?

Some wrongs seem unforgivable. Some find it impossible to forgive if the wrongdoer has not apologized and made amends. And crucially, some acts—mass murders, abduction of children, genocide—seem unforgivable if forgiveness implies halting legal consequences that otherwise would apply. In 1943 Simon Wiesenthal, while a slave laborer in a German concentration camp, was summoned to the hospital room of a dying young German soldier, who asked him as a Jew for forgiveness. Wiesenthal's later reflections and invitation to others to comment provide a rich and complex discussion of forgiveness and underscore the question: Who is in a position to forgive?[114] Amnesty is not available for those who allegedly committed crimes against humanity, war crimes, sexual abuse, or recruitment of minors.[115] A survivor of spousal abuse should not forgive the abuser unless the survivor now has genuine assurances of safety, which requires robust treatment and sometimes even separation from the abuser.[116]

Even in the less fraught area of debt, some wrongdoings seem outside the bounds of remission. Permanent grievance seems warranted against someone who obtains loans with no intention of repaying them and against a leader who gets loans to line his own pockets rather than to assist his community. But should unpaid student loans fall into the unforgivable category?[117] Exploring the topic of legal forgiveness is not saying it is always or even often warranted, but it should expose for debate when and how public authority should be used to support forgiveness between individuals and greater leniency in society.

In practice, legal actors and institutions withhold otherwise justified punishment for many reasons, including corrupt or discriminatory ones. Leniency may be racially biased, disrespectful of potential victims of misconduct, or otherwise inconsistent and unfair. These are dangers in the use of discretion by legal officials.

If courts or prosecutors forgo warranted legal consequences in favor of individualized forgiveness by legal actors, and if they use law to support or urge individual forgiveness, they could well risk undermining or jeopardizing the law's predictability, adherence to rules, deterrence, fairness, and objectivity. The rule of law aspires to equal treatment, restraint on government power, commitment to treat like cases alike, and the rational application of consequences. Some believe that using law to prompt forgiveness extinguishes the very trait that makes forgiveness distinctive: its exceptional, unconditional quality, far from the routine or mechanism of point-counterpoint exchange of legal arguments.[118] Then what happens to accountability? What happens to truth? Being particular rather than general can advance the goal of treating like cases alike.[119] Taking measures to guard against such risks must be part of determining whether any legal policies enacting forgiveness are warranted, worthwhile, or counterproductive.

As architects and tailors know, some materials (like wood and cotton) are more "forgiving" than others (like glass and silk charmeuse), which do not recover well from injuries.[120] Sometimes unforgiving materials better serve the craftsperson's purposes. Chapters 1, 2, and 3 explore similar issues for the materials of law. The selected topics are areas where some legal systems have taken steps that are called forgiving or could be seen as forgiving, letting go of justified grievances and sanctions.

The first considers forgiveness for a class of people who may attract more generosity of spirit than do others: minors. Chapter 1 looks, however, at minors who commit criminal offenses, sometimes serious ones. With a focus on child soldiers in international conflicts and juvenile offenders in the United States, the exploration in both instances examines when legal systems adopt restorative and other alternatives attentive to context and forces beyond the control of individuals and, in so doing, look to the future.

The second topic is a class of wrongdoing that throughout history has often given rise to informal and governmental forgiveness. Debt, and debt forgiveness, may seem quite different from criminal wrongdoing, and yet debt jubilees, along with amnesty for criminals, appear in the records of ancient Babylon and ancient Athens. Contemporary debates over debt forgiveness center on the debt of sovereigns, whether nations or cities, and the debt of American consumers, dealing with student loans and medical debt.

And the third topic is a method of legal forgiveness, amnesty, including executive pardons, with examples from around the world. This method, included within many legal systems, allows for a formal exemption from legal consequences for individuals or entire groups after wrongdoing ranging from criminal law to tax evasion, from immigration violations to bank misconduct.

Comparing and contrasting the possibilities of legal forgiveness for minors who commit crimes, and for people, entities, and groups with unpaid debts and other wrongful acts, this book asks why a fresh start is permitted in some cases but not others, and when and how forgiveness can be compatible with law's demands of predictability and equal treatment. The book closes with reflections, extensions to other fields of law, and further thoughts about seeking and confining forgiveness within law. Religious leaders, psychologists, friends, and family members acknowledge how forgiveness is a force for good, but it is complicated to make it part of formal legal practices. How can we do it right?

CHAPTER 1

FORGIVING YOUTH

—

Humanitarian workers too commonly assume that the remedy needed by children entangled in soldiering is an assurance of blamelessness. . . . Neglecting the likelihood that demobilized children may feel themselves very much at fault for their actions, regardless of their freedom from legal responsibility, is the rule rather than the exception. . . . In such situations, gaining access to legitimized systems of truth-telling and reparative justice can be a crucial source of relief and consolation.

—DAVID ALAN HARRIS[1]

MEMBERS OF THE REVOLUTIONARY UNITED FRONT (RUF), the rebel group leading a failed eleven-year insurgency in Sierra Leone, abducted a boy whom we'll call Emmanuel when he was seven years old.[2] He spent four years doing chores and then engaging in spying, fighting, and killing. When the war ended, he spent two years with a foster mother and then was reunited with his mother, grandmother, and uncle. Although his mother and grandmother forgave him, his uncle did not, and other community members would come and beat him. He once pulled a knife to defend himself against hostile community members. He dropped out of school, became involved in theft, and fell into a cycle of social rejection.

Another child taken by the RUF is a girl whom we'll call Tenneh, abducted when she was ten; she was abused, though not sexually assaulted, and she witnessed much violence, served as a human shield, and wounded or killed two people during her time with the rebels. Reunited with her mother, she had sleepless nights but focused on schoolwork. She told researcher Theresa Betancourt that "she has been able to forgive, but that the people who committed so much violence should be punished further and that their wrongs have not been put right."[3] A victim, she also aided those committing violence.

Armed conflicts often involve children in the work of war, as combatants, helpers, and sex slaves. The term *child soldier* refers to individuals drawn into roles supporting rebels or other violent groups who are still children when social and legal questions arise, who were children when they engaged in criminal acts but stopped before becoming adults, or who were children but became adults while continuously participating as combatants or supporters for combatants.[4] Under pressure or orders, they may have killed their parents, raped another child, or pressed other children into the same life of violence.

This chapter explores when and how child soldiers in armed conflicts should be forgiven. The larger political violence is not of their making, and for this very reason, local and global sympathy can often be marshaled to forgo punishment or accountability for them. Those who recruited or coerced them should be viewed as responsible, but the political and legal force and economic resources needed to do so are most often in short supply. Legal, cultural, and moral treatments of children have long struggled with the lack of a sharp line between childhood and adulthood, and the cases of child soldiers expose how crude are the tools and concepts at hand. Contrary to current international law and practice, someone should always be considered responsible for the conduct of child soldiers, be they the adult abductors or the young people themselves. At the same time, the malleability of youth, the larger forces bringing the youth to their actions during conflict, and their potential for change in the future warrant alternatives to retrospective, adversarial justice, alternatives that would assist their own growth and reintegration into their societies.

The coercion, pressure, and poor options experienced by minors caught up in armed conflicts are remarkably similar to those of American youth involved in gangs, drug trafficking, and other criminal activity. While child soldiers usually evade responsibility, American juveniles currently face punitive treatment. For both child soldiers and juveniles caught in crime, forgiveness requires acknowledging wrongdoing—and the societal response should include the creation of opportunities for constructive and meaningful lives and for restoring social relationships. Should the youth be forgiven for their conduct? How about the adults who drew them into it? In light of the systemic forces at work, legal forgiveness should be less concerned with particular victims than with remaking the rules and institutions that constrain the choices and opportunities for young people who enter the world.

DEBATES OVER THE LEGAL STATUS OF CHILD SOLDIERS

The project of international criminal justice can be traced to the 1970s, to post–World War II responses to genocide, to the rise of democratic revolutions in the eighteenth century, to the Enlightenment's philosophy of universal humanism,[5] to a 1474 atrocity trial conducted by the Holy Roman Empire, or to an even earlier treason trial addressing armed violence.[6] Substantial international rejection of the conscription and use of children as soldiers is new in the twenty-first century. But the potential liability for international crimes committed in armed conflict by individuals under the age of eighteen is less clear.[7] The legal and moral conceptions of condemnable conduct during war are shifting, as is the definition of *child*, which increasingly includes adolescents.[8]

Children continue to be abducted from the heart of their communities, then to be systematically manipulated, coerced, and socialized—sometimes under the influence of drugs—to become child soldiers. The emergence of lightweight, easily operated weapons facilitates children's transformation into ruthless killers.[9] Children are attractive to armed groups, extremist organizations, and governments because they are more easily conditioned into fearless killing and unthinking obedience.[10] Rebels, especially in long-lasting conflicts, may simply run out of sufficient numbers of adults, and hence turn to children.[11] In addition, children are recruited because they can be, and because the conditions of armed conflict increasingly permit them to play critical roles.[12]

International law and human rights enforcement have now

achieved the goal of punishing adults who involve children in armed conflict. The Rome Statute, the treaty embraced by 123 nations[13] that established the first permanent International Criminal Court (ICC), prohibits the conscription or enlistment of children under the age of fifteen into national armed forces or active hostilities.[14] In its first case, the ICC made history in the first prosecution and conviction for such crimes when it secured a fourteen-year prison sentence for Thomas Lubanga, a warlord in the Congo, for enlisting, recruiting, and using children as soldiers.[15]

The term *child soldiers* commonly includes both girls and boys; experts estimate that in some countries, up to 40 percent of children in armed groups are girls.[16] Girls "are targeted in armed conflict because of their vulnerability and their gender. They have been subjected to rape, mutilation, forced prostitution, forced pregnancy, forced combat, and death."[17] In the Central African Republic, the Lord's Resistance Army rewards commanders with girls to serve as domestic workers and sexual objects. The girls themselves increase their status and improve their treatment if they become mothers and "wives."[18] Child soldiers serve as fighters, porters, cooks, messengers, spies, medics, and sex slaves for both rebel and governmental groups.[19]

The treatment of child soldiers engaged in armed conflict raises new and perplexing issues of justice, morality, and international and domestic norms.[20] Under international law, a person eighteen or older is responsible for recruiting and overseeing child soldiers under fifteen;[21] no one is responsible for drawing young people who are fifteen, sixteen, and seventeen into a conflict.[22] The ICC has no power to prosecute

anyone under eighteen,[23] even though individuals under eighteen remain active participants in about three-quarters of all
the ongoing conflicts in the world.[24]

In 2012 the NGO Human Rights Watch identified fourteen countries that currently use child soldiers, either in their
own government's militaries or in armed groups,[25] including
Sierra Leone, Colombia, Angola, Chad, Côte d'Ivoire, the
Democratic Republic of Congo, Liberia, Sudan, Uganda, and
Nepal.[26] The Lord's Resistance Army of Uganda, South Sudan,
the Central African Republic, and the Democratic Republic
of Congo abducted and coerced young people to serve as soldiers.[27] Children are not a minor presence in many armed conflicts. In Liberia after 2002, half the soldiers fighting were or
had started as children.[28] Child conscription by rebel groups is
common in Burma, Nepal, and Sri Lanka.[29] The abduction of
children in some conflicts is itself a method of terror and punishment[30] or is rooted in the belief that children have special
protective powers.[31] Recruitment of younger children (twelve
to fourteen) pays off more than does recruitment of older children, who are more likely to desert and are less easily indoctri-
nated.[32] Living in captivity with constant threats to their lives
and safety produces obedience among most youth.[33]

Determining the legal responsibility of those who were
recruited as children to become soldiers is a challenge. Not only
is it hard to set the age or other trigger for criminal responsibility, but laws usually do not have a category for individuals who
are victims but come to engage in crimes and abuses of others.
When adults abduct, coerce, or entice children into assuming
the role of soldier—or sex slave—they victimize them, take

away their childhoods, and make them instruments of violence and lawlessness.[34] The Khmer Rouge in Cambodia forced children to kill members of their own families and coerced others into fighting and working for the regime.[35] The Lord's Resistance Army in Central Africa forcibly recruited masses of children, knowing they could control them more effectively than they could control adults who had grown tired of war.[36]

Should individual youths be forgiven because others are also to blame? Should they be forgiven because of their youth and vulnerabilities? Should those labeled as child soldiers be viewed solely as victims? What about those who joined rebel groups without being abducted or coerced, drawn by the ideology, or by chances for action and responsibility, or even by the thrill of the violence or being part of a political effort that could offer better opportunities?[37] Perhaps a new concept could be devised to acknowledge the complexity of individuals who have been both victims and perpetrators, who were abducted as children and then abducted other children.[38] Because no such conception currently exists, we should not be surprised to find ambiguity and controversy in international law.[39] How should any society view a returning soldier "who was made to give up childhood to become a combatant and whose resourcefulness (and luck perhaps) allowed him or her to survive, but whose resilient qualities are now ignored—or even rejected—by the community"?[40]

International law generally leaves such questions to individual nations,[41] but every nation except the United States has ratified the Rome Statute or the UN Convention on the Rights of the Child, which directs that state parties "shall take all feasible measures to ensure that persons below the age of 15 do not take part in hostilities."[42] In the United States, now the only nation that has not ratified the Convention on the Rights of the Child,[43] individual states set most rules governing minors, and many individual states also pursue the hard line on prosecution and punishment for minors who commit the most serious crimes.[44]

The hard line is illuminated in responses to terrorism. The U.S. Guantanamo military commission charged Omar Khadr with fighting for the Taliban against U.S. forces in Afghanistan when he was fifteen. Born in Canada to a fundamentalist Muslim family and raised to think of martyrdom as the highest aspiration, Omar spent much of his early teen years in an Al Qaeda compound, lived with Osama bin Laden for a time, and fought alongside his father against American and Northern Alliance forces in Afghanistan.[45] After Omar threw a grenade that killed an American Special Forces officer, he pleaded guilty to murder and attempted murder in violation of the laws of war, conspiracy, two counts of providing material support for terrorism, and spying. Khadr, at sixteen, was the youngest person incarcerated as a terrorist in the detention camp at Guantanamo Bay. Wounded and given medical treatment, he faced intensive interrogation. Many criticized the United States for its treatment of him. Radhika Coomaraswamy, the UN secretary-general's special representative for children and armed conflict, repeatedly requested rehabilitation services for him.[46] One commentator argued that Khadr should not be held responsible for being shaped by his terrorist parents and for being a young person without a fully developed brain, while others argued that being a child is not an absolute bar to prosecution, and Canada itself could have prosecuted him.[47] Although the U.S. government used Guantanamo to avoid application of the U.S. Constitution to the detainees held there, the Supreme Court ruled that at least some provisions of the Constitution did govern.[48]

As part of a plea bargain,[49] Khadr remained at Guantanamo for another year, then was transferred to his native Canada to serve the rest of his sentence there.[50] Canada has not only signed the Convention on the Rights of the Child but also particularly invests national identity in its endorsement of and advocacy for human rights. One commentator noted that Khadr's presence in Canada would test the nation's human rights commitments.[51] Khadr remained in prison in Canada until 2015, when the Canadian courts released him on bail, over the objection of the Canadian government, pending an appeal of the U.S. conviction.[52] Khadr apologized to the family members of his victim; after the Canadian Supreme Court ruled that his rights to "life, liberty and security of the person" under Canadian law had been violated, he received a settlement from the Canadian government, which acknowledged it had used information obtained from Khadr under "oppressive circumstances."[53] A survey of Canadians indicated disagreement with the settlement but also strong views that Khadr was treated unfairly.[54] In the United States, Khadr's case echoed how American states impose adult sanctions on juveniles.[55]

Putting to one side whether information used against him was obtained unfairly, perhaps societies across the world, in responding to someone like Khadr, should permit the use of defenses such as duress or arguments for leniency at sentencing.[56]

Such defenses operate as excuses or bases for reduced social condemnation and in a sense express forgiveness—letting go of justifiable grievances not by victims but by the legal system itself.[57] Letting go of criminal prosecution need not mean forgoing accountability; other methods of accountability can be devised that focus on changing behavior rather than assigning blame.[58]

Similarly, rather than blame child soldiers who are girls, drawn or forced into a conflict to become sexual slaves or "wives" for combatants, legal forgiveness or exemption from charges could be the norm. Yet these individuals commonly face special risks of rejection and stigma by their home communities in light of their assistance to the rebels and/or their sexual conduct, regardless of whether it was willing or coerced.[59] Studies suggest that female former child soldiers initially have more severe problems than do males, although over time, the boys may have increasing vulnerability to negative circumstances.[60] How should communities treat girls and young women returning from time as soldiers, servants, and "wives" of members of rebel forces? Should their involvement be forgiven because they have suffered? Is suffering by all child soldiers grounds for forgiving what they have done?

In the treatment of girls and indeed all child soldiers, domestic laws and social customs vary. The gap between international and domestic practices reflects ongoing disagreement over who is a child and when criminal responsibility attaches.[61] Excluding individuals under eighteen from prosecution for war crimes could lead to even more extensive abductions and recruitment by adults seeking to avoid prosecution themselves.[62] There are also practical problems for reintegration efforts for returnees who are not held accountable because they risk stigma and rejection.[63] Emerging international legal norms leave those under eighteen without culpability. The expense and challenges of criminal trials make it sensible to give priority to those most responsible for human rights violations rather than to minors swept up in hostilities. But forgoing any accountability may disserve former child soldiers as well as their home communities. Nonprosecution does not amount to forgiveness, and forgiveness by definition first needs acknowledgment of wrongdoing. Whether child soldiers have the degree of psychological and moral responsibility to be treated as wrongdoers—and whether ultimately they can be forgiven—remains the unsettled question.

Assessing Agency and Responsibility

Law alone cannot determine whether young people who participate in armed conflict are either entirely victims or entirely self-determining agents, for questions of psychological development and cultural practices matter. Psychological and public health field studies offer insights into post-traumatic stress syndrome, reintegration efforts, and adolescent moral development particularly relevant to child soldiers.[64] Differing cultural views about blameworthiness, selfhood, and choice also matter. Nonetheless, evidence from conflict settings and other contexts indicates that growth toward adult maturity takes time; that adolescents under the best of circumstances can both think like adults and be gripped by impulses and fears; and that even very young people can exercise intentional choices indicating their knowledge of right and wrong, self-interest, and the interests of others. There are problems with viewing former child soldiers or child sexual slaves as either perfectly autonomous actors or as actors without independent will and responsibility.[65]

Consider the story of Valentino Achak Deng, one of the "Lost Boys" of Sudan who fled their villages in the mid-1980s, pursued by militias, government soldiers, wild animals, and diseases. The author Dave Eggers channeled Achak's voice into the 2006 novel *What Is the What*, styling it as an autobiography of this boy refugee of the Sudanese civil war.[66] Although the perspective of the child soldier is obviously altered through the telling by a novelist, the book nonetheless offers details and insights.[67] Especially memorable are Achak's reflections on the pervasiveness of people being "used" in the world created by armed conflict:

> Of those boys with whom I walked, about half became soldiers eventually. And were they willing? Only a few. They were twelve, thirteen years old, little more, when they were conscripted. We were all used, in different ways. We were used for war, we were used to garner food and the sympathy of the humanitarian-aid organizations. Even when we were going to school, we were being used. It has happened before and has happened in Uganda, in Sierra Leone. Rebels use refugees to attract aid, to create the appearance that what is happening is as simple as twenty thousand lost souls seeking food and shelter while a war plays out at home.

Sympathy for children caught in wartime becomes another basis for exploitation: "*Aid bait*, we were sometimes called. Twenty thousand unaccompanied boys in the middle of the desert: it is not difficult to see the appeal to the UN, to Save the Children and the Lutheran World Federation."[68]

Aid workers could unwittingly ready children to enter armed militia:

> But while the humanitarian world fed us, the Sudan People's Liberation Army, the rebels who fought for the Dinka, were tracking each of us, waiting until we were ripe. They would take those who were old enough, those who were strong and fit and angry enough. These boys would trek over the hill to Bonga, the training camp, and that was the last we would see of them.[69]

When children are abducted, coerced, or enticed into serving illicit militias, they are victims, yet describing all minors involved in such militias as innocent obscures the complex and at times strategic decision-making by the children and youths. Some young people may go to militias due to a lack of good options; hunger or other kinds of deprivations may draw others.[70] Some search for social advancement and opportunity, like girl soldiers in Guatemala who found a chance to operate outside traditional gender roles.[71] Some exercise choice, if only briefly or occasionally, and show a capacity for rational decision-making that does not match the notion that children lack that capacity and so are not to be held responsible. A young person may act for self-preservation or self-advancement—to avoid punishment or gain rewards— without understanding the impact of those actions on others or on themselves. And some encounter and fall prey to power dynamics in refugee camps and with aid workers, revealing limited degrees of freedom even when they are released from armed combat.[72]

Although deserting a militia force is risky, some child soldiers find sufficient freedom and opportunity to do so.[73] One individual told a researcher that he planned to return to Liberia so he could claim the benefits available to demobilized child soldiers, but if he could not obtain sufficient support, he would return to fighting.[74] Many child soldiers in Côte d'Ivoire explained that they voluntarily left the militias because they believed that staying presented too great a risk of dying.[75] Others avoided killing by deliberately aiming incorrectly or otherwise permitting potential victims to elude harm.[76] How does the fact that some find it possible to do so affect our judgments about the culpability of others who do not?

Ironically, viewing child soldiers as innocent victims puts forgiving them beyond reach, because forgiveness is only for those who have committed a wrong. Forgiveness is not the right response to individuals who are inappropriately blamed because they lack capacities that would qualify them to be treated as free and responsible agents. Perhaps child soldiers could assert diminished capacity or developing capacity— short of full responsibility—and then obtain the legal benefit of an excuse or exemption from prosecution. But incapacity or diminished capacity seems inadequate to capture the experiences and capabilities of youth who are allowed to marry or who view themselves as capable of choice.

Precisely because they join the hostilities before adulthood, child soldiers operate within a social organization of domination and reciprocity; commanders offer young soldiers status and protection while ensuring their dependency.[77] Of course, adults, too, operate within complex and hierarchical organizations, but we tend to assume that they are less vulnerable than minors to developing psychological dependency on their commanders. For minors, psychological attachment to an armed unit replaces intimate ties ruptured by war.[78] Indeed, a young soldier's attachment to one or more adults substitutes for the bond with a parent. Socialized into the values and priorities of the armed group, some child soldiers experience friendship, mentoring, or even love for older soldiers as they develop loyalties and commitments threaded with both choice and constraint.[79] After surviving a terrible beating, an abductee of the Lord's Resistance Army found "moments of humanity and friendship" with the older man who treated his wounds and assumed a father-figure role.[80] Initiation rites and bonding through military training similarly offer child soldiers a sense of belonging and identity.[81]

How should one assess an individual's responsibility for actions chosen in these situations? In Colombia, the vast majority of child soldiers under study explained that they "volunteered," yet they also said they joined due to economic or social pressures.[82] Adults as well as minors experience coercion and desperation, conditions that may offer reasons to reduce punishment or even excuse liability for engaging in criminal activity. Indeed, some degree of leniency or even forgiveness may be warranted for anyone caught in a complex organization engendering psychological dependency.[83] Child soldiers can adopt different identities in different contexts, showing creativity in their self-protection and challenging the notion that they are helpless because of their age, the abuse they face, or the trauma they experience. Thus young persons may present themselves as tough combatants while they are with friends and former soldiers, then as traumatized innocents while they are with nongovernmental organization workers.[84] More than one young woman has navigated a war zone by swapping sex for safety in oppressive circumstances, demonstrating some degree of agency.[85]

Child soldiers should be seen as individuals struggling for meaning and needing to maintain or create a sense of their own moral agency, including recognition of past wrongdoing.[86] Many child soldiers may have a strong sense of self, linked to their survival and resilience.[87] Others may grapple with ambivalence and shame.[88] If social responsibility follows from individual choices, how should society treat child soldiers who navigate their challenging circumstances for personal advantage? Failure to hold accountable individuals who show at least some agency may be the practice of international criminal law, as prosecutors take limited resources to pursue those most responsible, but such prosecutorial decisions reflect financial constraints more than a careful assessment of former child soldiers' capacity to exercise choice or be held responsible.[89] Hence it is incorrect and unwise to assume that child soldiers have none of the capacities that warrant legal responsibility.

Doing so may even hamper rehabilitation efforts, for ignoring the choices that individuals make, and imposing no consequences for the harms committed by former child soldiers, may impair development over time of their own identities as moral agents.[90] Different views about all these matters arise within nations and between neighboring nations.[91]

A more profound issue around which cultures differ is whether an individual's moral responsibility is central or if the needs and interests of the community take precedence. The clash between the international human rights narrative of innocent child soldiers and some local communities' attitudes reflect in part local views of the centrality of community.[92] Reintegration programs pursued by international nongovernmental organizations may neglect specific cultural and national contexts.[93] Some former child soldiers are recruited again to join violent groups due to inadequate reintegration services and to ongoing poverty and community dislocation.[94] Returning from war as mothers of children, some former girl soldiers return to live with their former captors due to the social exclusion and stigma they experience at home.[95] One former girl soldier told international workers, "If we could go to school, the community would be nicer to us, we would get some consideration that would help a lot."[96] Anticipating ostracism, many such girls prefer to move to new environments rather than try to make the return to their home communities work.[97]

Members of some communities resent an international focus on rehabilitating child soldiers, because the operating view of children's rights challenges the status of children in that society.[98] Ironically, the Western conception of the primacy of the individual may neglect the needs and capacities of particular individuals involved. Western ideas of the individual support a focus on post-traumatic stress disorder and treatment, but a former child soldier's actual stress may result not from past trauma but from current living circumstances, fears of community retaliation, difficulties in family and community relationships, or worries about the future.[99] A particular risk is engendering resentment toward former child soldiers if special services and supports seem to privilege them compared with others or reward them for participating in violent activities.[100] At the same time, former child soldiers need help—therapy, cleansing rituals, opportunities to tell their stories—to deal with their own denial, anger, or blame toward others.[101]

Returning child soldiers who have not been held accountable may be viewed as dangerous "internal strangers."[102] Local attitudes about forgiveness, spiritual cleansing, and the importance of reconciliation can assist the reintegration of returning child soldiers, but this reintegration may seem to require treating the returnees as wrongdoers rather than as innocent victims.[103] Fifteen years after former child soldiers in Mozambique returned home, most of them—even without psychological treatment— were married, owned their own homes, and had had little difficulty gaining acceptance by their families and communities.[104] The researchers conducting this study concluded that psychiatric care interventions for returning child soldiers might do more harm than good by clashing with local cultural ideas about making peace with the spirits of the dead.[105]

Another scholar argues that recognizing child soldiers' criminal culpability is important for building peace and reconciliation after conflict, even if immunity for child soldiers makes sense on other grounds.[106] Yet in Uganda, international demands for prosecution of adults who had joined conflicts as minors seem at odds with traditional cultural practices favoring reconciliation and spiritual appeasement.[107] Elders reporting on cultural traditions may, however, be out of touch with the needs of youth and women.[108] Whether families and schools welcome former child soldiers back affects their adjustment and future prospects, but that willingness itself is complicated by cultural traditions about justice and blameworthiness.[109] It remains relevant to the interests of former child soldiers to discern whether holding them responsible for their actions advances peace and reconciliation. Perhaps there is a useful difference between being willing to accept more responsibility and being subject to judgments of legal responsibility.[110]

WAYS FORWARD: ACCOUNTABILITY AND ACKNOWLEDGMENT OF CIRCUMSTANCES

Turning a child into a soldier, a sex slave, or an aid to adults engaged in armed conflict is a crime, and serious efforts to disarm, demobilize, and reintegrate child soldiers are now part of peace accords, with the guidance of the Paris Principles developed by UNICEF.[111] Returning home either as adults or as minors, former child soldiers may connect with their families or communities or be rejected by them and be directed to camps or other communities. Quite apart from legal procedures, reintegration programs for former child soldiers can be effective especially if former child soldiers lead them.[112] And due to therapeutic supports, skills training, and the resilience of youth, many former child soldiers go on to productive and satisfying lives.[113]

But how should law respond? Should there be legal accountability, legal forbearance, or some other response? International criminal law and domestic criminal practices are often at odds over the age when individuals should be held responsible. Seeking accountability for the conduct of child soldiers while providing no collective response, internationally or collectively, creates its own problems. In northern Uganda, communities broadly accepted amnesties for combatants regardless of age and acknowledged that child soldiers were forced to kill, yet some community members remain upset and still think the returning soldiers should apologize.[114] When the High Court of Uganda tried eighteen-year-old Thomas Kwoyelo on fifty-six counts of war crimes and crimes against humanity, it elicited a wide range of responses from members of his community; some forgave him because he had been abducted and made to be a soldier at fifteen; others urged that he receive amnesty because punishment would not make him change; and still others urged that he be punished because he was a commander and should have known that murder was wrong.[115] The circumstances of different countries, different exposures to violence, and different experiences contribute to different pathways through adulthood.[116] Whether they are viewed as victims, perpetrators, or both, children who engaged in vicious killings, who aided others in armed conflict, and who were victimized by physical and psychological abuse, sexual assault, and circumstances are tools of violence organized by adults.

For many former child soldiers, the issue of forgiveness centers on whether they can forgive themselves for what they did and endured.[117] Emmanuel Jal, a former child soldier who became a musician/rapper, expresses his struggle for healing in these lyrics: "I'm in another war? This time / It's my soul that I'm fighting for."[118] Rather than offering former child soldiers blanket immunity from accountability processes, nations and the international community could offer them some kind of public process to acknowledge their participation in violence and lawlessness, as well as their experiences as victims and as perpetrators, and in so doing help individuals forgive themselves and construct new and productive chapters in their lives. One philosophical view emphasizes self-forgiveness as a precondition for forgiveness by others.[119] Surviving child soldiers report that they desire to socialize and find support networks.[120] Gaining a means to earn a livelihood and obtain medical assistance, having opportunities to denounce perpetrators safely and to document their departure from the militia groups, and undergoing mediation with community and family members who do not understand what has happened are particular requests from former girl soldiers.[121]

The design of public processes to handle offenses committed by child soldiers would differ from the standard approach to prosecution, legal culpability, retribution, and punishment. Many countries have established special juvenile justice systems that pursue social reintegration and individual rehabilitation in addition to accountability. Much could be learned from them. Another avenue would be to form truth commissions to attend to the particular issues and experiences of child soldiers. These restorative justice ideas focus on repairing harms, enhancing the future, and developing therapeutic insights. While restorative justice does not demand forgiveness, it invites an understanding of how the harm affected all involved; it gives victims a chance to express the impact of the harm on themselves and to ask for apology or restitution; and it allows victims, wrongdoers, and others to let go of negative emotions and trauma.[122] These alternatives connect former child soldiers with those they have affected and could complement the direct economic, social, and psychological services that promote reintegration.[123]

Devising special accountability processes for former child soldiers could assist them in dealing with their past and present while also creating vessels for the emotions and attention of the communities receiving them. Restorative justice mechanisms could acknowledge both the wrongs done to the young individuals and the wrongs done by them, while excusing them from adversarial criminal justice proceedings applicable to adults. Research indicates that restorative justice programs in the United States are more effective for participants in terms of reduced rates of reincarceration.[124] Existing legal and communal options either give overly simplistic blanket assertions of innocence or overly stringent assignments of blame. Distinctive restorative justice efforts, drawing on lessons from juvenile justice and from truth commission mechanisms, could also offer forgiveness rather than silence on the issue of accountability.

Juvenile Justice: Models and Warning Lessons

In the early nineteenth century, reformers in the United States recognized that children differ from adults in ways relevant to criminal responsibility and created houses of refuge for them.

By the turn of the twentieth century, jurisdictions across the nation established separate juvenile courts.[125]

In early nineteenth-century New York, Thomas Eddy and John Griscom founded the Society for the Prevention of Pauperism and argued against detaining children and youth in adult jails and prisons. Their work led to the establishment of the New York House of Refuge in 1825, to receive impoverished and homeless youth at risk of delinquency.[126] Later in the century, in Chicago, settlement house leader Jane Addams successfully lobbied for a separate legal system for juveniles, to be guided by challenges in the children's environment and their social, educational, and moral needs. In 1899 Illinois established the first juvenile court system.[127]

Emerging ideas about child and adolescent development supported these reforms, as did ideas about opportunities for guidance, therapeutic interventions, and holistic treatment.[128] Developing special juvenile justice processes for those who were children when they committed crimes recognized the ways children differ from adults for purposes of criminal responsibility. Children are less autonomous, more subject to coercion and pressure from others, prone to dependency, and potentially more resilient and corrigible. For more than a century, many nations have established special courts or processes to acknowledge these differences between minors and adults in the context of criminal acts.[129] As psychologists articulated the distinctive cognitive and emotional capacities of minors, juvenile justice in its ideal form integrated resources of law with psychology, social work, community, and religious engagement to focus on the whole person.[130] International human rights efforts articulate similar goals, with an emphasis on treatment and community service, rejection of life imprisonment, and alternatives to incarceration.[131]

Unfortunately, in practice, juvenile justice institutions have often fallen far short of the ideal and imposed severe restraints on children's liberty without delivering on the promise of psychological, educational, and other forms of help.[132] Moreover, buffeted by "tough on crime" pressures and reflecting voters' fears, American juvenile justice increasingly imposes severe punishments focused on the crimes rather than on the age and context of juvenile offenders.[133] Cycles of reforms, oscillating between leniency and stringency, support arguments for more fundamental improvements to avenues toward adulthood for all youth in society.[134]

Other experiments explore discussions between the youth and adults in the community about allocation of responsibility for wrongdoing and devise concrete actions as restitution.[135] Chances to narrate their experiences, make amends, learn skills, and develop connections with others in support of constructive lives in relationship to family members, work, and community could combine demands for accountability with support for a better future not only for the young people but also for those they affect. Resembling juvenile justice courts in looking to the future but involving more community members in a less adversarial process, a restorative justice approach tailored to former child soldiers could hold individuals accountable while adapting the fact-finding methods and consequences to their circumstances, with the aim of improving their chances for successful lives. Use of such a process would be especially worth considering for former child soldiers who have grown into adults while associated with the armed groups.

Former UN secretary-general Kofi Annan recommended that the Special Court for Sierra Leone create a special track to deal with individuals between the ages of fifteen and eighteen.[136] He acknowledged that despite the international legal norm against prosecuting minors, both the government and representatives of civil society wanted "to bring to justice children who committed crimes" against humanity and war crimes.[137] Yet even though the Special Court had statutory authority to prosecute juveniles,[138] such a juvenile justice track never emerged in Sierra Leone, partly because of a stalemate in the debate between those who wanted to deter young people from joining armed rebels and those who wanted to advance an emerging international norm against any criminal liability for those under age eighteen.[139] The panel's first prosecutor announced he would exercise his discretion not to indict child participants and instead would focus on prosecuting those "who forced thousands of children to commit unspeakable crimes" in Sierra Leone during its 1991–2002 civil war.[140]

With international tribunals thus far declining to pursue the juvenile justice route, domestic legal systems may potentially play a productive role, having the flexibility to devise special processes that embrace future reintegration while providing accountability. This would require investing resources and tempering desires for revenge. Given the domestic systems that are inclined to hold former child soldiers responsible as criminal perpetrators, not as victims, some form of accountability with restorative and forgiving features would be worth pursuing.[141] Former child soldiers could otherwise face severe sanctions, including the death penalty.[142] Members of their communities may be inclined to devote few if any resources to former child soldiers, given other pressing needs.[143]

Devising juvenile justice and restorative justice approaches would comport with the parameters of the UN Convention on the Rights of the Child.[144] The convention does not prohibit prosecution of minors; it simply calls for a fair process that accommodates the child's needs and vulnerabilities.[145] Rather than legally immunizing or legally ignoring former child soldiers, devising a special process to hold them accountable while assisting their reintegration advances international norms emphasizing "the best interests of the child," as well as the search for the acknowledgment that matters both to survivors and to their communities.[146] One risk, as discovered in the United States, is that focus on "the best interests of the child" may lead to inattention to due process and restraints on government power.[147]

A juvenile justice system designed for former child soldiers could emphasize reparative rather than punitive consequences.[148] Providing social services, educational opportunities, and other assistance to former child soldiers may be needed and warranted.[149] Yet caution should be taken to ensure that such aid does not engender new resentments by giving former child soldiers more than others in their communities receive.[150] For this reason, and also in acknowledgment of the trauma experienced by so many others in war-torn communities, reintegration efforts should be inclusive and part of larger social reconstruction. It is striking to consider how resonant these ideas are for communities like Chicago's South Side as well as for rural Uganda, suggesting the need for something quite different from a court.[151]

Truth Telling and Forgiveness Processes

A second alternative is to direct child soldier cases to a communal transitional justice process, enabling truth telling and forgiveness. This means more than government pronouncements or pressure on local community members to forgive returning ex-combatants. Civilians in Sierra Leone report that government and civil society actors urged forgiveness for ex-combatants as the "bitter pill" to swallow for the sake of peace.[152] Often treated as a unilateral process, in which victims forgive regardless of actions by the former child soldiers, a fuller version of forgiveness occurred when the former child soldiers engaged in interpersonal conversations and made apologies to others.[153] One community member described the experience not as forgiveness but as coexistence: "It is possible that one or two people really *have* forgiven, but most [are just] allowing those people themselves to live with [them]."[154]

Communal restorative justice initiatives emphasize victim participation and collaboration among affected individuals and the development of reparation strategies.[155] Although some complain about the futility of truth telling in the absence of more concrete efforts to rebuild ties and obtain genuine prospects for jobs and community involvement,[156] others find the idea of truth telling therapeutic for former child soldiers.[157] Attention to specific community needs and attitudes matter in the design and operation of any kind of transitional justice.[158]

Communal restorative justice could draw upon traditional cultural mechanisms, although efforts in Rwanda to stretch the traditional *gacaca* process to apply to war crimes achieved at best mixed results and lacked the protections for juveniles recommended by the Convention on the Rights of the Child.[159] Constructing an entirely new process, such as a truth and reconciliation commission or the creation of memorials, could involve former child soldiers in actions to benefit the community. Communal processes focus less on assigning individual guilt and innocence than on gathering the experiences and feelings of the former child soldiers, working on a shared narrative about the political and social contexts that make young people into soldiers and sex slaves, and pursuing rituals and practices that could restore their membership in larger communities.[160]

The question of whether to focus on the needs of former combatants or on the requisites of social peace and stability poses choices about how communities rebuild.[161] Finding paths that can achieve both ends challenges what may seem an either-or choice: to help those returning to the community or to help those who stayed and to address the past or to focus on the future. Some restorative justice efforts resist the labels *offender* and *victim* because they provide little room for growth and social reconstruction; instead, they deploy terms like *person harmed* and *person who caused harm*.[162]

A truth commission could be designed to allow former child soldiers the opportunity to address both aspects of their experiences.[163] Truth telling without punishment could offer healing opportunities for both the young people and their communities.[164] South Africa's Truth and Reconciliation Commission did allow children to testify, but not in public hearings.[165] In Sierra Leone, the statute authorizing the Special Court to prosecute minors directed the use of "alternative truth and reconciliation mechanisms."[166] Children participated as witnesses, gave statements, and contributed to a version of a truth commission report aimed at children.[167] The commission hired female statement takers to facilitate participation by girls and ensured that all participation was voluntary, assisted by informed consent, confidentiality, and anonymity.[168] Liberia's truth and reconciliation commission worked with child protective agencies to advance children's needs while involving children across the range of its activities.[169]

Truth telling processes could be part of a ritual of forgiveness, but that would press on former child soldiers to confess, apologize, and acknowledge wrongdoing rather than receive amnesty or simply move on.[170] Wresting confessions—even with a carrot of social approval rather than a stick of punishment—might produce the appearance of apology but undermine the genuine exchanges important to forgiveness.[171] Any doubt about the sincerity of statements made to avoid punishment raises concerns, especially when the people involved have faced trauma and learned to lie for self-preservation.[172] In northern Sierra Leone, a kind of "social forgetting" is a foundation for reintegration and healing for child and adult ex-combatants; a truth commission could undermine those efforts.[173] In many conflicts, others caution against involving youth in truth commissions, because testifying could force them to relive traumatic experiences or expose them to criminal prosecution.[174]

Nonetheless, in some communities, a truth commission would be welcome and helpful. A survey of the Acholi community in Uganda indicated that 58 percent of those responding did not support prosecutions for lower-level members of the Lord's Resistance Army, but an overwhelming majority sought some acknowledgment or apology as a prelude to granting amnesty.[175] Truth telling and confession could also help to answer community members' gnawing questions about what the child soldiers did and to whom.[176] A staff member with a nongovernmental organization in northern Uganda explained, "The biggest problem with the conflict is that no one knows who did what. . . . Deep in people's hearts, they keep thinking and remembering because no one said they committed the crimes, no one made an apology, and no compensation was provided."[177]

Alternatively, a community may adapt traditional rituals designed to cleanse and heal individuals of their crimes with a spirit of forgiveness and restoration for the whole community.[178] Traditional Acholi practices in Uganda deploy restitution and communal rituals, although historically these traditions were used following the abduction and forced recruitment of child soldiers.[179] Community members there have extended the tradition of *mato oput*—literally, "to drink bitterness from a tree and put the past in the past following a ceremony and compensation to victims."[180] These rituals may have particular relevance for those who were coerced into performing violent acts and those who were raped or turned into sex slaves or "wives."[181] Rituals in which individuals can shed the past and take on a new identity assist in their long-term mental health and social integration.[182] A truth telling social process might assist in the reintegration for those who stayed in hostilities long after they were abducted or joined as children, and perhaps even for those who joined initially as adults.[183] Use of the arts can also help develop empathic connections, discover and express remorse and self-acceptance, and express desires for community understanding and acceptance.[184]

Analogies Between Youth Gangs and Child Soldiers

The special problem of child soldiers bears analogy to children and youth in violent gangs and criminal syndicates. Like child soldiers, children and teens are drawn into violent activity in the United States and elsewhere when they have few other options, when they are threatened, and when adults induce them with money or ideology.[185] Across the United States, minors face laws that largely give up on rehabilitation and even the idea of crafting punishment to fit the crime. Danielle Allen of Harvard traced the experiences of her cousin, Michael, charged at age fifteen of attempted car-jacking, tried as an adult criminal defendant, convicted, incarcerated for eleven years—and caught in the "life-altering convergence of the drug business, gangs, and a newly unforgiving criminal justice system."[186] Michael—a talented boy who dreamed of becoming a writer and a firefighter—actually thought after his arrest that if he went back to the streets, he would end up in trouble, so he chose jail over bail, hoping for the protection of the criminal justice system rather than a gang. That he ended up killed a year after his release from prison remains beyond understanding to his philosopher cousin, but it has something to do with his adolescence spent in prison, in a system of no second chances.

Michael was one of tens of thousands of minors incarcerated in the United States.[187] The lack of forgiveness is especially notable in a system confining so many poor young people and African-American and Latino individuals.

In American schools, "zero tolerance" discipline policies and increased suspensions have not proved successful, according to research.[188] Many schools now pursue restorative justice methods for conflict resolution in hopes of building strong relationships and a sense of community that can prevent conflicts, curb delinquency, and disrupt the school-to-prison pipeline.[189] These labor-intensive initiatives focus on repairing injury following conflicts involving youth.[190] Efforts to develop restorative justice initiatives for juveniles are underway in several other parts of the world, including New Zealand and Canada.[191]

A moment of connection between the experiences of child soldiers and American youth offenders occurred when former Sudanese child soldier and author Emmanuel Jal visited a juvenile correctional facility in the District of Columbia.[192] The inmates had read Jal's 2009 book *War Child*, and he told them about taking orders to fight in a war that he did not understand and tried to escape. As he described this experience and explained that no one had been there to teach him to read and not to hate, "the heads started nodding. Yes, that sounded familiar." The inmates told him they found much to learn from his example. Jal saw the parallels between the inmates' stories and his own: "You put me in the orange jumpsuit, and I am one of you." He continued, "I need to go to more prisons. . . . They need to hear it from me. They need to realize that they make that change, up here [pointing to his head.] . . . Maybe they feel for me. For what I went through. . . . But right now, I feel for them." An observer noted that Jal "cried after meeting" with inmates, "which was the reverse of my expectations."[193]

Rather than making blanket assertions of innocence, an interactive process that is forgiving—that acknowledges the contexts of individual child soldiers and child "wives"—could afford meaningful transitions for the former children and for their communities. All children who end up as part of a war or a violent criminal organization have been wronged, but when they then proceed to inflict violent harms on others or to support those who do so, they contribute to further wrongs. Neither innocence nor guilt, all or nothing, fully offers the justice or the better future that individuals and societies need and deserve.

The general absence of resources for youth is a factor contributing to their involvement in rebel forces—and in domestic criminal activities. Unemployment and idleness among adolescents can be a powder keg, igniting violence.[194] Subjecting former child soldiers and youth offenders to terrible detention conditions and severe sanctions could stoke resentment and retaliation, seeding future waves of violence.[195]

In the United States, our unforgiving criminal justice system has produced the highest rate of incarceration in the history of the world.[196] The system also reflects the nation's racial and economic inequalities, consigning poor individuals of color to disproportionate arrests, police violence, judicial delays, inadequate legal representation, plea bargains in the face of prosecutorial overcharging, lengthy mandatory minimum sentences, jail and prison violence, and massive use of solitary confinement. Many young people of color are trapped in this unforgiving system.[197] Although recent U.S. Supreme Court victories allow people convicted of offenses as juveniles to petition for a case-by-case review of sentences of incarceration for life without parole,[198] the Court remains divided over what it takes to forgive such sentences.[199] Even those who obtain relief, shortening their incarceration, have no rights to education or psychological services. Arrests and incarceration of girls are mounting, chiefly for nonserious offenses—such as running away, truancy from school, and misdemeanors—but large numbers of the girls are themselves victims of sexual violence.[200] Criminal sanctions can impose significant harms and new trauma, when what is needed is greater knowledge of trauma symptoms and supportive services. But this is not likely without an attitude of forgiveness for their minor infractions.

—

WHAT WOULD IT TAKE for legal and political systems to embrace a degree of forgiveness for former child soldiers, for youth engaged in violent crime, and for youth involved in nonserious offenses? Restorative justice tools offer practical avenues for breaking cycles of violence and trauma. They emphasize mediation with victims and restitution by offenders, and they call for treating adolescents as responsible to some degree for their conduct and for recognizing the responsibilities of adults in creating a world that can exploit the young.

Maybe forgiveness for youth requires acknowledgment of the failures of adults. In Colombia, during Latin America's longest-lasting war, rebels, paramilitary leaders, and gang leaders forcibly recruited thousands of teens, but, in 2015, commanders of the largest rebel group, the FARC, announced they would no longer use fighters younger than seventeen, although they did not commit to releasing those already in their ranks.[201]

In a meeting organized by the government to promote reconciliation and lay the foundations for peace, Orlando Villa, a commander convicted of forcibly recruiting seventy-three youths, gave a public apology.[202] With government officials standing by, Villa said, "These recruited minors never wanted to be part of this war. They were totally tricked. For this, I ask for forgiveness." He continued, while surrounded by three heavily armed prison guards, "I harmed these youngsters, their families, and their entire communities. They lost the chance of becoming other people. I could have seen to it that they did not suffer harm but I didn't." Former child soldiers were present. One named Carlos later reported, "It felt like being back at the camp on the day I was recruited. I decided to forgive him once he apologized. I think he recognized the wrong he had committed. I later shook his hand and hugged him." Many other acts of reconciliation have followed meetings between civilian victims and FARC chiefs in peace talks. A senior official reasoned, "Public apology ceremonies are an important step towards reconciliation because the perpetrators recognize their responsibility for the damage they've caused, and it brings dignity to victims and contributes to their healing."[203]

Even though this episode raises questions about the motives for and authenticity of the apologies, it points to a path toward transition and perhaps personal release. Imagine if gang leaders, drug lords, and other criminal bosses in the United States apologized publicly for involving youth. Questions endure about what matters to those who lost their youth and innocence as soldiers, sex slaves, and workers for adults in wars and adults in crime. A crucial first step toward providing answers would be to listen to people who survived time as child soldiers and found ways to thrive.[204] One program connects former child soldiers in South Sudan refugee camps with relatives and potential mentors from the Sudanese diaspora abroad; its work suggests the resilience and power of connections.

Ishmael Beah, author of the 2007 best-seller *A Long Way Gone: Memoirs of a Boy Soldier*, about Sierra Leone, reflected specifically about the place of forgiveness in offering people in his position the opportunity to confront their past and to change:

> I was a kid when this happened. I wasn't psychologically developed enough to decide whether I would be a part of it or not, nor was there a choice in the situation. Nonetheless, I feel guilty about what I became and what I was forced to participate in or do or carry out.

He then explored the promise and limitations of forgiveness:

> What I think is you forgive and you forget so you can transform your experiences, not necessarily forget them but transform them, so that they don't haunt you or handicap you or kill you. Rather, you transform them so they can remind you, so that this doesn't happen again. They can prevent this kind of thing from happening to other people. You must do things positive with your experience rather than dwell on the negativity of it.

The idea of forgive and forget, it's not good for the perpetrator *or* the victim, whichever context you want to put it in. If for example your neighbor killed your family, if you keep seeing them as a perpetual murderer, you will never give them a chance to change; they will never feel at ease around you, and you will never feel at ease either. But when you transform that, when you think, *Okay, there was once a time they did that; perhaps they can change.* When you do that genuinely, you actually give them a chance to transform. Hence you heal. You're not afraid. This is what I think of forgiveness.[205]

Forgiveness in this sense offers recognition that individuals can change, even those who lost their childhoods to violent conflict and those who committed terrible acts. Finding hope in the lives of individuals like Ishmael Beah just might inspire societies to forge opportunities for others to build constructive futures.

CHAPTER 2

FORGIVING DEBT

~

The build-up of personal and collective debt in America and Europe should have sent warning signals to anyone familiar with the biblical institutions of the Sabbatical and Jubilee years, created specifically because of the danger of people being trapped by debt.

—Jonathan Sacks[1]

ALTHOUGH THE TERM *FORGIVENESS* has long accompanied treatments of debt, its moral dimension has seemed a quaint holdover from an earlier era. Yet when understood as a conscious, deliberate decision to forgo rightful grounds for imposing sanctions against a person or group who has committed a wrong or harm, the notion of debt forgiveness matches the actions of Norway in canceling the sovereign debt of several borrowing nations, and proposals in the United States to forgive college student loans.[2] Debt forgiveness is in fact a long-standing tool within legal systems to reduce the legal and practical barriers for individuals, communities, businesses, and nations in building a future. Historical and legal practices of debt forgiveness demonstrate the potential for achieving accommodation, for recognizing the larger context of a wrong, and for legitimately resetting affairs, allowing a fresh start. Objections to debt forgiveness—on the grounds that it encourages unwise financial behavior, redistributes costs to parties without blame, or escalates financial risk—are countered at times by objections to unfair lending practices or to traps for unwary consumers, students, low-income individuals, and small businesses. Ever since ancient Athens, when Solon authorized debt forgiveness and forgiveness of crimes, the legal practice of forgiveness has connected financial and criminal justice in worthwhile and at times unavoidable legal, political, and moral debates.

A debt may be the result of sheer poverty, improvident consumer spending, a failed business enterprise, a natural or economic disaster, or a financial sanction imposed by a government for misconduct. Mounting debt in the United States stems from the imposition of fines and fees by local courts and police, mortgages, credit cards, and medical care.[3] Globally, national governments can incur debt to make productive investments in infrastructure, national security, and development, but governmental debt can also indicate financial stress, corruption, and the risk of default, jeopardizing political and financial instability.[4] Debt also binds people together, connecting past, present, and future in promises, broken promises, risks, and needs. Forgiveness may come informally from the lender or through a legal process such as bankruptcy, amnesty, or legal reforms providing financial relief.[5]

Moral, religious, and legal approaches to debt forgiveness appear throughout history and across societies. Some versions of the Christian Lord's Prayer ask for forgiveness not of trespasses but of debts, "as we have forgiven our debtors."[6] Indebtedness may arise from circumstances beyond the control of the debtor and even reflect unfair behavior by lenders that justify their sharing responsibility for indebtedness. Laws can allow lenders and borrowers to negotiate privately to stretch payments for longer periods or alter the amount owed. They also can frame devices—including bankruptcy—to organize forgiveness of loans. Economic as well as legal and moral concerns come to the fore with potential forgiveness of debts.

When might debt forgiveness create incentives for further debt and further defaults? This question might push against ever forgiving debt. Yet punishing a person for nonpayment of debt is often futile and even counterproductive; consider how imprisoning parents who fail to pay child support, or terminating their driver's licenses, undermines the adult's ability to generate the earnings needed to pay child support.[7] Contrasting contemporary commitments to permitting a fresh start for some debts and not others can support the case for loan forgiveness, while taking steps to guard against inducing new, unwise debts. Bankruptcy, international sovereign loan renegotiation, and private philanthropic purchase and forgiveness of consumer debt are all legal tools of forgiveness critical to many crisis circumstances; they also offer important analogies and contrasts to debates over forgiveness of crime, immigration violations, and other legal wrongs.

DEBT, FORGIVENESS, AND BANKRUPTCY LAW IN HISTORY, MORALITY, AND ECONOMICS

Debt has been around for as long as people have been able to count. People past and present have failed to repay borrowed

resources; they have consumed in the present rather than wait-
ing to accumulate sufficient resources, and they have risked
financial obligations beyond their means. Across cultures and
time, forced labor or prisons have operated as sanctions for
nonpayment of personal loans, reinforcing social expectations
that individuals will have the personal integrity and responsibility to pay back debts.[8] Opposition to forced labor and peon-
age as punishments for nonpayment has stimulated ideas of debt
forgiveness as a possible alternative response.[9] Mosaic Law—
traditions written in the Hebrew Bible between the eighth and
seventh centuries BCE—provided for a Sabbatical every seventh year, forgiving loans taken by members of the community,
and a Jubilee every forty-ninth year, forgiving all debts.[10]

In the sixth century BCE, the statesman Solon, in response
to widespread serfdom and enslavement of debtors, enacted a
collection of laws called *seisachtheia* to authorize debt relief in
Athens, canceling all outstanding agricultural debts and eman-
cipating enserfed and enslaved debtors.[11] Solon explained that
a great shaking off of burdens was necessary to overcome the
ills of the city, ills of slavery for the indebted, war, and exile,
produced in part by the greed of the wealthy.[12]

Debt cancellation—like the biblical Jubilee and ancient
Athenian debt relief—do not have exact modern legal ana-
logues.[13] In the ancient world, governments could cancel debts
because most debts were owed directly to them. In complex
industrial and postindustrial societies, most debt is owed to
intermediary financial institutions. Property laws protect private creditors from government cancellations of debt. Nonetheless, governments can adopt debt relief policies, providing

financial assistance to homeowners in exchange for an interest in their assets. Similarly, governments can grant students relief from governmental and private loans in exchange for public service or a share in the individual's future earnings. Governments can create amnesties or cancel debts that they themselves create, such as fines for nonpayment of governmental fines.[14] And governments can create mechanisms—typically, bankruptcy—for debtors to restructure their relations with creditors, extend or reduce payments, or renounce the debt, accepting the consequence of a negative credit rating, and start afresh. Bankruptcy is a legal means by which debtors may let go of otherwise rightful claims against them, using the power of the law to bring to the table all the relevant parties to craft a solution that either terminates the entire debt or reduces the payments, selling the debtor's assets as needed.

The government of ancient Rome created a form of bankruptcy after years of punitive personal sanctions for debtors.[15] Scholars of bankruptcy acknowledge the origins of debt forgiveness in religious texts. Jewish, Christian, and Islamic texts called for releasing those enslaved by indebtedness.[16] The Qur'an provides for adjusting the time needed for an insolvent person to repay a debt. Procedures to allow an individual to declare insolvency and start afresh arose in the Mongolian Empire in the fourteenth century. Great Britain instituted a bankruptcy law in 1542. Bankruptcy is a practical legal response to debts that cannot be paid and an acknowledgment that unpaid debt has many causes and even some benefits; rigid enforcement of debts can have societal costs.

In *The Merchant of Venice*—written in the 1590s—William

Shakespeare gave a female character one of his most eloquent speeches: she pleads with the lender Shylock to forgive a debt, in words characterizing mercy as a blessing both for the one who receives it and for the one who gives it.[17] That the Venetian characters show little forgiveness toward Shylock is one of the Bard's commentaries on the law and on debt forgiveness, examining not law versus mercy but instead the complex relations among law, forgiveness, virtue, and vice.[18]

In the eighteenth and nineteenth centuries, joining binding rules and popular sentiments, preoccupation with debt and the difficult circumstances of debtors stimulated literary and political responses in England, Europe, and the New World.[19] In the nineteenth century, James Fenimore Cooper, Charles Dickens, George Eliot, and other American and British literary writers grappled with issues of debt and debt forgiveness, as well as when and how individuals should forgive.[20] In Eliot's *Middlemarch*, Fred Vincy has accepted credit from unreliable sources and must repay the debt or else the father of his true love will have to pay it; meanwhile Lydgate goes deeply into debt to accommodate his betrothed's desire to live an upper-class life. Perhaps then it is not surprising that Dorothea, the novel's main character, remarks, "It is surely better to pardon too much than to condemn too much." The novelist Margaret Atwood suggested in a 2008 review of debt in literature, "There's a pawnshop of the soul, it appears, where souls can be held captive, but then, possibly, redeemed."[21] Imagery and metaphors of debt run throughout Western literature.

Around the globe, political discussions and decisions have long addressed forgiveness of group or national debts as well as individual debts. May groups or nations ever obtain forgiveness for collective debts? In the years following the Revolutionary War, an enormous national debt plagued the new U.S. confederation of states, as they struggled to repay loans from France, Spain, and private investors in the Netherlands. The search for more power to raise taxes and manage the debt, previously left to the individual states, was no small part of the pressure to replace the Articles of Confederation with a Constitution providing for a stronger federal government. Even so, during many years in the 1790s, total expenditures exceeded revenues. Its heavy debt led the government to seize Indian lands, contrary to agreements, in order to generate funds. Perhaps because his own personal finances frequently led to debt, Thomas Jefferson believed that the debts of one generation should not burden the next, which should have a clean slate.[22] The principal author of the Declaration of Independence, a founding father of the United States, and later its third president, he had debts that were so great that his heirs had to sell much of his property.[23] Devising a legal framework for bankruptcy to deal with debt thus became a defining element in the founding of the United States.

The Constitution embraces the concept of bankruptcy by empowering Congress to enact national bankruptcy laws.[24] Congress authorized bankruptcy for individuals, businesses, and municipalities and made forgiveness of debtors routine rather than extraordinary.[25] A focus on debt also informed the post–Civil War constitutional revisions.[26] Since the 1930s, politicians, commercial actors, and consumer groups have debated the particular terms of bankruptcy law, with competing views of fairness and equality in balancing the rights and interests of debtors and creditors.[27]

Discharging debt through bankruptcy immunizes the debtor to lawsuits on those debts, with some conditions and limitations. U.S. bankruptcy law permits individuals and businesses to seek relief from debts by reporting to a court all property, debts, income, and creditors, as well as any security used to obtain loans. After considering any exemptions of property provided by state law, ensuring the return of security (such as a car obtained through an automobile loan), and verifying that the individual has completed courses on credit counseling and debtor education, federal courts then discharge the debts.[28] Alternatively, federal bankruptcy law oversees a process for an individual wage-earning debtor to pay creditors in installments, under the supervision of a court-appointed trustee.[29] A business can sell all its property and other assets to help pay its debts, or devise a repayment plan over an extended time under court supervision, or declare bankruptcy to reorganize itself or close itself down while terminating debts.[30] Individuals can follow similar procedures. Those who successfully discharge debts in bankruptcy must first pay filing and legal fees and face the loss of property (to be sold to repay the debt); even indebted individuals must pay fees to file for bankruptcy.[31] But after bankruptcy, the individuals and companies become free from remaining legal claims, although they will be viewed as a poor credit risk for future loans until they develop a record of making timely payments of bills for a decade or more. Individuals may mitigate these risks by using the liquidation and repayment elements of federal bankruptcy law.[32]

Only limited kinds of property—such as a family home—can be exempt from the claims of creditors, and some creditors avoid even that restriction if the home provides security for the mortgage. Moreover, the reputational costs of declaring bankruptcy are large, often making it difficult for the person or business to reestablish creditworthiness for a decade or more. Historically, bankruptcy has carried social stigma, underscored by social sanctions ranging from imprisonment to exclusion from public office, revocation of citizenship, and surrendering one's children to serve as slaves or servants.[33] In *The Merchant of Venice*, Shakespeare described one bankrupt individual as "a prodigal who dare scarce show his face at the Rialto."[34] Although in the United States the stigma associated with bankruptcy declined in the twentieth century,[35] bankruptcy continues to serve as a final resort, after renegotiation and other efforts do not work. Social resistance to loan forgiveness persists even in the face of widespread financial disasters.

Bankruptcy also represents costs for creditors, who, at best, receive just a portion of their legal claims. It legally forces forgiveness of debt—letting go of rightful claims—with the special feature of bringing together under one framework everyone having claims, including the debtor and all creditors. "Fairness for all" is the watchword, although the process gives priority to debts (such as child support and alimony) specified by public policies and to creditors whose debts are anchored by a legal security interest in the debtor's property. Bankruptcy is a better alternative to prison or slavery for debtors and also benefits creditors, who may gain access to some of the debtors' assets they otherwise would not find.[36]

Compared with the process in other countries, the bankruptcy process in the United States is a capacious and distinctive mechanism for forgiving debts of individuals and businesses, permitting greater opportunities for a fresh start than many other jurisdictions do.[37] Bankruptcy makes negative results from economic risk-taking less devastating and hence encourages innovation and entrepreneurship. At the same time, bankruptcy law elicits serious debate and political controversy because of the contrasting interests of lenders and borrowers, but also because of competing views about strict legal responsibility and forgiveness.[38] Some contemporary commentators reject construing the term *forgiveness* as having a religious or moral dimension in the context of debt, because legal frameworks permitting bankruptcy make the sentiments and attitudes of the debtor and the lender irrelevant.

Yet even if the term *forgiveness* is used only as a metaphor, its use underscores the humanity of those facing debt and the relevance of assessing right and wrong in the conduct of both the debtor and the lender. In the United States, the "power to reward the 'honest' but 'unfortunate' debtor with a discharge of debt" has a constitutional dimension.[39] Considerations of incentives, reward, and blame continue to animate debates over bankruptcy.

Is bankruptcy in the United States too readily available, leading individuals or businesses to shirk their duties to pay debts? Are the terms of bankruptcy too difficult for borrowers, providing them with inadequate relief, or too onerous for lenders, harming credit markets? Is society as a whole helped or hurt when bankruptcy is facilitated for individuals and businesses? Each of these possibilities may have some truth. Reliable assessments depend on understanding the causes of debt and the effects of responses such as sanctions and forgiveness.

The availability of bankruptcy relief may well induce some to take on more debt than they can handle. Individuals may take greater risks than they otherwise would because they believe they ultimately will not have to bear the costs. Called by economists the problem of "moral hazard," it may also lead those with insurance to fail to guard against risks, like those taking a cholesterol-reducing drug who fail to monitor their diet.[40] Many consumers, tempted by credit cards, borrow even when in long-term financial distress. Lenders deploy psychological research to draw consumers into credit card and other consumer debt, even when the consumer lacks sufficient resources.[41] Immediately after someone declares bankruptcy, credit card companies offer them new cards, enticing them into new debt at high interest rates because of the credit risk.[42] Even though the massive mortgage foreclosure disaster after 2008 resulted from the unscrupulous marketing of loans to financially weak and unrealistic borrowers,[43] concerns about moral hazard from forgiving outstanding mortgages trouble many people, though it is undeniable that lenders as well as borrowers deserve blame for the crisis.[44] Concern about moral hazard similarly may arise with possible forgiveness of child soldiers and people who commit criminal acts; in each instance, anticipation of exemption from legal consequences may lead to greater conduct violating legal norms.

Since 2005 U.S. bankruptcy law reforms, reflecting political judgments about who should benefit from flexibility and who should have more rigid consequences from unpaid debt, have made it more difficult than previously for individuals and small businesses to pursue bankruptcy.[45] Student loans are exempted from bankruptcy relief. So are individual states, although municipalities can declare bankruptcy. Revisions designed to protect creditors have made it more expensive for individuals in debt to pursue bankruptcy and have also removed the tool of reduced payments on a mortgage for a primary residence.[46] The timing of the reform exacerbated the housing market crash of 2008, leaving many homeowners no choice but to walk away from a home and leave it to the creditors, who themselves were not set up to manage and resell homes. Placing tighter restrictions on bankruptcy, some argue, is too blaming and unforgiving of debtors, especially when the debtor has been not irresponsible but unlucky. Catastrophic medical costs, unemployment, divorce, and other challenges beyond individuals' control are major factors in personal bankruptcy.[47] The law reforms paid less attention to the risky behavior of lenders than to the acts of debtors, even though at least some lenders engaged in predatory or oppressive practices.[48] Creditors who try to get around protections for debtors pose risks not just to their immediate customers but to the larger society.[49]

Setting the optimal balance between encouraging and discouraging debt is challenging, from the vantage points both of individual borrowers and of society. Biblical norms and medieval rules against usury—lending on exorbitant terms—favor debtors, reflecting long-standing concerns about those with assets taking advantage of those experiencing economic challenges.[50] Also favoring debtors are economic and historical assessments that debt itself is not a bad thing; it can fuel investment, productivity, and human welfare. When people borrow to build a business or renovate a house, they create value for the society as well as for themselves. For inventors and entrepreneurs, debt accompanies creativity, and debt forgiveness can encourage more creativity.[51]

But pervasive and high debt loads with little hope for repayment can stymie growth, dry up markets for credit, and trap large numbers of people in miserable circumstances. In addition, the terms on which debt is structured—the ways loans are marketed and interest is compounded—can be unfair, misleading, or manipulative. An economy predicated on consumer purchases can go off the rails when those purchases depend on perpetual indebtedness or are made at inflated prices that anticipate high default rates on consumer credit. Similar dangers can arise for nations that borrow, and even more pronounced dangers and abuses grow from corrupt leaders who divert resources borrowed in the name of the nation for their personal benefit.

Markets assist in the allocation of debt and credit through prices, but they are not always sufficient to set the balance for borrowers, creditors, and the world at large. Professional lenders know they always risk nonpayment, and they build that risk into the terms of their loans and portfolio of loans. In this respect, debt forgiveness involves a different kind of power relationship than forgiveness of criminal violations. In instances of violence, the wrongdoer often has had access to more power than the victim. In instances of debt, the one who breaches a promise to pay often has fewer resources and opportunities than the lender. Even lenders outside business contexts by definition have resources that borrowers do not have.

In a fundamental way, bankruptcy law acknowledges that debt has a societal dimension beyond the lender-borrower relationship, as it provides a socially structured way for a debtor to start over after failing to repay debts. It also acknowledges that creditors usually have more freedom—more power—than do lenders, and it sets the legal consequences to even the playing field. Bankruptcy laws help signal that creditors need to take caution in lending money, given the risk that they will not be paid in full or at all. This, in turn, puts brakes on cyclical tendencies of economies to move between boom (when people with easy credit spend too much money) and bust (when people do not spend enough to keep the economy operating). Thus, debt forgiveness has benefits beyond mitigating a particular borrower's difficulties. Like restorative justice in the criminal context, bankruptcy looks to the future of the broader community, not just at a specific past problem. When Shakespeare's Polonius advises his son, "Neither a borrower nor lender be," he shared his knowledge that both borrowers and lenders can create resentment and culpabilities.[52]

When consumers and businesses within a society accumulate severe amounts of private debt, nations consider reducing the percentage of debt by printing new money (at the risk of inflation) or even by linking access to newly minted dollars to requirements that individuals pay off mortgages and credit card debts.[53] High levels of citizens' debt endanger the financial health of a nation, slowing or halting their spending and investment.[54] Forgiving debt may be essential, then, not just for individuals but for society at large, yet it creates the moral hazard of debtors taking on more debt than they can handle. When nations themselves are debtors, similar dynamics become more complex and can jeopardize global financial markets, political relations, and peace. Hence legal mechanisms for debt forgiveness can be important to individuals, communities, companies, nations, and the world. When debt forgiveness is not available—due to legal rules, political dynamics, social disapproval, or the sheer poverty of affected individuals—negative consequences can escalate. Debt forgiveness is often unavailable for governmental debts, consumer and student debts, and debts created through criminal justice practices, and each of these areas may call for more fundamental consideration of legal forgiveness.

Special Issues Posed by Governmental Debt

In 2014 the British government acknowledged that Britons were still paying interest on obligations incurred in 1720, when a financial crash following the South Sea Bubble led the government to accept a bailout, placing an enormous debt on its books.[55] Refinancing governmental debt in light of shifting interest rates can keep even very old debts around for decades or centuries, without indicating financial danger or imprudence if the nation is otherwise economically productive. Entire nations may incur debt far larger than the national domestic economy; territories, states, and municipalities may incur severe debts with no apparent path toward solvency. Special difficulties arise with forgiving debts of sovereigns: there may be no operative rules, or no basis to enforce them; and the need to borrow again on reasonable terms may determine the viability of the sovereign.

National governments have tools for dealing with debt that private actors do not—tools that include printing money and taxing to build revenues. These options pose further challenges, both financially and politically. A national government may collapse and repudiate its prior debts, but economists argue that it would then face severe difficulties obtaining future credit and respect among other nations. Within the United States, following the economic crisis of the 1830s, Arkansas, Florida, and Mississippi repudiated prior debts; after the Civil War, the federal government repudiated the debts of the Confederacy and amended the Constitution to establish repudiation of debts due to insurrection or rebellion.

Nations have no option of bankruptcy because no international tribunal exists to authorize and supervise it. Individual nations are unlikely to surrender elements of their sovereignty sufficient to enable such a process.[56] Hence the only lawful ways to work down sovereign debt are to repay it or renegotiate it.[57] External creditors—other nations, international bodies, and private lenders—can exert their own priorities as they buy national bonds.

Nations have often declared insolvency, and repeated declarations of insolvency are historically common.[58] The economist William Easterly notes that "from the two Greek city-states who defaulted on loans from the Delos Temple in the fourth century BC to Mexico's default on its first foreign loan after independence in 1827 to Haiti's 1997 ratio of debt to exports of 484%, debt servicing difficulties have been a feature of the world economy throughout history."[59] Although borrower nations that default face difficulties obtaining credit, developing nations have recently found many potential sources of loans, including global businesses, other nations, and international financial institutions such as the World Bank and the International Monetary Fund. Yet new loans can build up sovereign debt that goes unpaid. Some nations may not only declare insolvency but seek to repudiate their debts as immoral or otherwise not worthy of recognition.

Repudiation of Odious Governmental Debt?

As South Africa transitioned from the apartheid regime to a full government, its new leaders considered repudiating approximately US$20 billion of sovereign debt incurred by the former regime. In 1997 calls to repudiate that debt mounted in nongovernmental organizations and religious circles; they made the case that the apartheid regime had inccurred the debt to strengthen its economy, security, and defenses without the political or moral approval of the nation's majority, who hence should not be weighed down by it. What would the international legal community, across law and finance, do with such repudiation?

Nonpayment of a promise to repay is a wrong. But debtor nations often argue that a loan itself was wrong—in its shape, terms, or even purpose—thereby justifying a revision or nonpayment. Perhaps the terms of the loan were unfair, or the debt was incurred by unscrupulous and undemocratic leaders without benefiting the people. On these grounds, some have proposed the creation of a doctrine of international law that can forgive some or all national debt, when the citizens are not to blame, as "odious." Arguments that odious debt should become a doctrine of international law have not succeeded in mobilizing global public opinion, so continued discussion of the idea could be rhetorical and chiefly serve to call on creditors to offer compassion in adjusting or forgiving debts.

Arguments for recognizing "odious debt" seek to soften the negative consequences when a debtor nation defaults on repayment or pursues more favorable repayment terms. Simply calling the debt "odious" is a step in attempting to gain public support. Odious debt advocates may also anticipate that default and repudiation risk ruining the borrower nation's future access to credit. Requiring repayment of odious debt punishes the citizens for bad behavior by their leaders, without doing anything to halt or deter lending to horrible regimes; an odious debt doctrine could redirect international capital to more productive and transparent uses.[60]

Aristotle long ago articulated grounds for nonpayment of debts incurred by a tyrant, because such a leader served only his own interests.[61] Similar moral arguments can be made today for repudiation of national debts incurred by deposed leaders, and against global banks and nations imposing onerous terms. Some argue that odious debts should not be repaid because they were undertaken for purposes at odds with the interests of the people who are expected to repay them. Despite the usual rule in international law and civil law of *pacta sunt servanda* (agreements must be kept even after a transition of government), forgiveness of odious debt would excuse nations from repaying debts undertaken by a prior regime that were contrary to the interests of the society.

The modern articulation of odious debt is credited to Alexander Nahum Sack, commonly but erroneously identified as a former tsarist minister. In 1927 he suggested that, for a given territory:

> when a despotic regime contracts a debt, not for the needs
> or in the interest of the state, but rather to strengthen
> itself, to suppress a popular insurrection, etc., this debt is
> odious for the people of the entire state. The debt does not
> bind the nation; it is a debt of the regime, a personal debt
> contracted by the ruler, and consequently it falls with the
> demise of the regime.[62]

The concept of odious debt remains just that—a concept, not a doctrine of international law, although in 2006 Norway unconditionally canceled approximately $80 million in obligations owed to it by Ecuador, Egypt, Jamaica, Peru, and Sierra Leone, based on its own assessment that these debts were not legitimate because they did not serve the borrowers' needs.[63] There are many examples of repudiated debt, nonpayment of debt, modified debt, or disputed debt following regime changes, as in Cuba, Britain, South Africa, post–World War I Germany, and interwar Latin America. In many of these instances, some of the loans were repaid. Similarly, the United States repudiated Texas's debts as it entered the Union, Mexico repudiated its Austrian debts, and the Soviet Union repudiated tsarist debt.

For a legal precedent, advocates of an odious debt doctrine point to Costa Rica's refusal to honor debts owed to the Royal

Bank of Canada incurred by the dictatorial regime of Federico Tinoco (1917–19) because the United States and Britain did not recognize his authority as legitimate. When Costa Rica then faced threats of an international commercial boycott, the successor regime agreed to international arbitration conducted by William Howard Taft, former U.S. president and then chief justice. Chief Justice Taft found that Tinoco had exercised effective control, and hence his thirty-month military regime should be treated as a sovereign state, and that its successor was subject to its continued contractual obligations. At the same time, he concluded that repayment of the debt should not be enforced, because the funds were used not for governmental purposes but for the personal support of Tinoco and his brother—and the lending bank knew or should have known this would be the case.

With this case as a precedent, contemporary advocates argue that creditors should not be able to demand repayment from nations that undertook debt solely to benefit their rulers. Demonstrators and some political leaders in Greece, Spain, and Italy blame their crushing sovereign debts for the euro debt crisis and denounce them as odious or illegal.[64] It may be possible to articulate a definition for odious debt,[65] but using such a concept in practice would raise a host of problems. The case of a successor regime repudiating a debt on the grounds that it is odious requires making an exception to the usual rule that a nation's debts continue regardless of who is in office;[66] would such an exception be available if the new officeholders also served in the prior regime? Would debt forgiveness predicated on a shift in regime create new incentives for regime change, even if faked for this purpose? If the prior regime was not organized as a democracy, does lack of a democratic structure leave every action of the regime without the popular consent needed to make a debt legitimate?[67] Also hard to assess is whether the borrowed funds obtained were spent for ends contrary to the interests of the nation.[68] Even if a loan went into a tyrant's bank account, funds are fungible, so the lenders could object to application of the doctrine if the tyrant's government provided national security or other services.[69]

Fundamentally, arguments for a doctrine of odious debt argue that it would urge international lenders to avoid supporting corrupt or oppressive regimes. But who is well situated to identify oppressive regimes? Perhaps a public international institution such as the United Nations could be charged with determining whether an entire regime is "odious," whatever that means; would that regime therefore in effect become ineligible for future loans?[70] Such an assignment is probably beyond the competence and political capacity of the United Nations or another international body to make.[71] Also, odious debts can be "laundered" by international financial institutions.[72]

Against the compelling moral arguments to forgive odious debt lies the fact that the existence and implementation of the doctrine over time would prevent more loans from taking place, burdening those most vulnerable, such as starving people living under an oppressive regime.[73] Although meant to help a struggling nation, a legal rule allowing nonpayment of odious debt would diminish the pool of creditors to a small, unscrupulous group.[74] Even more troubling, there is no good way to prevent a regime from concealing information that would be relevant to a finding of odiousness before the loan is granted.[75]

Many who are interested in the notion of odious debt seek to shift blame to creditors for taking advantage of impoverished nations or for funding corrupt leaders and regimes.[76] Some even suggest that the creditors should seek forgiveness for their complicity and responsibility.[77] In this sense, exploring odious debt could broaden the inquiry into the contributions of various actors to the problem, the harms, and possible solutions. To be precise, though, odious debt as a doctrine would not operate as loan forgiveness but rather would amount to a position that the creditors and the larger credit market behaved so badly that they do not deserve to be repaid.

In this light, the huge debts of many developing nations invite consideration of the responsibilities of other governments and of international financial institutions, as well as revision of international lending and borrowing policies.[78] These larger issues came to the fore when leaders in South Africa contemplated repudiating the apartheid-era debt. In 1997 the archbishop of Cape Town, Njongonkulu Ndungane, urged South Africa to use the "Doctrine of Odious Debt" because "its foreign and domestic debt was incurred, by and large, under the apartheid regime, and should . . . be declared odious and written off."[79] As it turned out, President Nelson Mandela chose instead to pay back the debts. At that time of political transition, the nation would have been highly vulnerable to political ostracism, especially as it sought the end of anti-apartheid sanctions. In addition, Mandela and his advisers understandably cared about preserving and strengthening South Africa's access to credit and capital markets.

A global recognition of the unfairness embedded in its apartheid-era debt would have made a difference. After the transition, the amount of national debt fell from nearly 50 percent of the country's gross national product to less than 45 percent in 2017, but it remained high, and in early 2018, the nation's debt again grew closer to 50 percent of GNP.[80]

Even if the doctrine of odious debt receives no further formal endorsement, the rhetorical arguments supporting it could improve voluntary routes for renegotiating and restructuring debt.[81] Electronic fund monitoring could make such efforts more effective now than in the past.[82] A registration and monitoring scheme for creditors, enhanced by electronic data sharing, social networking, and citizen monitoring, could link loans to the conduct of nations in terms of corruption, successful development projects, citizen disagreements with the uses of loans, and other measures that exist or could be developed.[83] Another option would be to create a legal presumption against enforcement of a limited class of loans, such as those used for the personal enrichment of a former leader, or for the purchase of arms used to suppress popular uprisings, or for resources to maintain an oppressive regime.[84] Nongovernmental organizations could develop robust voluntary standards to spur aggressive monitoring, to rate creditors along these and similar dimensions,[85] and to evaluate sovereign borrowers with the aim of reducing loans for improper purposes.[86] Public and private actors could offer technical assistance to debtor nations so they could stretch out payments and take advantage of shifts in interest rates and in the value of relevant currencies, just as lender nations do.[87]

Over time international financial bodies or collaborating national governments could authorize a structure to oversee a kind of international bankruptcy process to recognize the futility of seeking repayment of loans from destitute nations. The process could operate like bankruptcy for individuals and businesses, offering a fresh start and a sense of hope for nations struggling to recover from political and financial disaster.[88] A bankruptcy-like process ideally would bring together all creditors and the government of the debtor nation to negotiate extending time, reducing payments, and sharing current and future assets, with fairness to all in mind. Nations currently can renegotiate debt terms with banks; a routinized bankruptcy-like proceeding could offer a less disruptive alternative than relying on markets for distressed sovereign debt,[89] with the associated risks of litigation and transaction costs. Banks may even come to accept reasons for nonpayment or reasons to forgo interest, given specific details about the circumstances. The recent experience of Argentina, which spiraled downward through a series of defaults on sovereign debt, has been exacerbated in litigation by holdout creditors seeking to derail a negotiated restructuring of the debt.[90] Some practices of global creditors lead advocates to argue for extending the notion of odious debt to democratic nations and territories burdened by predatory loans.[91]

In the absence of international bankruptcy or a recognized odious debt doctrine, poor and emerging nations struggling with debt cannot declare bankruptcy. Nor can they renegotiate debt arrangements with the help of a bankruptcy-style framework. Developing nations are often reluctant to default, not only because that would injure their creditworthiness but also because such actions can drive up costs or destroy the international market for loans for nations in their situation. As a result, for many struggling nations, voluntary forgiveness by creditor nations and private lenders remains the most promising option.

Nongovernmental organizations such as the Jubilee Network, which links 75 U.S. institutions and more than 650 faith groups around the globe, are pursuing such voluntary action. Drawing on the biblical notion of a Jubilee year wiping away all debts, the Jubilee Network claims credit for achieving "critical global financial reforms and more than $130 billion in debt relief for the world's poorest countries."[92] The Committee for the Abolition of Illegitimate Debt, a global initiative that started in Belgium, now pursues debt cancellation for developing nations; between 1998 and 2000, it collected 24 million signatures in 166 countries on a petition to this end. Pope John Paul II and Bono have used moral arguments and their high visibility to press "first world" nations to drop enforcement of debt of developing nations. In seeking to alleviate world poverty through political pressure and religious and ethical appeals, these efforts helped persuade international financial institutions to undertake the Multilateral Debt Relief Initiative. Some creditors have also offered to exchange national debt enforcement for commitments to invest domestically in environmental conservation or economic development. National and international laws could provide incentives and rewards for such voluntary efforts.

Special Issues for Territories, States, and Municipalities
Under U.S. law, individual states cannot declare bankruptcy. Pension obligations and unpaid bills lead some states—currently Illinois—to explore whether Congress or the courts might extend bankruptcy law to include them.[93] With its bonds downgraded to the lowest rating, Illinois may have to explore the possibility of defaulting on its obligations, as Arizona once did, or seek special congressional authority to restructure its debts.

Puerto Rico, an unincorporated territory without even the self-governance powers of a state, lacks control over its finances and economy; receives much less in federal support—for health care and other programs—than do states; regularly loses businesses and citizens who depart for better opportunities elsewhere; and about a decade ago, lost a beneficial tax rate when Congress repealed it.[94] A large amount of Puerto Rico's economy operates illegally, avoiding taxation. Economic mismanagement may contribute to the island's difficulties. Puerto Rico began to default on its debts and then enacted a bankruptcy act, but a federal court ruled that federal law superseded it—and federal law provided no basis for Puerto Rico to declare bankruptcy.[95]

With its economy in free fall, Puerto Rico and its bondholders pressed the federal government for a solution, and Congress created a board authorized to control the budget and restructure Puerto Rico's debt.[96] Then a natural disaster—Hurricane Maria—exacerbated the problem.[97] President Donald Trump initially suggested that the federal government would forgive Puerto Rico's debt but then changed course.[98] Although the federal government could improve the island's

finances by providing disaster relief, increasing federal benefits, and restoring a preferential tax rate for businesses, it is
not clear that it has the power to forgive the debts, which are
held by a variety of investors, bond funds, hedge funds, and
middle-class Puerto Ricans. Only a negotiated settlement of
claims under a bankruptcy-like process could obtain adjustments from bondholders, pension holders, and businesses,
with sufficient order and legitimacy to produce plans for all to
let go of some of their rightful claims.[99]

American cities do have the legal ability to use bankruptcy
relief, but they face complex political and financial considerations. One mayor contemplating bankruptcy for his city
explained to me he worried it would betray the city's citizens.
Cities that consider bankruptcy have to navigate their subordinate status to state governments, defined by the particular
terms of their state's constitutions and case law. Detroit became
the largest U.S. city to undergo a bankruptcy, after a nine-day
trial determining that it was eligible, insolvent, and could not
achieve results through negotiation.[100] Amid Detroit's more
than one hundred thousand creditors, including unions and
pension funds, some people argued for selling paintings held by
the Detroit Art Museum, but Detroit's bankruptcy proceeded
within the confines of federal law, which does not allow liq-
uidating a city or selling its parts.[101] The governor of Michigan appointed an emergency manager to address economic
disaster in Detroit following the collapse of the automobile
industry, which triggered objections for bypassing its demo-
cratically elected government,[102] but the strategy—and negotiated contributions by almost all affected by the city's financial

collapse—helped lead to encouraging signs of Detroit's economic recovery.[103] After the court accepted Detroit's petition for bankruptcy, Lynn Brimer, representing Detroit's retired police officers, announced, "Perhaps it's fair to say the fight has just begun."[104] Detroit mayor Dave Bing then commented, "There's going to be a lot of pain for a lot of different people, but in the long run, the future will be bright."[105]

Connecticut recently directly forgave $755 million in debt payments owed by the City of Hartford, even though Connecticut itself has a heavy debt.[106] The city narrowly avoided declaring bankruptcy and breaching its promises to pay pensioners, bondholders, and others to whom it held obligations. Some analysts have criticized such debt forgiveness because of the moral hazard and recommend instead policy changes to alter the conduct that produces municipal debt.[107] To avoid similar debt crises, Rhode Island and Pennsylvania have instituted emergency managers or receivers; Michigan has required municipalities with underfunded pensions to fix the situation.[108] In these instances, the political judgment at the state level trumps voter choice at the municipal level. Unfortunately, these political dynamics often have racial and class dimensions, given the overrepresentation of impoverished people who are also members of racial or ethnic minorities in the jurisdictions (including Puerto Rico, Detroit, and Hartford) laboring under governmental debt. The fates of impoverished communities lie at the hands of voters and decision makers outside their communities.

Municipal debt crises present challenges to democratic governance as the mechanism to resolve tensions among creditors, debtors, residents, and political leaders. Even if debt forgiveness by a state or municipality is legally possible, the risks of corruption or incompetence by officials in charge make judgments about handling municipal debt especially difficult. A city or territory dealing with overpowering debt likely depends on an all-hands-on-deck approach, including help from the state and private sector. Emergency responses can go only so far. Reliance on an emergency manager may have helped Detroit turn around its financial situation, but it was emergency managers whose decisions gave Flint, Michigan, lead-contaminated water.[109] Governance reform, not only financial relief, is a critical part of dealing with and preventing insolvency and its functional equivalents for cities, states, and territories.[110] Financial disaster within a governmental entity signals problems that very often require reforms, which themselves need external forces in order to overcome internal logjams.[111]

As impoverished nations and struggling states, territories, and municipalities tackle governmental debt, debt forgiveness remains a powerful rhetorical theme, even if not always a feasible or desirable action. In their struggles to deal with collapsing economies, sovereign nations and parts of the United States must grapple with the absence of an overarching authority that could forgive their debt. There is no bankruptcy authority at an international level; there is no existing mechanism for Illinois to declare bankruptcy; and there is no easy way for even a U.S. president to undo Puerto Rico's obligations to its public and private creditors. Yet bankruptcy or structures like it provide the only comprehensive framework for bringing all those affected together to forge a solution. The political will for a bankruptcy-like procedure for Puerto Rico, a bankruptcy and an emergency manager in Detroit, and a bailout of Hartford by the Connecticut government grew because of compelling need and widespread recognition of the multiple causes behind the indebtedness in each instance. Rather like restorative justice, the comprehensive financial restructuring of a government shares responsibility across people and entities that can claim to be part of the problem or its effects. Recognizing that larger communities are implicated in debt is important also for effective responses to debt that crushes individuals and warrants explorations of debt cancellation, restructuring, or forgiveness.

CONSUMER AND STUDENT DEBT IN THE UNITED STATES

In the United States, older people are facing higher levels of debt as financial risks shift from government and employers to individuals. Individuals bear the burdens of diminishing resources in social safety nets, increased health care costs, and reduced incomes.[112] As a result, the rate of bankruptcy filings by people aged sixty-five or older tripled between 1991 and 2013, although many others in similar positions do not pursue that option.[113]

At least these older individuals have the choice of declaring bankruptcy, and they may be better able to manage the hit to their credit rating than young people are, starting out their adult lives. Consumers burdened by credit card and other debt also can pursue bankruptcy, although it carries immediate financial costs, damages their credit rating for seven to ten years, creates difficulty obtaining loans, and may generate adverse publicity, loss of property, and difficulty finding and keeping employment.[114] Students with college debt cannot discharge it through federal bankruptcy law except in instances of total disability, death, or some kinds of public service.[115] This is a serious problem for individuals and for the country as a whole. Student debt has doubled over the past ten years, approaching $1.4 trillion. Millions of Americans have failed to repay their loans on tuition that itself increased dramatically over the same period.[116] Apparently, fewer than five hundred people have sought to discharge student loans through the "undue hardship" provision in the bankruptcy law.[117] Calls for reform come from many quarters. Some seek to restrict loans to students in academic programs that are likely to generate remunerative jobs, while others press for loan forgiveness in the face of forces beyond the students' control.[118] Arguments to preserve and expand forgiveness programs build on governmental programs such as Pay As You Earn.[119] Revamped in 2011, it forgives federal student loans after borrowers have paid a certain percentage of their income for a specified number of years.

The Department of Education under President Trump requested public comment about the calculations of hardship under the bankruptcy law, but staff members also suggested ending a long-standing program that forgives school loans for individuals who take up public service employment.[120] The federal department has delayed or halted relief for students who claim they were defrauded by for-profit colleges.[121] Some of those colleges may have used predatory lending practices. Meanwhile those for-profit colleges are eligible for bankruptcy protection—and the defrauded former students are not.[122]

According to current court filings, some creditors that generated student loans lost the paperwork documenting the loans, but borrowers still owe on those debts and risk harm to their eligibility for further credit if they fail to repay.[123]

By some estimates, about half of the bankruptcy petitions filed by Americans stem from medical expenses.[124] Medical debt is the most frequent reason that debt claim collectors contact consumers.[125] A study by the Urban Institute found that between 2013 and 2015, after the enactment of the Affordable Care Act, the percentage of American families that reported having trouble paying their medical bills declined from 22 percent to 17 percent, but such relief depends on the viability of state and federal health insurance.[126]

Especially in times of large student debt, consumer debt, medical debt, and mortgage debt, reformers call for wiping the ledger clean for those with terrible financial burdens. Lenders raced to sell subprime mortgages, approving them even for individuals lacking financial means because of the apparent rises in real estate values and the resale markets for mortgage-backed securities and in the process produced a financial bubble that burst in 2008. Many homeowners lost their jobs and savings and also the hope of using equity in their homes in the face of financial troubles. Even for those who were able to meet their mortgage payments, the home's loss of value often rendered those payments less than financially rational. So following the 2008 global financial disaster, massive numbers of homeowners defaulted. The problem was not the fault of the homeowners alone, although they had chosen to undertake the debt. The exuberant real estate market, aggressive marketing of mortgages that bypassed conventional credit requirements, shifting risks through derivatives and credit default swaps, inadequate regulatory oversight, and financial institutions (due to complexity, arrogance, or short-term thinking) taking on too much risk all contributed. Many of those with wealth and sophistication avoided having to absorb losses, but others had put their savings and creditworthiness into their primary residence and then faced bad options.

Many private creditors restructured and forgave elements of home mortgages, only to trigger tax liability because forgiven loans are largely treated as taxable income in the United States. In response to public demand, Congress extended the short-term Mortgage Forgiveness Debt Relief Act of 2007, which was in effect through 2012, and then was extended through 2017. It allowed homeowners to refinance their mortgage without having to pay taxes on any debt modification or forgiveness that they received (up to $2 million per year).[127] Congress extended the Act repeatedly to avoid financial crises—and perceptions of unfairness—for underwater homeowners who owed more than their homes were worth, due to mortgages that had been pressed on them when real estate values were rising. Lacking equity in their homes, these homeowners without congressional relief would have faced significant difficulties paying income tax on debt forgiven through the postcrisis adjustments.[128]

Legal changes in each of these areas could help balance the interests of debtors and creditors and address the unstable financial markets, unfair or predatory lending practices, and misrepresentation or fraud that contributed to the debt. Federal guarantees—with some student loans and some home mortgages—would allow federal regulations to better oversee

negotiated adjustments of payment schedules and terms, or make
loan payments conditioned on investigation of complaints about
misrepresentation, fraud, or unfair practices. Tax relief could be
ensured for those borrowers receiving adjustments that would
otherwise be treated as taxable income, and tax incentives could
encourage lenders to offer such adjustments when warranted.
Consumer protection departments of state attorneys general and
state and federal legislators should monitor patterns of bankruptcy filings and public complaints to ensure investigations of
and responses to problems of the sort producing the subprime
mortgage crisis, the inflating rates of college tuition and thus
of student loans, schools' misrepresentations of graduation and
employment rates, scams targeting senior citizens facing debt,
and similar defects in the lending markets.

Commercial debt collection companies purchase bad debts
and collect pennies on the dollar by garnishing wages and
harassing debtors; in 2013, taking a page from their book, supporters of Occupy Wall Street started Rolling Jubilee to purchase consumer debt and forgive it.[129] Having raised more than
$700,000 by July 2017, the group was able to buy and forgive
$32 million worth of people's medical bills, student loans, and
consumer debt, while expressing compassion for "distressed
debt" as a human problem.[130] The effort has also given tools to
student loan borrowers to manage the collateral consequences
of their debts and to dispute them.[131] A former debt collec-
tor launched a nonprofit organization, RIP Medical Debt, that
uses philanthropic donations to purchase and forgive distressed
medical debt.[132] For just ten dollars, a collection agency can

purchase $1,000 worth of debt, an amount that increases at 12 percent interest annually, then pressure the debtor to pay the full amount. Conversely, the nonprofit organization purchases $1,000 worth of medical debt for ten dollars and forgives it. The comedian and television host John Oliver purchased $14.9 million in distressed medical debt for $60,000 and publicly forgave the debt on his television show, *Last Week Tonight*.[133]

These are instances of private players using the discounts in the secondary market in debt to leverage philanthropic dollars to forgive the debts of consumers and students. Governmental policy could encourage such activities; civil society should honor them. Beyond offering a fresh start for individuals, these efforts demonstrate the potential for financial institutions, public policies, for-profit colleges, and others to make causal and remedial contributions to reducing the indebtedness of individuals. Even when bankruptcy is neither an available nor a desirable solution, it contributes the idea of a fresh start for borrowers over their heads in debt and models a solution that broadens the focus from the debtor to the multiple parties able to improve the situation for all. The point is not to undo warranted and reliable protections for lenders but to even the balance of power of less sophisticated borrowers, prevent lenders from off-loading so much risk onto secondary markets that they do not take appropriate precautions in lending, and involve other public and private actors when either the problem or the solution implicates broader circles of people and institutions. Can those same elements come into play with debt imposed by the government on impoverished people caught up in the criminal justice system?

CRIMINAL LAW AND DEBT

When the Department of Justice investigated the 2014 police killing of Michael Brown, an unarmed African-American teenager who lived in Ferguson, Missouri, it uncovered a widespread practice of fines and fees used by the local justice system to fund its activities, largely on the backs of poor residents. Similar practices across the country have now become central concerns for reformers who recognize the unfairness of threatening jail for poor people who cannot pay fines and fees imposed by the local police and courts.[134] Further studies exposed often byzantine layers of charges for room and board, court time, public defense, judicial supervision, and more, all imposed on low-income individuals as the jail and prison populations grew over the past decade.[135] Despite a Supreme Court ruling forbidding the use of incarceration for debt, such practices proceed with the notion that those who do not pay government-imposed charges are in contempt of the law, justifying the threat of imprisonment.[136]

When Texas processes an individual in the criminal system, it always assesses fifteen categories of court costs and an additional eighteen discretionary fees, including fees for being committed to or released from jail. In Washington State, a defendant with a single conviction is subjected to twenty-four fines and fees.[137] The criminal justice process creates financial obligations that include costs and fees associated with legally required supervision of the individual following conviction as well as fines and forfeiture of property, intended as a form of punishment or restitution to victims. Such financial obligations

can prevent the targeted individual from ever climbing out of
debt and entanglement with the legal system.[138]

One study found that 20 percent of formerly incarcerated
individuals take out loans to cover the costs charged by government.[139] Such fees are regressive and disproportionately affect
members of racial and ethnic minorities. In many instances,
governments lose rather than raise money through such fines
and fees because of the costs of administration, court time, and
collection efforts.[140] The civil rights lawyer Alec Karakatsanis,
who has challenged such practices successfully in court, concludes, "The vast majority of these cases are not there for any
legitimate [reason] let alone any rigorous public safety concern.
They're there because so many people have come to depend on
the everyday metastasizing of this bureaucracy for their own
livelihoods and to make a profit."[141] It is tempting to borrow
the notion of "odious debt" from international legal debates to
describe this swirl of fines and fees that entraps some of society's
most disadvantaged people.

Promising reforms are not hard to identify. Local governments could publish the fees and fines for public notice
and end traps for the unwary—easy steps to take.[142] States
could require hearings about an individual's ability to pay
before imposing fees or fines, or enact amnesty periods, or
offer penalty-free extended time for payments.[143] Communities could permit community service as an alternative to probation or prison, prohibit jail time for unpaid fees, connect
poor defendants to job training programs and social services,
cap the revenue that can be raised through fines or fees, and
eliminate debt imposed on juveniles.[144] Ending suspension of

drivers' licenses for nonpayment, providing legal representation, and helping poor families with financial education or coaching are other longer-term responses.[145] Broadening the focus beyond the individual debtor opens the door to many solutions; so does the fundamental idea that people should have a chance at a fresh start, even when they have done something wrong.

—

BANKRUPTCY AND BANKRUPTCY-LIKE PROCEDURES are long-standing legal tools for forgiving debt. They give individuals, businesses, and governments a second chance while providing for the orderly resolution of outstanding obligations. They thus combine practical concerns and aspirations for release from otherwise justifiable claims. The market mechanism of selling distressed debt is another tool that increasingly finds philanthropic participants who buy consumer debt at vast reductions and then forgive it. Because U.S. tax law likely treats such acts as taxable income, the government could itself be forgiving and exempt such loan forgiveness from taxation; incentives for such private effort could also guide governmental policies. It could take account of the risks of wrongly encouraging people and entities to take on new debt with no ability to repay it, while also acknowledging that creditors make loans that can be onerous or that carry risks of default that creditors have to bear. Sometimes other actors—including government and philanthropy—need to step in and absorb some of the losses. The deep histories of debt cancellation and bankruptcy reflect repeated recognitions that debt has multiple causes, perpetual indebtedness causes social harms, and that focusing on individuals' fresh starts benefits everyone.

Legal rules can and should preserve the governmental, economic, and communal environment that encourages risk-taking, acknowledges the realities of impoverishment, and recognizes the participation of actors on many sides of transactions in a world of risks, enterprise, and chance. Arguments that some debts should be deemed so odious that they need not be paid have not prevailed in international law, but defaults by sovereign nations, just like defaults by individuals, remain an option that nations can use to press for more cooperative solutions. But when a government itself imposes fines and fees that make individuals into debtors—and threatens imprisonment for nonpayment—that government is blameworthy in ways that are difficult for any to forgive.

CHAPTER 3

AMNESTIES AND PARDONS

———

President Gerald R. Ford was never one for second-guessing, but for many years after leaving office in 1977, he carried in his wallet a scrap of a 1915 Supreme Court ruling. "A pardon," the excerpt said, "carries an imputation of guilt," and acceptance of a pardon is "a confession of it."

—SCOTT SHANE[1]

THEY WERE CALLED THE "THIRTY TYRANTS." In the summer of 404 BCE, after Sparta defeated Athens in the Peloponnesian War, they led a political coup, producing a repressive and brutal oligarchy during their eight-month rule. During that time, they killed between 5 and 10 percent of the citizens and expelled more than half of the population. Afterward the leaders of Athens, restoring democracy, adopted an amnesty. This kind of removal from legal liability protected all participants of the former regime from exile or legal accountability, except for the highest officials.[2] Apparently, these efforts helped ancient Athens avoid the cycles of revolution and counterrevolution familiar in other areas.[3] The amnesty was not just a political expedient but evidence of admirable moderation and character.[4] Aggrieved

individuals even in unrelated lawsuits could introduce character evidence about the behavior of their opponents during the
tyrants' rule, as an outlet for continuing resentments.[5]

This use of amnesty represents a classic example of a legal
mechanism for clemency, canceling past grievances, and offering a fresh start for all.[6] In court speeches for years thereafter, speakers crafted the story of the amnesty as evidence of
Athenian forbearance, generosity, reasonableness, and wisdom.[7]
Jurors and leaders swore oaths marking conciliatory attitudes
toward those who did not directly cause them harm.[8] Transitions could be peaceful and could strengthen the rule of law
even without truth telling or direct sanctions against most of
the perpetrators of the mass violence.[9] Offers of amnesty might
accelerate the end of a war or strengthen chances of a durable
peace.[10] Offers of amnesty, combined with community service
or rituals and truth-telling efforts, might provide a fair tool in
assisting former child soldiers and their communities.

As the nation that incarcerates more people than any other
society in history,[11] the United States could do well to consider making greater use of forgiveness mechanisms, but so
far the yearly ritual of a presidential Thanksgiving pardon
for a live turkey has had more cultural resonance than pardons or commutations for prison inmates. The spirit of second chances embedded in bankruptcy shows a long-standing
legal and cultural embrace of forgiveness in the context of
economic breaches. Why not build more avenues for second
chances into the legal treatment of criminality—not only for
those charged for crimes when juveniles but also for adults,
through clemency?

Amnesty is a device available through legislation; through the executive power of a king, president, or governor; and through courts. It can be used to ease a political transition, to acknowledge a shift in policy, to recognize service or rehabilitation, or indeed for any reason, given its origins in political power and in the divine right of kings. In 2016 Tajikistan marked the twenty-fifth anniversary of its independence from the Soviet Union with a criminal justice amnesty, releasing more than three thousand inmates from prison, pardoning four thousand people with suspended sentences, and shortening the sentences of five thousand others.[12] King Norodom Sihanouk of Cambodia granted amnesty in 1996 to nearly all prisoners, including perpetrators of Khmer Rouge atrocities,[13] with the stated motivation of fairness and the unstated context of a peace process following civil war and political transition. President Ronald Reagan and Congress orchestrated the 1986 amnesty for undocumented immigrants, allowing 2.7 million people to apply for jobs, open bank accounts, build credit, and buy homes if they had lived continuously in the country before 1982 and applied for a green card, while paying a $185 fee.[14]

The immigration amnesty generated highly positive economic results for the nation but also produced backlash and resentments, perhaps because it led to a surge in illegal immigration, illegal hiring of undocumented individuals, and demographic shifts that altered the political landscape.[15] In 2018 the St. Louis City Municipal Court established a warrant amnesty program, allowing anyone with an outstanding warrant for violating certain city ordinances to pay their original fines without late penalties.[16] A California amnesty administrative program tries to help certain companies avoid bankruptcy by excusing labor law violations.[17]

Amnesty is an instance of clemency, mercy, compassion, or forgiveness for a legal or moral violation. Tempering the rigors of legal rules, clemency derives from the prerogatives of monarchs. *Amnesty* has come to mean allowing a group to avoid legal consequences, while a grant limited to one person is commonly known as a *pardon*. Founding father Alexander Hamilton justified extending the royal power pardon in the new U.S. Constitution because he predicted that a "well-timed offer of pardon . . . to the rebels" could "restore the tranquility of the commonwealth."[18] President John Adams pardoned participants in an early rebellion, and President Andrew Johnson pardoned Confederate leaders after the Civil War; Presidents Thomas Jefferson, James Madison, and Andrew Jackson also extended pardons to individuals who deserted the army.[19] As in ancient Athens, amnesties and pardons can quiet social or political antagonisms. The U.S. Supreme Court has commented that amnesties usually deal with "crimes against the sovereignty of the State" and "political offenses," with "forgiveness being deemed more expedient for the public welfare than prosecution and punishment."[20] Whether admirable or troubling, amnesties and pardons are thus long-standing legal mechanisms for letting go of justified accountability. Their use may either lessen or increase resentments. When are they justified? When are they misguided—in undermining the evenhandedness of the law, or in excusing the inexcusable, or in encouraging future lawbreaking? What, if any, guardrails should limit amnesties or pardons?

Particularly promising are amnesties designed to assist a political transition and let go of grievances against the losing side; pardons, too, may play that role, or acknowledge a shift in governmental policy, or recognize an offender's change of heart. Forgiveness inside of law could be strengthened through comparisons across fields and contrasts across legal systems. When local communities change laws criminalizing possession of marijuana, but some people remain sentenced under the prior law, should the legal system find a way to forgive violations of the old law? And when particular laws divide the nation, might amnesties for violators help forge a path forward for the whole society?

Much more troubling are amnesties and pardons that shield the powerful from accountability, cover up wrongdoing, or reward gifts or support. Like all forms of legal forgiveness, amnesties and pardons carry the risk of undermining respect for law and its commitment to equal and neutral treatment. The pros and cons must be weighed in particular circumstances. What some see as unfair immunity given to corrupt or privileged individuals, others may see as a valuable way to turn the page on a past regime. Either description could fit a debated 2017 amnesty for business leaders in Tunisia following a change in leadership.[21] The U.S. Department of Justice, with no formal issuance of amnesty, refrained from prosecuting bankers involved in the subprime mortgage crisis; instead, to the dismay of many, it simply extracted financial settlements from the banks, holding no individuals responsible.[22]

Perhaps the most famous pardon in recent memory followed one of the most serious national political crises in U.S. history.

President Gerald Ford, hoping to quell political divisions, exercised the presidential pardon power on behalf of his predecessor,
Richard Nixon. President Ford, the first person to become U.S.
president without ever having been elected either as president or
vice president, became vice president following the resignation
of Spiro Agnew, who left office when he was charged with tax
evasion and corruption.[23] Eight months later President Nixon
resigned in the face of the Watergate scandal—extensive illegal activities against the Democratic National Committee that
came to light with a bungled burglary of DNC headquarters in
the Watergate Hotel. This and other illegal activities, including
wiretapping, stealing, firebombing think tanks, making physical assaults, and covering up all of these acts, prompted a Senate investigation and the appointment of a special prosecutor.
The House initiated an inquiry into whether to vote to impeach
the president. After President Nixon directed the firing of the
special prosecutor, and the Supreme Court ordered the release
of White House audiotapes, the House Judiciary Committee
voted to impeach Nixon, but he resigned before the full House
had a chance to vote on the matter. Gerald Ford was sworn in
as president. The new president declared, "Our long national
nightmare is over."[24]

A month later President Ford issued a pardon for Nixon
for offenses against the nation during his time in office that
could have given rise to prosecution. There is no question about
his constitutional authority to do so. The presidential power
to pardon expressly excludes only impeachments, and if the
Senate follows impeachment with a conviction, removal from
office is the remedy.[25] The pardon occurred after Nixon was

out of office and after the House halted inquiry into whether to vote to impeach him.[26] The presidential pardon power can reach all federal criminal offenses at any time, and pardons may be granted even before any legal proceedings have begun. But accepting a pardon entails admission of guilt.[27]

President Ford said he chose to announce the pardon on a Sunday to emphasize that it was an act of mercy, not of justice.[28] He stressed his hopes to avoid further political division as the nation moved beyond the Watergate scandal, while suggesting that Nixon had already lost much in giving up the presidency.[29] It was a forward-looking act for the nation if not for Ford's own political interests. Political leaders in both parties sharply criticized the pardon, and the president's press secretary resigned in protest.[30] The Republican Party thereafter suffered massive electoral losses; the failure of President Ford's reelection bid may well have stemmed from this pardoning of Nixon. If so, that fulfilled the constitution's design: elections are the accountability mechanism in response to presidential actions.[31]

President Ford nonetheless defended the decision as an effort to heal wounds. Years later the journalist Bob Woodward, who had played a pivotal role in exposing the scandal, suggested that the pardon had "an aroma of a deal: that Nixon would resign with the guarantee that he would get a pardon and Ford would get the presidency."[32] Yet even Woodward concluded that Ford's pardon "was an act of courage, rather than the final corruption of Watergate."[33] Others who initially opposed the pardon later concluded it was a compassionate move and respected that President Ford genuinely believed it was good for the country, even at the cost of his own reelection. Opinion polls shifted from a majority opposed in 1974 to a majority in approval by 1986.[34] This entire experience underscores the potential power of presidential pardons in periods of national change or uncertainty.

President Ford granted another amnesty around the same time that reflected his efforts to assist a transition. He offered amnesty to all individuals who had avoided the draft during the Vietnam War, though he conditioned it on public service. Later President Jimmy Carter, fulfilling a campaign promise, eliminated the public service condition in order to "heal our country" after the politically divisive war.[35] Some one hundred thousand Americans had moved outside the country to avoid the draft; others had hidden at home; some in the military deserted; and over five hundred thousand risked criminal prosecution for violating draft laws.[36]

Congress, academic conferences, religious organizations, and other groups had been debating the possibility of amnesty. A report by the Ford Foundation (unrelated to Gerald Ford) studied the possibility of granting amnesty to draft evaders, deserters, and veterans with dishonorable discharges. It acknowledged that an amnesty would anger some and could encourage future draft dodging, but about 60 percent of its survey participants supported a conditional amnesty. Accordingly, the report argued for amnesty, defining it as "an act of grace by the state in which persons guilty of crimes are released from the penalties set by law."[37]

> In cases involving long and bitter civil dispute, amnesty often
> has served as a useful and legal means through which magna-

nimity, rather than punishment, was exercised in the broad interest of reconciling a divided society. Although the act of granting amnesty waives the normal course of the legal process, it at the same time reaffirms the legitimacy and the underlying strength of that process.[38]

Observing some thirty-seven prior uses of amnesty (all conditional) in U.S. military matters and other examples in other countries, the report cited compassion as a reason for granting amnesty to draft avoiders who had faced difficult choices between legal compliance and personal conscience.[39] The report also acknowledged the widely articulated arguments against U.S. involvement in the war.[40] The report recognized that two big concerns worked against amnesty: the potential for future resistance to military conscription and service, and the risk of implying disrespect for veterans who made the sacrifice to serve and who already faced serious obstacles to reintegration.[41] These considerations may well have informed President Carter, who excluded military deserters when he ended the condition of community service in exchange for those receiving amnesty.

Despite contemporaneous controversy, the pardon of Richard Nixon and the Vietnam-era amnesties seem in retrospect to have helped the nation while relieving individuals of punishment. Yet they raise two enduring questions about the use of such forgiveness devices: the danger of corruption—a pardon or amnesty given in exchange for personal advantage or self-dealing—and the risk of encouraging future violations because of the possibility of forgiveness. Both problems deserve attention, especially in exploring possible guardrails for using the powers. Even though both the pardon power and the conscription amnesty fall within the lawful authority of the U.S. president, political and moral debate and pressure could influence uses of the power or, at minimum, identify and object to abuses.

CORRUPTION

The first set of risks is corruption: unethical behavior by one in power, typically for personal gain. Geoffrey Chaucer's fourteenth-century *Canterbury Tales* satirized the abuse of religious practices, as church officials raised money by selling pardons and forgiveness, known as indulgences.[42] His pardoner announces: "Intent is only for to win, And nothing for correction of sin."[43] In the sixteenth century, Martin Luther critiqued high-living clergy in the Roman Catholic Church for selling indulgences as relief from sin; in so doing, he launched reforms focused on good works and generated many branches of Protestant Christianity.[44] Luther declared, "Those who believe that they can be certain of their salvation because they have indulgence letters will be eternally damned, together with their teachers."[45] Ever since, selling forgiveness has had a particularly odious reputation, but that does not mean it has stopped. In the seventeenth century, according to some accounts, King James II sold pardons for two shillings.[46]

In 1923 the Oklahoma State Legislature impeached and removed Governor John Calloway Walton for charges including improper use of the pardon power and some alleged bribery, but the charges may also have been trumped up in light of his aversion to the death penalty and to the Ku Klux Klan.[47] In the 1970s in Tennessee, criminal convictions were brought against several top aides of Governor Ray Blanton for selling pardons in a scheme that did not reach the governor (who was, however, later impeached for a different corrupt scheme).[48]

Corruption will remain a challenge as long as the executive pardon power is unlimited and unreviewable. Issuing a pardon in exchange for money, political support, or personal advantage abuses the public office and the pardon's purposes of social healing, correcting overzealous punishment, or recognizing rehabilitation of the wrongdoer. A quid pro quo exchange for a pardon exemplifies corruption and the wrongful confusion of public power with personal gain.[49] The political tools of impeachment and criminally charging subordinates may help check the risk of corruption in the granting of pardons and register ongoing public disapproval of exchanging pardons for personal advantage.

As a recent example, consider how a president of Peru pardoned his imprisoned predecessor shortly after a group of that predecessor's supporters helped the current president avoid impeachment.[50] In 2009 President Alberto Fujimori was convicted of bribery and human rights abuses and sentenced to prison. His "imprisonment was a landmark for Latin America, a message that all should be equal before the law in a region where the norm has too often been impunity for the rich and powerful," wrote *The Economist*. In December 2017 President Pedro Kuczynski faced impeachment over his ties to an allegedly corrupt construction firm. But Fujimori-affiliated legislators, including Fujimori's son, declined to impeach him. Three days later Kuczynski pardoned Fujimori. [51] This pardon seemed especially unwarranted as Fujimori faced declining health and probably would have died in prison. He showed no remorse, and establishing accountability through an independent judiciary remains a work in progress in Peru and in South America generally. Hence the pardon seemed, as editorial writers at the *Economist* put it, "like a sordid bargain to let the president [Kuczynski] survive."[52]

How should we view pardons that reflect political calculations? Should we extend our disapproval of personal gain in pardon-granting to Gerald Ford's pardon of Richard Nixon, especially if Nixon agreed to resign, promoting Ford to the presidency, in exchange for a pardon? The facts remain shrouded in history and politicized accounts, but even if an explicit exchange took place, personal benefits to Ford seem overwhelmed by the larger benefit of a swift close to a national scandal. Concerns about a quid pro quo diminish when the pardon releases a wrongdoer from a rightful punishment in order to benefit society—considerations largely missing in the instance of Fujimori. In a 1927 Supreme Court decision, Justice Oliver Wendell Holmes reasoned that a pardon "is part of the constitutional scheme. When granted, it is the determination of the ultimate authority that the public welfare will be better served by inflicting less than what the judgment fixed."[53] The framers valued the assurance of freedom for the executive pardon power, immune from judicial or legislative review, and they even accorded the president the authority—subject only to the political sanction of the electorate—to abandon otherwise-prescribed criminal consequences in pursuit of other benefits to society.

No such benefits surrounded President Bill Clinton's last-minute pardon for Marc Rich, whose former wife had donated $1.4 million to Democrats, including Bill and Hillary Clinton: $450,000 for the Clinton Library, $10,000 for Clinton's legal defense fund, and a pair of coffee tables and chairs with a market value of $7,375 for the Clintons.[54] Although Bill Clinton, when he was no longer in office, defended the pardon as a correction for prosecutorial overreach, others emphasized that the pardon power should not be used to excuse a fugitive who had been charged with tax evasion and illegal commerce with Iran, while Iran held American citizens hostage.[55] Appearing to reward someone who had donated dollars for the president's personal and political gain, the pardon of the unrepentant swindler Marc Rich insulted all those affected by Iran's brutality toward the United States. Marc Rich's crime hurt American interests as well as the nation's commitments to law. There were no good reasons for this pardon and plenty of bad ones. No wonder the pardon infuriated many of Bill Clinton's own supporters; it spotlighted suspect ethics of a president who already faced questions on that score.[56]

For decades, U.S. presidents have relied on the Department of Justice to engage in an administrative process and delegated review of potential presidential pardons. This practice ensures that many eyes see a pardon application, and it offers some protection against corrupt abuses of the pardon power. Such efforts can slow what otherwise might be a hasty or ill-considered pardon, expose risks of corruption, and even insulate the executive branch from pressure and temptation. That extra care was absent in the lead-up to Clinton's last-day pardon of Marc Rich, which occurred outside the established Department of Justice review.[57]

The benefits of the administrative process are undone, however, if they permit the kind of corruption that may arise with recent practice at the Department of Justice.[58] As administrative review shifted to a subordinate official responsible for liaison with prosecutors, pardon recommendations grew to reflect the views of prosecutors, who are committed professionally to defending convictions rather than reconsidering them.[59] This administrative structure, combined with the independence of prosecutors, arguably undermines the use of the pardon power as a check on the severity of the criminal law.[60] It is understandable that prosecutors may view the pardon as a challenge to law enforcement, but if so, their influence reflects a corruption—a departure from the original design—of the executive power to pardon and individualize justice.

During the debate over the U.S. Constitution, Alexander Hamilton defended giving essentially unfettered pardon power solely to one person, because "undivided" responsibility would help the holder of that power focus on the arguments for mitigating law's rigors.[61] Arguing against granting the Senate power to review presidential pardons, Hamilton emphasized that locating the power solely in the president would help incline the officeholder against actions that might lead to "being accused of . . . connivance." Apparently the danger of collusion with another branch of government seemed greater than other risks of corruption.[62] When Hamilton concluded that "one man appears to be a more eligible dispenser of the mercy of government, than

a body of men," his words captured the risks arising from delegating administrative power to those responsible for criminal justice enforcement.

The most extreme corruption of the pardon power would arise if an executive used it to forgive him- or herself. Rather than offering a cleansing, forwarding-looking fresh start, a self-pardon would further embroil the government in accusations of corruption and scandal. As a literal matter, the constitutional texts of the pardon power of the U.S. president, of governors, and of leaders in other countries typically do not include a prohibition on pardoning oneself, despite the old adage "one cannot be a judge in one's own case."[63] Nonetheless President Donald Trump floated the idea of pardoning himself, his aides, or his family members. Scholars and pundits acknowledged that he might legally use the pardon power this way, although there are counterarguments based both on tradition and on ethics. The Constitution explicitly imposes only "cases of impeachment" as a limit on the presidential pardon power. When constitutional language is clear, it usually means what it says.[64] The exclusion of impeachment may point to an implied limitation on self-pardons, especially in face of an actual or threatened impeachment. Another constitutional provision, the Emoluments Clause, forbids payments from foreign powers and implies a limit on self-dealing.[65] Combining the emoluments clause with the exclusion of "cases of impeachment" from the presidential pardon power especially suggests limits on a president's power to pardon him- or herself. A few state governors appear to have pardoned themselves.[66] The political fallout of a self-pardon, though, could be severe, and impeachment or failure at reelection could follow.[67] If the pardon impedes an impeachment process, the pardon itself could amount to a new impeachable obstruction of justice. In addition, in the federal system established by the Constitution, the president does not have pardon power over state criminal charges, so a self-pardoning president who commits offenses defined by state law could still be criminally prosecuted and convicted.[68] Self-pardon by a president, governor, mayor, or other official is the ultimate self-dealing, violating aspirations of fairness and objectivity.[69] It should be rejected morally and politically.

The risk of self-pardoning highlights the tension lying in wait since the prerogative of royalty was transformed into a power of the executive in a constitutional democracy committed to the view that no one is above the law.[70] Unlike in the United States, South Africa's Constitutional Court directs that an executive power must comport with the nation's constitution and hence is reviewable by that court.[71] South Africa's Constitution also commits executives to follow the rule of law, which generally bars anyone from being the judge in his or her own case.[72] South Africa further permits pardons only after prosecutions have proceeded through to convictions, after justice "has run its course."[73] Even where the pardon power has involved no limits, a watching public is capable of disapproval and protest and may well object to its use in particular cases, which can provide some check on corruption.[74]

INDUCING LAWBREAKING

A second concern about the use of pardons and amnesties is that it risks encouraging others to disobey the law. This danger resembles a "moral hazard,"[75] the risk named by economists that people will increase their risk-taking when they are insured because they are insulated from consequences, notably if bankruptcy forgiveness is provided too often and too leniently.[76] Opposition to President Ford's amnesty for Vietnam-era draft resisters warned that it would encourage future resistance to military conscription and service. Conservative media and polls emphasize a fear that granting amnesty to immigrants who entered the United States without legal authorization would encourage others to follow in their footsteps.[77]

Placing conditions on amnesty can reduce the risk that future lawbreaking will result. Such conditions may require people to disarm, to reveal the facts of their lawbreaking, to obtain drug treatment, or to participate in community-based justice mechanisms.[78] Alternatively, the amnesty may include restrictions, such as confiscating assets or forbidding recipients from holding public office or receiving pensions.[79] Clemency may be conditioned on swearing allegiance to the country or performing acts of service.[80] Forgiveness judgments must always consider the jeopardy to the rule of law and to the fair treatment of others who obey the rules.

To tamp down encouragement of lawbreaking, a government may craft relief that falls short of a full pardon. It may simply provide a reprieve, a temporary postponement of punishment, or remission of fines or forfeitures.[81] A commutation adjusts a punishment, reducing the length of a sentence or replacing a death sentence with imprisonment, without relieving the offender of significant legal consequences for the offense.[82] Commutations do not restore other rights lost upon conviction, such as voting, jury service, or parental status.[83] Yet these and other collateral consequences of conviction, compounded by poverty and racial attitudes, produce lifelong effects even for people who have served the punishment set by the criminal justice system.[84]

Decisions about amnesties, pardons, commutations, and reprieves can be unpredictable and slow. President George W. Bush hoped to avoid the pressure from well-connected felons that affected President Clinton; his reliance on the slow-moving review process in the Department of Justice frustrated members of his staff, who sought ways to demonstrate compassionate conservatism.[85] Well into his second term, President Barack Obama had given few pardons, and his team, too, seemed frustrated by the review process in place.[86] As a result, he spurred intensive review of federal criminal convictions and enlisted private groups to assist a clemency project. What resulted was a set of restrictive criteria, confining relief to nonviolent, low-level offenders whose sentences were much longer than would have resulted due to intervening changes in the law.[87]

Even with this streamlined procedure, giving priority to individuals convicted of drug-trafficking offenses whose sentences exceeded what subsequent law would authorize, the resulting scope of legal forgiveness was narrow, and the numbers affected remained limited.[88] Some 4,000 volunteer lawyers screened requests from 36,000 inmates; only 1,225 of those who met the criteria received clemency.[89] White House counsel Neil Eggleston explained that "those receiving pardons have shown they have led a productive and law-abiding life after conviction, including by contributing to the community in a meaningful way. . . . These are the stories that demonstrate the successes that can be achieved by both individuals and society in a nation of second chances."[90]

This commutation process took steps to mitigate the unfairness of so many people serving time under sentencing rules that Congress had later rejected.[91] The 2010 Fair Sentencing Act had revised the dramatically more draconian punishment for possession of crack cocaine compared with powder cocaine, but it left untouched the many individuals already punished under the prior sentencing regime.[92] When President Obama launched the clemency review effort, critics warned it was cumbersome and too limited and cautioned that it could exacerbate the risk of racial or other biases because it involved subjective factors such as levels of remorse.[93] The Department of Justice said it would study the racial patterns in the clemency review initiative, but it did not release results.[94] Reform of the clemency process used by the president could and should be designed to preserve the administrative review needed to guard against political corruption but also to protect against conflicts with the interests of prosecutors and law enforcement.

Another limited form of legal forgiveness is expunging or sealing criminal records—limiting who may have access to them. Such measures can help people move on with constructive lives after serving their sentences. This process generally permits restoration of civil rights, limits inquiries by employers and licensing boards about criminal histories, and prohibits exclusion of individuals based on an expunged conviction or arrest record.[95] Cities, counties, and states across the United States have adopted "ban the box" rules, removing conviction history from job applications to postpone consideration of this factor until late in the hiring process.[96]

Indiana has enacted an expansive law making expungement and sealing of records mandatory for records where there has been no conviction. For most misdemeanors and less serious felonies, expungement is mandatory upon a determination of eligibility; serious felonies are also eligible for expungement through a discretionary decision.[97] Expungement restores civil rights (including firearms rights in all but domestic violence cases), limits employer and licensing board inquiries about criminal history, regulates background checking practices, prohibits licensing and employment "discrimination" based on an expunged conviction or arrest record, and protects employers from liability for negligent hiring based on an employee's criminal record. In all cases, the law states that an expunged conviction shall be treated "as if the person had never been convicted of the offense."[98]

The supervising prosecutor in one Indiana county emphasizes, "Our goal is to encourage success and make ex-offenders productive members of society." For this prosecutor, expungement introduces no worries about enlarging incentives for lawbreaking and instead underscores the layers of punishment that have extended beyond criminal sentences. Juries and even judges involved in sentencing are often unaware of such additional negative consequences, yet they hamper people's reintegration into society after completing their criminal sentences. Other Indiana prosecutors object to felony expungements even of low-level offenses, where expungement is mandated by statute for those who meet the criteria. Struggles to implement the law demonstrate contrasting views about forgiveness among prosecutors and judges in the state, even as the courts step in to implement the law and pro bono lawyers offer help.[99]

Granting relief from collateral consequences of criminal convictions is another remedy that stops short of a full pardon and might spur more illegality but nonetheless offers real benefits. Convictions can make people ineligible for many jobs and licenses, public housing, voting rights, jury service, military service, and governmental aid, including student loans.[100] Partial or conditional pardons at the federal or state level can relieve individuals of these burdens.[101]

Twenty-three states have recently broadened second-chance legislation, enhancing opportunities for reentry and reintegration in a nation with a massive number of convictions.[102] Two cities in California recently decided to forgive old convictions for marijuana possessions, following the state's legalization of recreational use of marijuana.[103] Even without requests from affected individuals, the district attorney in San Francisco automatically erased convictions; San Diego's government proceeded either to clear or to downgrade the convictions from felonies to misdemeanors.[104] Other states that have approved recreational marijuana now allow people with prior convictions for possession to apply to vacate or clear them.[105] These efforts, like pardons by presidents and governors, offer forgiveness in light of changes in public opinion and in criminal law, and they acknowledge that "mistakes can be remedied, broken lives can be repaired, and rips in the national fabric can be mended."[106] In spirit and in practice, such efforts sound the themes of restorative justice—repair relationships, strengthen the community, offer people fresh starts, and support positive steps for the future.

Amnesties or pardons granted with conditions, and lesser relief such as commutations and expungements, may actually reduce incentives for others to disobey, because unlike full pardons, they limit forgiveness for past violations. But it is fair to expect that forgiving attitudes toward disobedience may inevitably encourage disobedience. This can be a worthy gamble, in exchange for the benefits of amnesties and related relief. The potential benefits include not only reintegration of past offenders but also the healing of social or political divisions and recognizing individual contrition and good works. Yet another important benefit is building respect for and trust in legal institutions, for those who view the law as unfair or biased; by communicating that law can be forgiving rather than mindlessly rigid, amnesties and pardons can convey connection with such concerns.

Perhaps more controversially, another possible benefit is allowing room for a certain amount of disobedience. In a democracy, disobedience can be a way to express substantive disagreement with particular laws; violations by individuals can also give occasion for legal and political checks and balances to work. Acts of disobedience can gain attention and generate legal responses by courts, legislatures, and the public.

Civil disobedience was an essential tactic of the 1960s civil rights movement. Initially, the legal system was unforgiving: a state court punished Dr. Martin Luther King, Jr., for leading a march in violation of a court order even when the underlying ordinance was itself found unconstitutional.[107] The Supreme

Court affirmed the punishment despite arguments on King's behalf that the order had been issued without giving him a chance to be heard and that the order, based on the ordinance, was itself unconstitutional. In so doing, the Court enforced the unforgiving "collateral bar rule," created in the Alabama state courts. The collateral bar rule forbade any judicial consideration of a challenge to the substance of a court order by someone who disobeyed the order before coming to court to challenge it; hence the rule prevented Dr. King from attacking the constitutionalization of the ban on his march even as a defense once he had been charged with contempt of court for violating it.[108] In a typical criminal case, a defendant can raise legal objections to a law even after violating it, but the collateral bar rule prevents this kind of challenge. The decision in *Walker v. Birmingham* remains troubling, especially because the Court itself identified an exception where the court order is "transparently invalid."[109] This would seem to be precisely such a case,[110] given that, in a lawsuit brought by another minister who did not violate the order, the Supreme Court later found both the denial of a parade permit and the injunction forbidding the march—the antecedents of Dr. King's contempt punishment—to be constitutionally defective.

In the long term, the acts of civil disobedience led by Dr. King fueled political and legal change. He used his time in prison to write "Letter from Birmingham Jail." There, he defended direct action as necessary to create change and justified violating the unjust laws. He closed his letter, addressed to eight white religious leaders who had questioned the movement's tactics, with a request for forgiveness:

If I have said anything in this letter that is an understate-
ment of the truth and is indicative of an unreasonable
impatience, I beg you to forgive me. If I have said anything in this letter that is an overstatement of the truth
and is indicative of my having a patience that makes me
patient with anything less than brotherhood, I beg God
to forgive me.[111]

Dr. King's "Letter from Birmingham Jail" was a pivotal document of the 1960s civil rights movement, a stirring, internationally known affirmation of disciplined civil disobedience
and moral judgment.

The power to forgive legal wrongdoings acknowledges the
potential imperfection of law itself. To consider amnesties and
pardons is to examine and halt mistakes in norms, procedures,
or applications of law. One reason executives should retain
and use the pardon power is to check overly zealous or biased
prosecutions, excessively punitive rules, and simply mistaken
policies. The founders of the United States and the state constitutions planned that executive power could correct wrongs,
heal divisions, and temper justice with forgiveness.[112] George
Washington pardoned participants in the Whiskey Rebellion and expressed some sympathy for the farmer-distillers on
Pennsylvania's southwestern frontier who resisted payment of a
federal excise tax on whiskey. Although he authorized military
force to put down the rebellion, he pardoned convicted rebels
in the interest of the public good, with as much "moderation
and tenderness which the national justice, dignity, and safety
may permit."[113]

President Trump's Pardon of Sheriff Arpaio

Pardons and amnesties, available in many legal systems, can be used to release individuals from otherwise justified sanctions and to help communities and societies let go of grievances. Executive pardon power can be a corrective to mistakes by others. But sometimes the grant of a pardon or amnesty generates new resentments and even condemnation. Although early negative reactions may be overtaken with the passage of time, the firestorm after President Donald Trump pardoned Sheriff Joe Arpaio is not likely to dissipate.

President Trump pardoned the former six-term Arizona sheriff whose practices gave rise to a 2011 lawsuit in which he was ordered to stop unconstitutional racial profiling in detaining and harassing residents of a predominantly Latino neighborhood. In the same year, a federal Department of Justice investigation concluded that Arpaio had engaged in "unconstitutional policing" through discriminatory police practices, jailing, and retaliation against people who made complaints.[114] In 2016, in the face of evidence that Sheriff Arpaio continued these practices, a federal judge found him in civil contempt of the court and, after further disobedience and a five-day trial, found him guilty of criminal contempt.[115] In 2016 Arpaio ran for reelection and lost. As an early and vocal supporter of candidate Donald Trump, Arpaio also became a focal point at campaign rallies where the candidate revved up his supporters, asking: "Do the people in this room like Sheriff Joe? . . . So was Sheriff Joe convicted for doing his job?"[116]

President Trump chose Arpaio for the first pardon of his

presidency, which unleashed public disapproval from a wide range of people and triggered new questions about the scope of the presidential pardon power. Senator John McCain criticized the pardon because it "undermined the president's claim for the respect of rule of law."[117] Senator McCain also focused on Arpaio's lack of remorse.[118] In fact, the sheriff claimed he had done nothing wrong. Confronted with Arpaio's acts and lack of remorse, critics argue that President Trump's pardon itself was legally faulty, despite historic traditions treating the pardon power as free of constraints.[119] Some call President Trump's pardon of Sheriff Arpaio an impeachable offense.[120] A legal challenge framed by the advocacy group Protect Democracy argues, contrary to conventional wisdom, that this pardon exceeded the president's constitutional power; although the pardon power initially was largely unconstrained, subsequent constitutional amendments guaranteeing equal protection and due process have modified it, with the guidance of equal protection and due process.[121]

What makes President Trump's pardon of Sheriff Arpaio so wrong? At a very basic level, it used the exceptional pardon power to reward a prominent campaign supporter. Short only of an exchange for a cash bribe or a pardon of oneself, this pardon-to-a-supporter is a direct form of self-dealing.[122] Here it smacks of President Clinton's pardon for Marc Rich, whose wife had contributed substantially to Clinton campaigns.[123]

Further, the pardon of Arpaio signals to other supporters that this president is willing to use the pardon power in this manner.[124] Given the simultaneous investigations by Congress and by an independent counsel appointed by the Department of Justice into possible collusion between President Trump's campaign and Russian officials, the Arpaio pardon communicates "to Trump's current and former aides that, if they are threatened with contempt for refusing to testify, he will pardon them too."[125]

But the wrongness of the Arpaio pardon goes deeper. It is shocking because of the thorough documentation not only of illegal conduct but also of cruelty and gross mistreatment under Arpaio's command. Nearly all the deaths in the jails he ran are unexplained; jail staff denied medical attention to inmates, including a pregnant woman, who lost her baby.[126] Journalists documented Arpaio's racist tirades and efforts to humiliate people;[127] his establishment of a "jail" (known in the community as a "concentration camp") using army surplus tents in sweltering heat with minimal food, excessive force, and restraints; and his sweeps stopping cars, looking for "illegal immigrants."[128] No one has challenged the findings that his practices violated statutes, regulations, and the Constitution. All this makes the pardon appalling.

How should we assess the risk that pardons increase incentives for people to disobey the law? The pardon of Arpaio for judicial contempt—he had disobeyed a direct order to comply with the law—not only flouts the law itself but is a direct invitation for disobedience. Pardoning someone who constantly manifests disrespect for law compounds this risk. Arpaio's disrespect for courts made him infamous among other law enforcement officials. He disregarded direct orders to halt his illegal practices. And in this instance, his disregard was not a single act but a consistent mode of operation. Found first in civil contempt and then, after continuing violations, in criminal contempt for his violations of direct orders to halt his practices, Arpaio remained disdainful of the judiciary and of the law. To pardon someone who gives no showing of remorse is unusual; to pardon a law enforcement official who so thoroughly disdained the law is to excuse or honor that attitude of disrespect for law and for the courts.

Pardoning a law enforcement official who disrespects the law further degrades the law and the judiciary, but here it was the president himself who disrespected law.[129] While still a candidate, Trump repeatedly questioned the fairness of federal Judge Gonzalo Curiel, who presided over a fraud suit against Trump University, because Curiel is "Mexican" (although actually he was born in Indiana, in the United States, and has always been a U.S. citizen) and because Trump planned a border wall.[130] Unlike other presidents who disagreed at times with court rulings, Trump openly attacks the integrity of judges and of the judiciary.[131] After a terrorist assault in Manhattan, on October 31, 2017, President Trump attacked the courts as "a joke and a laughingstock" and stated "no wonder so much" terrorism takes place in light of the courts. His pardon of Arpaio expresses a similar attitude.[132]

The Arpaio pardon may in fact encourage others to flout official authority and disobey any law. That it does so specifically in the context of constitutional civil rights protections marks a disturbing rejection of crucial successes in the nation's long journey toward civil rights enforcement. With a constitution that embraced rather than rejected slavery, a bloody civil war leading to slavery's end, and a subsequent century of legal struggles to effectuate rights for African Americans, the United States has made progress largely through judicial action that restricts state and local violations. State officials vowed "massive resistance" to court-ordered desegregation, but federal court decisions prevailed. President Trump's pardon of Sheriff Arpaio expresses contempt for this long struggle and gives comfort to any who would disregard civil rights and judicial enforcement. It is starkly different from Dr. Martin Luther King, Jr.'s, nonviolent disobedience of a court order that was later found to be unconstitutional. King was a private individual, resisting illegally conducted state power, while Arpaio was a state law enforcement official, disobeying a federal court order protecting the rights of others.

While the Arpaio pardon was still only a suggestion made by candidate Trump, Vanita Gupta said that it would "not be a dog whistle to the so-called 'alt right' and white supremacists, but a bull horn." Lawyers at the American Civil Liberties Union said a pardon for Arpaio "would just be the latest injustice to befall the countless people wronged by his years of racism, lawlessness, and abuse."[133] The actual granting of the pardon to Arpaio follows in a line of actions by President Trump that condone white supremacy and deploy the distinct power of the office of the presidency to do so.[134]

But even a pardon does not erase history. Indeed, because accepting a pardon means conceding guilt, Arpaio sought to vacate (undo) the contempt judgment. U.S. District Judge Susan Bolton declined, reasoning that a pardon does not "revise the historical facts" of the case. Quoting the basic reference text, *Black's Law Dictionary,* she explained that a pardon "releases the wrongdoer from punishment and restores the offender's civil rights without qualification," but "it does not erase a judgment of conviction, or its underlying legal and faculty findings."[135] The pardon relieved Arpaio of punishment, but did not change the facts of his crime. Forgiving is not forgetting.

Yes, the presidential pardon power as stated in the U.S. Constitution is almost limitless. Pardons and amnesties can introduce needed generosity, avenues for peacemaking, tempering of rigid retribution, recognition of repentance and good deeds, and practical measures to help individuals and communities let go of grievances, even well-justified ones. The legal devices of forgiveness, pardon, amnesty, commutation, and reprieve can check overreach by government, erect escape valves for social division, or create avenues for debate and social change.[136] But even pardons and amnesties can go wrong, and those granting them should be held accountable and restrained by law and morality. Pardons and amnesties risk inviting corruption, discriminatory use, unpredictability, and unfairness. Any pardon or amnesty could encourage further illegality.

The legal tools of forgiveness can themselves be abused, but that should not be a reason for less forgiveness in the law. Instead, it should be a reason for developing rigorous, reasoned analysis about when forgiveness is and is not warranted. Pardons should not be used where the underlying crime demonstrates absolute disregard for the rule of law; it also should not be used to excuse violations by government officials of the civil rights of others. Developing procedural and substantive guideposts for using the pardon power would strengthen it, not weaken it, especially if those guideposts guarded against corruption and conflicting interests. Other nations, with constitutions written centuries after the U.S. founding document, set limits on executive pardon power.[137] Some give the power to a multiperson council; some combine such a council with an executive.[138] Several nations reserve pardon authority for legislatures or require participation by multiple branches of government.[139] A recent trend authorizes judicial review of clemency, making the act of forgiveness subject to standards of fair process and the check of judges' consideration.[140]

Justice Anthony Kennedy once called for a reinvigoration of the atrophied pardon process because "a people confident in its laws and institutions should not be ashamed of mercy."[141] Forgiveness within the law, exercised wisely and fairly, strengthens the law and justifies people's faith in it.

CHAPTER 4

REFLECTIONS

❦

I WROTE A BOOK a while back on using law, art, memorials, and other social resources to trace a path between vengeance and forgiveness.[1] Ever since, people have asked me: Why seek an alternative *between* vengeance and forgiveness? Why not promote forgiveness itself? Forgiveness by individuals, groups, and even governments affords a valuable resource in responding to wrongs, so why shouldn't legal systems use it explicitly? Societies make and enforce laws because human beings have great capacities to hurt one another. We should not be surprised to find that the law itself can do damage.

But harms can come not only when law goes awry but also when it is carefully and accurately implemented. Fully enforced criminal laws produce much punishment but not necessarily better people or a better society, and perfectly enforced laws can recover financial debts but not end indebtedness. Law professor Grant Gilmore put it well: "In heaven there will be no law, and the lion shall lie down with the lamb. . . . In Hell there will be nothing but law, and due process will be meticulously observed."[2]

Elaborating the point, Gilmore stressed that law reflects the moral worth of a society, and more law is needed in societies that are less just.[3] Forgiveness in law adjusts imperfections within the rules and those that implement them; it can also acknowledge larger social failures to prevent misery, restrain power, or realize justice. Forgiveness offers wrongdoers a fresh start; it wipes the slate clean.[4] The legal procedure of bankruptcy does that; amnesties and pardons can, too. How about taking this idea on board more fully to limit the collateral consequences of criminal punishments; to enact general norms and design dispute systems that focus on the future as they work to resolve conflicts; and to allow legal officials to use their discretion to act with leniency when justified?

Promoting legal forgiveness, however, may jeopardize the predictability, reliability, and equal treatment sought by the rule of law. Using legal processes to coerce individuals to forgive would be abusive and even counterproductive, although adversarial legal processes may also influence people's emotions in unproductive ways. The challenge is to amplify law's support for forgiveness while preserving the rule of law. Law needs sufficient respect for those who have suffered harms and for those who have caused harm in order to attend to the past and prepare for the future.

Looking back at the examples pursued in this book, we may conclude that individuals who became child soldiers should not be subject to international criminal sanctions; nor should they be categorically exempted from accountability.[5] Forgiving them requires acknowledging their wrongdoing. Domestic and international institutions could construct distinctive means both to acknowledge the wrongdoing and to assist the individuals and their societies in constructing positive next steps. The former child soldiers could become involved in devising juvenile-justice-style hearings, truth commissions, or other formats for acknowledgment, while also performing community service and receiving educational and therapeutic help. Youth involved in gangs and illegal drug trades, like child soldiers, are caught in webs made by their elders; they, too, could become part of restorative justice efforts that educate the community and assist their own transition toward constructive adulthood.

As for sovereign debt, it should be eligible for forgiveness and restructuring through legal frameworks that function like domestic bankruptcy procedures; similarly, tax incentives provided by domestic governments could promote nongovernmental buybacks to help relieve crushing student and consumer debt. Mechanisms for forgiving consumer debt in this country deserve more attention.

By analogy to the fresh start afforded through bankruptcy, what would enable a fresh start after a criminal conviction? For someone who has already served a criminal sentence, collateral consequences such as being barred from holding occupational and drivers' licenses, and excluded from housing and from voting, prevent a fresh start. Expungement of records and reentry programs could help. So could "ban the box" initiatives directing employers to consider a job candidate's qualifications first, apart from a criminal record.[6]

Other legal fields afford further perspectives. Take naturalization and immigration. In September 1944, Louis Repouille, an immigrant to the United States, sought to become naturalized—to become a U.S. citizen. The governing law, then as now, requires that such applicants demonstrate "good moral character" during the five years prior to the application;[7] no evidence about conduct prior to the previous five years matters. Unfortunately, four years and forty-nine weeks before his application, Repouille engaged in an act that led to his prosecution for manslaughter.

What was the act? He used a chemical compound to put one of his five children to death. This child, then thirteen years old, had severe brain damage; he was blind and unable to communicate, control his bodily functions, feed himself, or move. Repouille was indicted for manslaughter in the first degree, a serious offense but one treated as less serious than murder because of mitigating circumstances. The jury, after hearing the evidence and arguments submitted during the trial, both agreed and disagreed: It convicted Repouille of manslaughter in the *second* degree (meaning the killing reflected recklessness or negligence rather than intention). The jury wrote the judge a note recommending the "utmost clemency." The judge, in turn, stayed the sentence—suspending any punishment—and then placed Repouille on probation, which he served. That ended the criminal case. Four years and forty-nine weeks after he killed his son, Repouille applied to become a U.S. citizen. What would you do, if presented with his application? How should we view his manslaughter conviction in light of the legal standard requiring the applicant to demonstrate "good moral character" for the prior five years? As so often happens, the litigation turned complex issues of fact, law, and morality into a yes-or-no question: Did Repouille demonstrate good moral character, enough to become a naturalized citizen—yes or no?

Repouille's naturalization case raises at least two questions:[8] Should the jury's or judge's positions in the criminal case express a kind of understanding—a kind of forgiveness—of his act of killing that should lead to a judicial grant of U.S. citizenship? Was the best answer to grant or to deny him citizenship—or find some other response?

As the naturalization case proceeded, the trial judge at the federal district court found that Repouille had demonstrated good moral character and ordered the government to grant him citizenship. The district attorney appealed the decision. The three judges on the Court of Appeals for the Second Circuit wrestled with whether "good moral character" should be defined through deference to experts in ethics, public opinion polls, or some other method, and they concluded, in less than crystal-clear prose: "Left at large as we are, without means of verifying our conclusion, and without authority to substitute our individual beliefs, the outcome must needs be tentative; and not much is gained by discussion."[9] They basically said, "It's too hard! We cannot decide, and because it is unclear, Mr. Repouille fails; we are not persuaded either way, and he loses because he had the burden to persuade us."[10] But the appeals court opinion did not stop there. It specifically told Repouille that he could file again later, putting more than five years between the act of killing and the application for citizenship. Presumably the government would look at the uneventful intervening five years and grant him citizenship.[11]

The decision, authored by a distinguished judge with the unusual name of Learned Hand, illuminates multiple points in a legal case when forgiveness can be granted as well as ambivalence about doing so. The dictionary defines *forgiveness* as "allowing for a degree of imperfection." The court noted that the jury imposed a verdict for something less than the charged crime and also recommended utmost clemency; the judge exercised discretion to stay execution of the sentence and prescribed probation only. The appellate court did not forgive the mistake made by Repouille, or more likely by his lawyer, in applying for naturalization shortly before the five-year period had lapsed. But it did offer a kind of forgiveness in allowing Repouille to file a new petition five years following the killing; it dismissed the present naturalization case "without prejudice" against a later filing—and thus permitted a clean slate for purposes of litigation. A broader element of forgiveness is present in the five-year cap itself, through which Congress allowed those like Repouille to start afresh. The legislature might have adopted the five-year period for demonstrating good moral character in order to limit the burden of fact-finding needed for the naturalization decision or to allow people room to make mistakes and recover from them. Either way, the statutory framework, for purposes of citizenship applications, lets go of potential blame for bad moral conduct arising before that time.

Imagine what a court would do with a petition from a genocidal leader who waited nearly five years after the genocide before filing citizenship; it is hard to believe that a court would say, "What the heck, wait a few weeks and file again."[12] Even if such a person waited until after the five years had passed, would a court ignore the past and treat the naturalization law as excluding prior genocidal acts? Or would a court creatively interpret the law to permit evidence of acts taken more than five years previously, or effects of those actions falling within the more recent years?

In the United States, contemporary debates over immigration have made questions of forgiveness central in presidential elections and in high-profile litigation, but here the violations at issue concern immigration law.[13] Restrictions on immigration are a prerogative of every sovereign nation. Enforcing them is challenging in a nation with multiple and long borders. In addition, inconsistent enforcement may reflect inconsistent public policies, especially in countries that need, or that exploit, the relatively cheap labor of undocumented workers to fill jobs that citizens do not want.[14] During World War II, needs for labor increased sufficiently that Congress approved a partnership with Mexico to permit temporary employment for Mexican workers.[15] After labor organizing efforts and strikes exposed poor working conditions, the program lapsed, perhaps because some employers concluded that they could pay less for undocumented workers, and perhaps because resentment by U.S. citizens grew. In the meantime, American farming became partly dependent on immigrant workers, and many noncitizen families came to expect periodic work opportunities in the United States.[16]

Efforts by both Presidents George W. Bush and Barack Obama to enact comprehensive reform of immigration laws failed in Congress but gave rise to a particular focus on the children of undocumented immigrants, nicknamed "Dreamers," following the unsuccessful Development, Relief, and Education for Alien Minors (DREAM) Act. Their presence in the country stemmed from decisions not of their own making; many came as very young children with no experience in their parents' home country; and all attended American schools. All told, they were appealing candidates for exceptions to immigration laws criminalizing their presence in the country and exposing them to risks of prosecution and deportation. In 2012, toward the end of his second presidential campaign, President Obama issued an executive order giving undocumented immigrants under the age of thirty authorization to be lawfully employed and to avoid deportation, but with no path to citizenship.[17] Called Deferred Action for Childhood Arrivals (DACA), the program offered temporary amnesty to the Dreamers; the program in a practical way codified the president's informal discretionary power to direct the use of limited resources for immigration law enforcement, including to the benefit of undocumented individuals. By transparently declaring the forgiving policy as a general order, President Obama pursued political benefit but also triggered a firestorm of objections.

Through court action, critics challenged President Obama's 2014 effort to launch a similar program, Deferred Action for Parents of Americans and Lawful Permanent Residents (DAPA), affording protections to the parents of U.S. citizens.[18] Critics challenged the executive order in court by asserting that the president lacks constitutional authority to change the practice of the law without changing the legislation.[19] While running for the presidency, Donald Trump vowed to end DACA, but when he tried to do so after the election, defenders of the program successfully brought lawsuits to halt his action,[20] amplifying polarized political views over temporary immigration law amnesties.

Like child soldiers and gang-involved youth, the Dreamers did not create their situations and instead are caught in larger forces. They seem especially worthy of legal forgiveness, because their only culpable voluntary act was failing to leave the country of their families, their schooling, their friends, and their imagined futures. In all these instances, the youth have some degree of choice, but debates over their legal status should be broadened to address the larger power plays and policy conflicts produced and shaped by adults who direct and at times coerce minors. That context should matter. A report of experts warned against blaming individuals who carried out violent attacks without exploring the social and political contexts for the violence: "Put simply, an exclusive focus upon naming the 18-year-old paramilitary who carries out a sectarian or racist murder obfuscates the role of the sectarian or racist demagogue who inspired him to take up an AK47 or a machete in the first place."[21]

To pursue forgiveness in law is to focus on building a better future. Often this involves shifting from a focus on a specific violator and specific victim to use of a wider lens— not to negate the violation and its immediate harm but to understand the broader patterns and consider fair paths forward for all. This wider lens is often accompanied by forgiveness, because letting go of even warranted grievances permits empathy, understanding, and interest in what contributes to past problems and future solutions.

Concentric circles of people, incentives, and causes influence violations of the law. Restorative justice efforts broaden the focus from the wrongdoer and victim to these concentric circles and explore the effects and contributions of others, in the school or community, past and future. They do so not to excuse the person immediately responsible but to clarify the interconnections between people, forces, and structures that contributed to the wrong, as well as connections to those who can make a difference in the future. Especially in the context of civil war and massive violence, letting go of the past may call for recognizing responsibilities beyond those of the individuals immediately at fault. Michael Ignatieff, an expert on centuries of violent Balkan conflicts, challenges the "myth of blamelessness,"[22] the idea that everyone with a grievance is only a victim and never contributed to centuries of civil war with plenty of blame on both sides. The South African political philosopher and activist Wilhelm Verwoerd, who has worked on truth and reconciliation processes in Northern Ireland, calls for "inclusive moral remembrance."[23] Acknowledging the concentric circles of people who influenced violence and lawbreaking, recognizing that even victims might have contributed to a problem, and seeing that even those who did not cause a problem may have the ability to ease its consequences—these perspectives help individuals, groups, and nations let go of grievances and move forward.

Alternative means of dispute resolution, such as mediation to address employment disputes and settlement conferences for complex litigation, can create contexts where apologies and reparations contribute to solutions, allowing people to move forward with their lives. Forward-looking processes can even address serious human rights violations with occasions where parties can collaborate.[24]

Discharging debt through a bankruptcy process addresses larger patterns: It brings together multiple parties who look to the future while remedying broken promises. It not only acknowledges and adjusts the behavior of the immediate parties, the debtor and creditors, but also implicates the larger credit market and even the bad luck that influences debt. Methods of forgiving sovereign debt could have similar elements: they could involve multiple parties, respond to broken promises, address the future, and recognize the elements of luck and ripple effects in credit markets. Broadening the frame of law could locate consumer debt, student loans, and sovereign debt inside broader patterns of conduct by credit card companies, for-profit schools, international lenders, government pension managers, and other actors who contribute to defaults on debt. The point is not to deny the responsibility of the debtors but to develop modes of prevention and reform that reflect others' contributions to the problem, as well as potential solutions. Similarly encompassing the society's needs, amnesties for Vietnam War resisters and for undocumented immigrants reflect the bigger forces within which individuals make decisions that bring them in violation of the law.

Cultural contexts affect the resonance of legal and social practices that make room for forgiveness by the government or by the individuals directly involved. A group of social scientists asked Latin Americans (all from Uruguay) and western Europeans (all from France) about forgiveness and found that a majority from both regions value it, even without assuming a change in heart or repentance by the violator.[25] Interestingly, those in Latin America were more likely than those in western

Europe to accept someone other than the offended person as the forgiver: someone like a family member or even an institution such as a church.[26]

No one should assume that what works well in one society will work in another. Nonetheless, the legal and social practices of diverse societies around dispute resolution and their avenues for forgiveness within law offer potential contrasts and possibilities. The use of a review process for pardons from punishment in some communities has inspired others to consider adopting or adapting it. Many countries provide for judicial review or participation by a board or cabinet of advisers.[27] Even if there is no prospect for judicial review or other oversight of executive parties in the United States, the fact that other nations do provide such a check challenges claims that pardons lie outside reasoned justifications. Perhaps, even with no change in the structure of power, the United States could develop a jurisprudence of pardons, articulating acceptable and unacceptable grounds and circumstances for granting them. Enforceable by public approval and ultimately by elections, a jurisprudence of pardons would create expectations of acceptable reasons for particular exercises of official discretion, which could provide a needed check against abuses and unequal treatment. The details of these suggestions are less important than their possibilities for devising legal rules and practices that support forgiveness without forgoing fairness. Extending these approaches across different fields can afford perspectives that help move beyond blame games. Including forgiveness within law requires broadening the time frame to include future considerations as well as past actions and attending to patterns of effects with both generosity and commitments to fairness.

Perspectives that include forgiveness while adhering to norms of equal treatment are needed now more than ever, as the techniques of statistical prediction, machine learning, and other features of artificial intelligence become tools for law. Some people hope to restrict discretion of judges and other legal officials by using artificial intelligence, analyses of past decisions, and predictive algorithms. Human discretion would still be part of the design of such approaches. The real promise of computer-assisted decision making is the pressure to make explicit the factors at work—and to audit the results in light of public values.[28] Journalist Julia Angwin highlights risks of "unjustified forgiveness" as algorithms are used to devise risk scores as tools for making decisions about bail, probation, sentencing, or parole. The algorithms may overestimate the percentage of repeat offenders among black defendants and underestimate the probability of white recidivism.[29] Feeding the algorithms data that reflect disparate (or biased) law enforcement practices will repeat or amplify problematic practices. Rather than replacing human judgment, machine learning can push human beings to be more explicit and self-reflective about their judgments, predictions, biases, and use of discretion.[30]

—

THE NATION OF BHUTAN—which originated the concept of Gross National Happiness—recently opened its first law school.[31] As it teaches future lawyers, the law school prepares students to handle disputes in a formal court system founded on rights and adversarial views, as well as dispute resolution through village elders, which is predicated on conciliation to maintain social harmony.[32] Professor Stephen Sonnenberg decided to begin the first contracts class at the new school with:

> a series of preliminary in-depth interviews with village elders *before* diving into the more standard contracts class-room doctrine. We then spent a fair amount of the remaining semester comparing "formal" doctrine with what we found in the field. One of the major take-aways in that comparison between contract law doctrine on paper, and contract law as practiced in customary [settings] was the loss of the forgiveness element in how people thought about contractual remedies. It was fascinating to hear elder testimony about the rigidity (and injustice) of the modern legal system, as opposed to their more traditional approach.[33]

Further study can illuminate whether the traditional approaches burdened some, such as women, more than others, and whether the modern system can make room for traditional elements of forgiveness.

Cultural practices and religious traditions contributed to the resonance of forgiveness at South Africa's Truth and Reconciliation Commission. Victims decided for themselves whether to forgive perpetrators, who applied for amnesty by providing full disclosure of their actions; some felt pressured to forgive; others found it helpful to hear what had happened to their loved ones. TRC chair Archbishop Desmond Tutu drew upon both Christian and traditional African notions of forgiveness and social repair, but not everyone in South Africa shared his commitment to social reconciliation.[34] The psychologist Pumla Gobodo-Madikizela, who worked with the TRC, before becoming a university professor, reported that Eugene de Kock, former chief of the death squad, asked to meet with the widows of two black policemen he had killed with a bomb. At the meeting, he apologized. One widow, Mrs. Pearl Faku, later recalled:

> I couldn't control my tears. I could hear him but I was overwhelmed by emotion, and I was just nodding as a way of saying yes, I forgive you. I hope that when he sees our tears he knows that they are not only tears for our husbands, but tears for him as well. . . . I would like to hold him by the hand and show there is a future, and that he can still change.[35]

After the 1994 Rwandan genocide, official policy, churches, and nongovernmental organizations pressured individuals to forgive, which triggered criticism and resistance by some people. Working with traumatized refugees as a psychotherapist, Esther Mujawayo refused to forgive the perpetrators, even though tempted by survivor guilt, fear, empathy, and external pressure. Some survivors may be disturbed by the lack of authentic apology from the perpetrators and concerned about submitting to the governmental policy of forgiveness. Resisting the temptation to forgive may be an important expression of personal dignity, even by one who recognizes the wrongdoer's humanity and wonders, as Mujawayo did. She noted, "who knows what we could have done in their place."[36]

Resisting the impulse to forgive is a theme emerging as the

international #MeToo movement against sexual predators and sexual harassment exposes the misconduct of men in positions of authority across business, entertainment, academia, and the judiciary.[37] Attorney Jill Filipovic comments, "The seriousness of a man's conduct must guide what his penance looks like, but every man currently in the limelight for behaving badly toward women (and the many who aren't in its glow) have an obligation to act like adults and recognize that their actions have consequences."[38] In the context of offenders in the entertainment business, one survey indicates viewers can be forgiving.[39] Thordis Elva contacted her rapist, Tom Stranger, and after eight years of communicating by mail, they met in person to explore reconciliation and forgiveness.[40] Their book prompted protests by critics who claimed it glamorized a rapist; their TED Talk garnered over four million views.[41] Investigative reporter Katie J. M. Baker reflected, "We can't require every rape survivor to not just talk with but collaborate with her rapist. Yet the interest in their story is a testament to people's hunger for a new approach"—a kind of restorative justice model. Baker continued:

> In restorative justice, victims, communities and wrongdoers together discuss the crime committed and what should be done to make amends. Restorative justice is complex and imperfect. It relies on perpetrators to first admit wrongdoing; facilitators aren't always neutral parties; and it often requires victims to communicate with their assailants. But its emphasis is on repairing and preventing harm, not indefinite, often ineffective punishment.[42]

Should legal proceedings encourage people to forgive wrongdoers? To explore forgiveness is to acknowledge that some wrongs are unforgivable. That is undeniable as a description of human beings responding to the Holocaust, other genocides, murders, or abductions of children, acts so unspeakably horrific that even asking about forgiveness can seem an insult to both victims and survivors. Legal systems around the world assign no statute of limitations for murder. The philosopher Hannah Arendt claimed that we cannot forgive absolute evils that are too large and radical to punish.[43] Others, though, press for forgiveness precisely at such a moment in order to create a parting from a terrible past.[44] Even an act that lies beyond forgiveness need not lie outside accountability.[45] Is it possible to make room for the possibility of forgiveness in the corridors and edges of formal proceedings, without using the power of the state to pressure people who have been victimized to forgive?

Forgiving under government pressure is not really forgiveness, and it places further burdens on people already victimized. Legal procedures that require apologies also undermine genuine expression of remorse. Precisely because individual forgiveness is so admirable, care should be taken to avoid false or pressured performances of it.[46] Making legal room for individuals to forgive those who have harmed them should not mean pressuring them to forgive. For some, choosing not to forgive is a source of strength and integrity; for others, mourning—not forgiveness—is the path toward letting go of resentment.[47] Some people simply have to learn to live with being unforgiven,[48] yet it remains possible to see the wrongdoer as human.[49] Accountability for others is a crucial step before forgiveness can be possible.[50] And then there is Oscar Wilde's wisdom: "Always forgive your enemies; nothing annoys them so much."[51]

———

I HAVE EXPLORED how child soldiers and other adolescents accused of criminal law violations may not be entirely innocent, but neither are they responsible for the social conditions in which they make their choices. The same can be said of individuals who are drowning in consumer debt or student loans, and even of sovereign nations, cities, and states in debt. Each is to blame when they violate promises to pay back loans or laws against violence, but each also is embedded in larger social patterns that construct limited and often poor options.

To ask how law may forgive is not to deny the fact of wrongdoing. Rather, it is to widen the lens to enable glimpses of these larger patterns and to work for new choices that can be enabled by wiping the slate clean. Making more opportunities for forgiveness within law might help law grow toward justice; it might also nudge individuals and societies toward the respect and generosity expressed through apology, restitution, and forbearance from law's most stringent demands. Law, in one way or another, affects emotions. It could support forgiveness as much as it can support revenge.

We should guard against turning to forgiveness solely because more robust justice is unavailable. Let us be careful not to deploy the power of the law to distort private emotions, and let us not elide the differences between individuals and groups. Yet let us consider how and when law can usefully express forgiveness and let go of grievances. Even and especially when law adjudicates the past, we hope it will make for a better future.

Paul Boese, a man who loved to craft sayings that would be quoted, wrote before Twitter, but he would have loved it. I will end with one of his quotations that I like so much: "Forgiveness does not change the past, but it does enlarge the future."[52] Ultimately, forgiveness points toward the future, not just toward the past, and thus it offers an important dimension for designers and agents of the law.

ACKNOWLEDGMENTS

I DON'T THINK OF MYSELF as a particularly forgiving person, but I am a profoundly grateful one, especially toward the wonderful people who have made this book possible. Anthony Appiah suggested I write it; Roby Harrington patiently waited for it, as my attention turned to duties as a dean, and then provided invigorating and invaluable comments and support. Because of the efforts of the amazing dean's staff at Harvard Law School—Liberty Kenneally, Catherine Claypoole, Cherisa Ellis, and Kelsey Ryan—I was able to pursue the initial work reflected in this book. And due to the heavenly Radcliffe Institute, led by the superb Dean Liz Cohen and by the indefatigable Fellowship Program director Judy Vichniac, the book came to fruition with daily encouragement and suggestions from the most generative fellows and most gracious staff. In particular, I thank Professor Kathryn Sikkink for thorough and thoroughly generous comments; Jane Lipson and Samantha Power supplied critical fortification.

Writing this book would not have been possible without the support of my friend John Manning as deputy dean and now as

Harvard Law School dean. Rachel Keeler expertly helped with multiple transitions, including moving this book from drafts to completion. Copy editor Janet Biehl and the team at Norton provided excellent work, turning the draft into this book.

I am so grateful for the invitation to share my work at the Brennan Center Jorde Symposium, October 20, 2014 (University of California, Berkeley) and January 8, 2015 (University of Chicago), published as Forgiveness, Law, and Justice, 103 Cal. L. Rev. 1615 (2015), https://scholarship.law.berkeley.edu/cgi/viewcontent.cgi?article=4307&context=californialawreview. During the symposium, I learned from all the participants and especially from commentators Kathryn Abrams, Aziz Huq, Christopher Kutz, and Martha Nussbaum. Versions of the Introduction received crucial comments and inspiration from participants at the Grand Forum of the Most Honorable Jurist, Renmin University, Beijing, China, on June 29, 2013; at Vassar College, Poughkeepsie, New York, February 12, 2014; at the Annual Reconciliation Lecture at the University of the Free State, South Africa, February 24, 2014; at the University of Buenos Ares, Argentina, May 15, 2017; at the Aspen Institute-Rodel Fellowship Program for elected leaders in Washington, D.C., on October 8, 2017; and at Harvard's Advanced Leadership Initiative, in Boston, Massachusetts, on May 16, 2018. Along the way, for what is now the Introduction, Lara Berlin, Marissa Brodney, Zoe Brennan-Krohn, Trevor Dodge, Taylor Poor, Julia Ratner, and Jake Weissbourd offered helpful insights and research.

An invitation to receive an award from Trinity College History Society in Dublin, Ireland, on November 13, 2012, provided an invaluable setting to explore the themes of Chapter 1. I remain deeply grateful for that invitation and for the lively discussion it engendered. Material in Chapter 1 also reflects the questions and criticisms of Professors Fionnuala D. Ní Aoláin, Gabriella Blum, Jennifer Chacon, Jack Goldsmith, Gerry Neuman, Diane Orentlicher, and Gerald Quinn, as well as the substantial and crucial research assistance of Sima Atri, Lara Berlin, Ming Cheung, Sarah Dorman, Gillian Grossman, Sharon Kim, Taylor Poor, Melissa Proctor, Derecka Purnell, Julia Ratner, Jacob Steiner, and Domonique Worship. The comments of Camilla Barker and Mindy Roseman, and of participants in the Harvard Human Rights Program workshop, made a real difference. Invaluably, Jonathan Wroblewski shared his deep knowledge of criminal justice and so thoughtfully commented on the entire manuscript; Michael H. Ryong Jung shared his analytic precision, legal expertise, and passion for justice for young people; and Theresa Betancourt's spectacular work in the field and abundant advice taught me more than I can say about the experiences of and prospects for former child soldiers.

Turning to earlier versions of Chapter 2 on debt, particular thanks go to Terry Aladjem, Bill Alford, Lauren Anstey, Tom Brennan, Justin Cahill, Anna Gelpern, John Coates, Charlie Donahue, Charles Fried, Chris Hampson, Donna Harati, Seth Klarman, Bill Rubenstein, Aime Salazar, Steve Shay, Holger Spamann, Brandon Storm, Cass Sunstein, Roberto Unger, and Jonathan Zittrain for helpful comments and questions, and to the Social Studies community at Harvard University who attended my Navin Narayan Memorial Lecture at Harvard on October 29, 2014.

Adriaan Lanni's scholarship and comments gave vital insights into the historical material in Chapter 3; Roy Kellenberg provided a reminder to think about hope for a different future when forgiveness does not seem quite right. For that chapter, and indeed for the entire book, my remarkable Radcliffe research fellows Carissa Chen, Isabel Espinosa, Blessing Jee, Hilda Jordan, Flora Li, and Luke Minton brought powerful questions, materials, and enthusiasm. Over multiple years, my creative and unflagging research assistants Ariel Eckblad, Trevor Dodge, Travis Edwards, Jon Gould, Chris Marks, Sonia McNeil, Morgan Meagher, Daniel Morales, Paloma O'Connor, Sylvanus Polky, Daniel Saver, Jeanne Segil, Alexander Rodney, Hannah Solomon-Strauss, and Jake Weissbourd offered rich and detailed comments, sources, questions, and insights.

For the project as a whole, my emphatic thanks go to Danielle Allen for arranging the Harvard Safra Center workshop on the book draft on May 16, 2018, and to Cheryl Bratt, John Goldberg, Jonathon Gould, Nien-hê Hsieh, Tommie Shelby, Carol Steiker, Danielle herself, and other participants for their spectacular comments and advice. Thanks also to my colleagues at Harvard Law School who shared ideas and insight during faculty workshops and informal conversations. During 2018, Liz Lerman shared her creativity and wisdom and brought together talented artists for a collaborative inquiry into forgiveness and law as a subject for dance; what a gift this has been and will continue to be. For support both intellectual and personal, my deep thanks go to Bill Alford, Larry Blum, Mary Casey, Nancy Gertner, Gish Jen, Randy Kennedy, Rabbi Jonathan Kraus, Liz Schneider, Molly Shanley, Vicky Spelman, Rick Weissbourd, and my spectacularly forgiving family. Mira Singer's fine, meticulous editorial hand appears on every page. Indeed, in exploring the best ideas here, demonstrating the give-and-take of generous listening, and offering the best diversions and escapades, none are better than Joe Singer, Mira Singer, Jo Minow, Newton Minow, Mary Minow, Nell Minow, and David Apatoff.

Throughout this project, my students have been constant, challenging, and kind interlocutors. How illuminating to learn alongside the engaged students in the spring 2013 Harvard Law School Reading Group on Law and Forgiveness and the convivial students at the Richardson Law School at the University of Hawai'i January 2018 course on law and forgiveness (thanks to Dean Avi Soifer for the opportunity and advice!); how invigorating to talk with students willing to engage in serious debates about law and forgiveness at welcome events at Harvard Law School between 2010 and 2016; and how grateful I am to students, past, present and future, for inspiring my hope in the possibilities of both fresh starts and concentric circles of care and responsibility. I am most thankful for this chance to say thanks.

NOTES

Introduction

1. Jill Stauffer, A Hearing: Forgiveness, Resentment, and Recovery in Law, 30 Quinnipiac L. Rev. 517 (2011–12).

2. "Forgiveness offers something that punishing cannot give: in forgiving, we allow the wrongdoer to make a genuinely fresh start; the slate is wiped clean." Lucy Allais, Wiping the Slate Clean: The Heart of Forgiveness, 36 Philos. & Public Aff. 33, 68 (2008).

3. Hannah Arendt viewed forgiveness as the human faculty for undoing deeds and words that have been spoken, and "the necessary corrective for the inevitable damages resulting from action." Hannah Arendt, The Human Condition 215 (1958). Her work, following World War II, sounded notes resonant in the later American civil rights movement and in post-apartheid South Africa. Elisabeth Young-Bruehl, Why Arendt Matters 110–14 (2006).

4. For a thoughtful treatment of legal forgiveness, see John D. Inazu, No Future Without (Personal) Forgiveness: Re-examining the Role of Personal Forgiveness in Transitional Justice, 10 Hum. Rts. J. 209 (2009) (viewing legal forgiveness as the state's cancelation of a debt that it is owed, and distinguishing personal, group, and political forgiveness).

5. Donald H. Bishop, Forgiveness in Religious Thought, 2 Stud. Comp. Relig. (1968), http://www.studiesincomparativereligion.com/uploads/ArticlePDFs/38.pdf. For detailed discussion of the multiple discussions and meanings of forgiveness in Jewish and Christian traditions, see 9 Encyclopedia of the Bible and Its Reception 436468 (2014). The Christian tradition teaches, "If your brother or sister sins against you, rebuke them, and if they repent, forgive them. Even if they sin against you seven times in a day and seven times come back to you saying 'I repent,' you must forgive them" (Luke 17:304). Buddhist practices of letting go and forgiveness clear out vengeful feelings. See Thanissaro Bhikkhu, Three

Tactics from the Buddha to Forgive Without Feeling Defeated, Tricycle (Feb. 17, 2018), https://tricycle.org/trikedaily/three-tactics-forgive-without-defeat/. Jewish tradition teaches: "From where do we know that it is cruel to not forgive? For it says, 'Abraham prayed to G-d and G-d healed Abimelech.' (Bereishit [Genesis] 20:17). Mishna in Baba Kamma 8:7. Jewish Law (Halacha) requires one to ask forgiveness from anyone whom you may have harmed, whether the harm was physical, financial, emotional, or social. Also, one is required to be gracious in granting forgiveness." Forgiveness, Ahavat-Israel, http://www.ahavat-israel.com/am/forgive. See also Mishnet Torah Teshuva 2:10 ("When asked by an offender for forgiveness, one should forgive with a sincere mind and a willing spirit.") Hindu teachings emphasize that "the act of seeking (prar-thana) forgiveness (kshama, daya, krupa) may be carried out unilaterally, without the presence, permission, or expectation of the other side. The act of extending deliverance (anugraha-pradana) or forgiving (karunya, advesha, ab-haya) may also take place unilaterally without the presence, permission, or expectation of acceptance from the other side." Forgiveness in Hinduism, What-When-How, http://what-when-how.com/love-in-world-religions/forgiveness-in-hinduism/. See Gita Rad-hakrishna, The Law and the Concept of Forgiveness, 1 Asian J. L. & Governance 313 (Autumn 2011).

6. Allais, supra, 33, 62. See also Lisa Belkin, Unforgiveable: Why Is It So Hard to Apologize Well—And Sound As If You Mean It? N.Y. Times (July 2, 2010), https://www.nytimes.com/2010/07/04/magazine/04fob-wwln-t.html.

7. Christina Baldwin, Life's Companion: Journal Writing as a Spiritual Question (1990).

8. See June Hunt, How to Forgive When You Don't Feel Like It (2007).

9. Nelson Mandela Transformed Himself and Then His Nation, L.A. Times (Dec. 6, 2013), http://articles.latimes.com/2013/dec/06/nation/la-na-tt-nelson-mandela-20131206.

10. For example, Jewish teachings stress that harms against people can be forgiven only by other people, not by divine authority, and they direct wrongdoers to apologize and take actions of reparation and repentance. Solomon Schimmel, Wounds Not Healed by Time: The Power of Repentance and Forgiveness (2004). See Yoma 86b ("For Resh Lakish said that repentance is so great that premeditated sins are accounted as though they were merits"). Many Christian sources encourage forgiveness even if the wrongdoer has not apologized or repented. See, e.g., Luke 23:34; Matthew 6:15; and Peter 3:8–9. See also R. T. Kendall, Forgiving the Unrepentant, Christianity Today (Mar. 9, 2005), https://www.christianitytoday.com/ct/2005/march/forgiving-the-unrepentant.html. On one view, forgiveness calls for a change of mind by the wrongdoer, and then often the one who forgives also has a change of mind, giving up earlier feelings of vengeance or unwillingness to forgive. Young-Bruehl, supra, at 103.

11. Allais, supra, at 33, 68.

12. See Jean Hampton, Forgiveness, Resentment, and Hatred, in Jeffrie G. Murphy and Jean Hampton, eds., Forgiveness and Mercy 80–81 (2010).

13. Some advocate forgiveness as a way to change attitudes toward the other, not to alter the balance of wrongdoing by punishment or repentance; see Allais, supra, 67–68.

14. Mayo Clinic Staff, Forgiveness: Letting Go of Grudges and Bitterness, Mayo Clinic (2017), http://www.mayoclinic.com/health/forgiveness/MH00131; Lecia Bushak, How Forgiveness Benefits Your Health: Forgiving Wrongdoers Can Expand Physical Fitness, Medical Daily (Jan. 7, 2015), https://www.medicaldaily.com/how-forgiveness-benefits-your-health-forgiving -wrongdoers-can-expand-physical-fitness-316902. For research on forgiveness, see, e.g., William Bole, Drew Christiansen, and Robert T. Hennemeyer, Forgiveness in International Politics: An Alternative Road to Peace (2004); Pumla Gobodo-Madikizela, Forgiveness and the Maternal Body: An African Ethics of Interconnectedness (2011); Charles Griswold, Forgiveness: A Philosophical Exploration (2008); Michael Henderson, Forgiveness: Breaking the Chain of Hate (1999); Aaron Lazare, On Apology (2005); D. Tibbits, G. Ellis, C. Piramelli, Fred Luskin, and R. Lukman, Hypertension Reduction Through Forgiveness Training, 60 Journal of Pastoral Care and Counseling 27–34 (2006); Leonel Narvaez, ed., Political Culture of Forgiveness and Reconciliation (2010); Margaret Walker, Moral Repair (2008); and E. L. Worthington, Jr., The Power of Forgiveness (2006). In 1998 the John Templeton Foundation launched a philanthropic program supporting research on forgiveness: A Campaign for Forgiveness Research, http://www.templeton.org/what-we-fund/grants/a-campaign-for-forgiveness-research.

15. See Angela Haupt, How to Forgive, and Why You Should, US News & World Report, Sept. 29, 2012, http://health.usnews.com/health-news/articles/2012/08/29/how-to-forgive-and-why-you-should; and Nara Schoenberg, A Journey to Forgive Daughter's Murderer, Chicago Tribune 15 (Dec. 27, 2017) (Barbara Mangi overcomes fear, anger, and suffocating sadness after forgiving her daughter's convicted murderer). Physical and psychological well-being can be enhanced by forgiving and letting go of the stress and burdens of holding a grievance. Dr. Robert Enright, a developmental psychologist at the University of Wisconsin, identifies forgiveness therapy with the phases of uncovering anger, deciding to forgive, working on forgiveness, and release from emotional constraint. He found that cardiac patients pursuing forgiveness therapy had improved outcomes when compared with others who received only the standard medical treatment and counseling. See Martina A. Waltman, D. C. Russell, C. T. Coyle, R. D. Enright, A. C. Holter, and C. Swoboda, The Effects of Forgiveness Intervention on Patients with Coronary Artery Disease, 24 Psychology and Health 11–27 (2009); and Megan Feldman Bettencourt, The Science of Forgiveness: "When You Don't Forgive You Release All the Chemicals of the Stress Response," Salon (Aug. 23,

2015), https://www.salon.com/2015/08/23/the_science_of_forgiveness_when_you_dont_forgive_you_release_all_the_chemicals_of_the_stress_response/ (describing research by Enright and others, supported by the Templeton Foundation Campaign for Forgiveness Research).

16. Kent Matlock, Pay the Grace Forward, N.Y. Times (Oct. 2, 2011).

17. Harold S. Kushner, How Good Do We Have to Be: A New Understanding of Guilt and Forgiveness 107 (1996).

18. Jodi Picoult, The Storyteller 438 (2013).

19. See Forgiveness: A Sampling of Research Results, American Psychological Association (2006), http://www.apa.org/international/resources/forgiveness.pdf. For websites devoted to research on forgiveness in varied fields, see http://www.forgiving.org/campaign/research.asp. See Hampton, supra.

20. For thoughtful explorations of the risks of forced forgiveness, see Adam Grant, Give and Take (2013); Carol Greenhouse, Praying for Justice (1989); and Deborah Shurman-Kauflin, Why You Don't Always Have to Forgive, Psychology Today (Aug. 21, 2012), https://www.psychologytoday.com/blog/disturbed/201208/why-you-dont-always-have-forgive.

21. Rebecca Saunders, Questionable Associations: The Role of Forgiveness in Transitional Justice, 5 Int'l J. Transitional Just. 119, 136–40 (2011).

22. See, e.g., Fyodor Dostoevksy, Crime and Punishment (1866); Charlotte Brontë, Jane Eyre (1847); Ayn Rand, Atlas Shrugged (1957); J.R.R. Tolkien, The Fellowship of the Ring 56, 627 (1954); The Two Towers 347, 467–69 (1955); The Return of the King 947 (1955).

23. A few examples include: Brian Adams, "Please Forgive Me," https://www.youtube.com/watch?v=7x8wPt8xarE; Adele, "Hello," https://www.youtube.com/watch?v=YQHsXMglC9A; Christina Aguilera, "Hurt," https://www.youtube.com/watch?v=wwCykGDEp7M; John Lennon, "Jealous Guy," https://www.google.com/search?q=john+lennon+jealous+guy&ie=utf-8&oe=utf-8&client=firefox-b-1.

24. James Wright, D.C. Area Mother's Tea Focuses on Forgiveness, Preventing Violence, Afro (Sept. 2, 2015), http://www.afro.com/d-c-area-mothers-tea-focuses-on-forgiveness-preventing-violence/; Michelle Boorstein, At the Willard, Tea and Empathy, Wash. Post, Sept. 2, 2008, http://www.washingtonpost.com/wp-dyn/content/article/2008/09/01/AR2008090102542.html.

25. See Jeffrie G. Murphy, Forgiveness and Resentment, in Jeffrie G. Murphy and Jean Hampton, Forgiveness and Mercy 33 (1988).

26. See Jules Coleman, Adding Institutional Insult to Personal Injury, 8 Yale J. Reg. 223, 224 (1990).

27. On transitional justice, see, e.g., Tricia D. Olsen, Leigh A. Payne, and Andrew G. Reiter, Transitional Justice in Balance: Comparing Processes, Weighing Efficiency (2010); and Ruti G. Teitel, Transitional Justice (2002).

28. Dullah Omar, the minister of justice at the time, explained, "a commission

is a necessary exercise to enable South Africans to come to terms with their past on a morally accepted basis and to advance the cause of reconciliation." "Tutu and His Role in the Truth & Reconciliation Commission," South African History Online (2016), http://www.sahistory.org.za/article/his-role -truth-reconciliation-commission. The TRC Act directed the commission to consider, in each application for amnesty, whether the applicant admitted fault (possibly with excuse or justification), whether the violation was associated with a political objective and the act was proportional to that objective, and whether the applicant made a full disclosure of all relevant facts. Brandon Hamber and Steve Kibble, From Truth to Transformation: The Truth and Reconciliation Commission in South Africa (1999), http://www .csvr.org.za/publications/1714-from-truth-to-transformation-the-truth-and -reconciliation-commission-in-south-africa.html.

29. Desmond Tutu, No Future Without Forgiveness 272 (1999).

30. Id.

31. Alex Boraine, A Country Unmasked: Inside South Africa's Truth and Reconciliation Commission (2001). Boraine more recently mourned the descent of democratic South Africa into instability and corruption: Alex Boraine, What Went Wrong?: South Africa on the Brink of Failed Statehood (2014).

32. Trudy Govier, Forgiveness and Revenge 144–45 (2011).

33. Priscilla B. Hayner, Unspeakable Truths, Confronting State Terror and Atrocity 144 (2001); Pierre Hazan, Measuring the Impact of Punishment and Forgiveness: A Framework for Evaluating Transitional Justice, 88 Int'l Rev. Red Cross 19, 41 (Mar. 2006), https://www.icrc.org/eng/assets/files/other/ irrc_861_hazan.pdf.

34. The anti-apartheid activist Steven Biko led the Black Consciousness movement, and his brutal death in prison inspired further challenges to the regime. See Donald Woods, Biko (1991); and the 1987 film Cry Freedom.

35. Paul Van Zyl noted, "The fact that both former and current rulers were distressed by aspects of the TRC's final report is perhaps the strongest evidence that the TRC fulfilled its mandate in a fair and impartial manner." Paul van Zyl, Dilemmas of Transitional Justice: The Case of South Africa's Truth and Reconciliation Commission, 52 J. Int'l Aff. 648 (1999), http://center .theparentscircle.org/images/d96de38c44bc4080be6d8ffe2a172ccc.pdf.

36. Hugo van der Merwe and Audrey R. Chapman, Did the TRC Deliver?, in Audrey R. Chapman and Hugo van der Merwe, eds., Truth and Reconciliation in South Africa: Did the TRC Deliver? 241 (2008).

37. Audrey R. Chapman, Perspectives on the Role of Forgiveness in the Human Rights Violations Hearings, in Chapman and Van der Merwe, supra, at 80.

38. The operations of the TRC exposed ambiguity and multiplicity within the very idea of reconciliation, which can refer to relationships between individuals, construction of an integrated political community, or building a narrative of unity regardless of the realities on the ground. See Tristan Anne Borer,

Reconciling South Africa or South Africans? Cautionary Notes from the TRC, 8 Afr. Stud. Q. (2004), http://asq.africa.ufl.edu/v8/v8i1a2.htm. Roy Hellenberg, a South African educator, explained to me that the TRC left lasting questions about whether political forgiveness and reconciliation were right concepts or whether personal mercy and attention to structural injustice made more sense. He also found Nelson Mandela's personal acts of will and control of his resentments more appealing than Archbishop Tutu's efforts to convince others to forgive. Personal conversation, Aug. 30, 2018.

39. Priscilla Hayner, Unspeakable Truths: Transitional Justice and the Challenge of Truth Commissions (2011).

40. Susan McKay, Bear in Mind These Dead 296 (2008).

41. Id.

42. Jay A. Vora and Erika Vora, The Effectiveness of South Africa's Truth and Reconciliation Commission: Perceptions of Xhosa, Afrikaner, and English South Africans, 34 J. Black Stud. 301 (2004).

43. James L. Gibson, The Contributions of Truth to Reconciliation: Lessons from South Africa, 50 J. Conflict Resolut. 409 (2006), http://www.arts.yorku.ca/politics/ncanefe/courses/pols4255/pdf/Week%209%20Gibson.pdf; David Backer, Evaluating Transitional Justice in South Africa from a Victim's Perspective, 12 J. Int'l Institute (Winter 2005), http://hdl.handle.net/2027/spo.4750978.0012.207 (reporting study of Cape Town residents).

44. United Nations, International Convention on the Protection of All Persons from Enforced Disappearance, Resolution A/RES/61/177; see Article 24.

45. Howard Zehr, Changing Lenses: Restorative Justice for Our Times (2015); Marilyn P. Armour and Mark S. Umbreit, The Paradox of Forgiveness in Restorative Justice, in E. L. Worthington, Jr., ed., Handbook of Forgiveness (2004).

46. Rosemary Thompson, Helping Communities Heal, Chicago Bar Association News 1213 (Feb./Mar. 2018).

47. University of Michigan, Office of Student Conflict Resolution, Restorative Justice Circles, https://oscr.umich.edu/article/restorative-justice-circles.

48. Amos Clifford, Center for Restorative Process, Teaching Restorative Practices with Classroom Circles (prepared for San Francisco Unified School District), https://bit.ly/2OhhsNK.

49. John T. Whitehead and Steven P. Lab, Juvenile Justice: An Introduction 343–54 (8th ed. 2015). More challenging issues arise if the offender has not ever been a member of the community.

50. See Heather Strang and Lawrence W. Sherman, Repairing the Harm: Victims and Restorative Justice, 15 Utah L. Rev. 15 (2003).

51. Joanna Shapland, Forgiveness and Restorative Justice: Is It Necessary? Is It Helpful?, 5 Oxford J. L. & Relig. 94 (Feb. 2016), https://academic.oup.com/ojlr/article/5/1/94/1752338.

52. Whitehead and Lab, supra, at 357.

53. See Institute for Restorative Justice and Restorative Dialogue, https://irjrd .org/our-initiatives/.

54. UNICEF, Toolkit on Diversion and Alternatives to Detention, https://www .unicef.org/tdad/index_56370.html;Ted Wachtel, My Three Decades of Using Restorative Practices with Delinquent and At-Risk Youth: Theory, Practice and Research Outcomes, delivered at the First World Congress on Restorative Juvenile Justice, Lima, Peru, Nov. 5, 2009.

55. Desmond Tutu, No Future Without Forgiveness 271 (1999).

56. Robert W. Taylor and Eric J. Fritsch, Juvenile Justice: Policies, Programs and Practices 313 (4th ed. 2014).

57. Id., at 431. "Crime severs bonds between victims, offenders, and families. It breaks down the basics of security and trust on which community is built. Although offenders must take full responsibility for restoring mutual respect, the entire community must be involved to provide understanding and sup- port" (432).

58. Tameside Metropolitan Borough, Youth Offending: Restorative Justice, https://www.tameside.gov.uk/yot/restorativejustice.

59. See Derrida, supra (quoting a victim speaking at the TRC). See Cláudia Perrone-Moisés, Forgiveness and Crimes Against Humanity: A Dialogue Between Hannah Arendt and Jacques Derrida, HannahArendt.net (2006), http://www.hannaharendt.net/index.php/han/article/view/90/146. Der- rida suggests that a state can judge but only people can forgive.

60. See Martha C. Nussbaum, Anger and Forgiveness: Resentment, Generosity, and Justice (2016) (urging avoidance of anger, and arguing against forms of forgiveness that require a performance of contrition as a condition for letting go of anger following injurious conduct).

61. I am indebted to Alexander Rodney, who developed these ideas by building upon work of philosopher Thomas Scanlon and work in public international law. See Alexander J. Rodney, Law and the Forgiveness Narrative: The Path from Corrective Justice to Reconciliation and Moral Repair, LL.M. Paper, Harvard Law School, Apr. 2012 (supervised by myself and T. M. Scanlon).

62. The Code of Hammurabi, ¶¶ 48, 117, http://www.constitution.org/ime/ hammurabi.pdf.

63. George Burton Adams, The Origin of English Equity, 16 Colum. L. Rev. 87, 91, 97 (2016).

64. The Domestic Violence Survivors Justice Act Challenges Double Punish- ment, Correctional Association of New York (June 19, 2017), https://www .correctionalassociation.org/news/the-domestic-violence-survivors-justice -act-challenges-double-punishment.

65. Forgiving and Forgetting in American Justice: A 50-State Guide to Expunge- ment and Restoration of Rights, Collateral Consequences Resource Center 2–25 (Oct. 2017).

66. Id., at 17–23.

67. Louise Mallinder, Amnesty, Human Rights and Political Transitions: Bridging the Peace and Justice Divide 4–5, 160–82, 185–89, 399 (2008).

68. Id., at 369 (quoting Tom Winslow, Reconciliation: The Road to Healing? Collective Good, Individual Harm? [1997] 6 Track Two).

69. Alicia A. Caldwell, Today's Immigration Debate Rooted in Reagan "Amnesty," Experts Say, PBS NewsHour (Aug. 23, 2016), https://www.pbs.org/newshour/nation/todays-immigration-debate-rooted-reagan-amnesty-experts-say.

70. Offer in Compromise, IRS (2018), https://www.irs.gov/payments/offer-in-compromise; Liz Weston, Why Debt Forgiveness Isn't What It Seems, NerdWallet (Dec. 7, 2017), https://www.nerdwallet.com/blog/finance/debt-forgiveness/.

71. Juliet Bennett Rylah, Retired Parking Enforcement Officers Claim City Uses Illegal Quotas, LAIST, May 12, 2014, http://laist.com/2014/05/12/retired_parking_enforcement_officer.php; Stephanos Bibas, Rewarding Prosecutors for Performance, 6 Ohio St. J. Crim. L. 441 (2009); Edward P. Stringham, Prosecutors Are Rewarded for Convictions, Independent (May 22, 2007), http://www.independent.org/newsroom/article.asp?id=2024.

72. Anna Pratt and Lorne Sossin, Brief Introduction of the Puzzle of Discretion, 24 Canadian J. L. & Soc. 301 (2009).

73. Carol Steiker, Passing the Buck on Mercy, Wash. Post (Sept. 7, 2008), http://www.washingtonpost.com/wp-dyn/content/article/2008/09/05/AR2008090502971.html ("How did we scale the soaring peaks of mass incarceration? The decline of mercy has played a leading role. With the noble intent of bringing rationality and order to what had often been a chaotic and even discriminatory system of criminal justice, reformers at every stage of the justice system have sought to limit the power of discretionary actors to say no to punitive policies.")

74. Paul H. Robinson, Sean E. Jackowitz, and Daniel M. Bartels, Extralegal Punishment Factors: A Study of Forgiveness, Hardship, Good Deeds, Apology, Remorse and Other Such Discretionary Factors in Assessing Criminal Punishment, University of Pennsylvania Public Law and Legal Theory Research Paper Series, Research Paper No. 11–12, https://www0.gsb.columbia.edu/mygsb/faculty/research/pubfiles/5664/extralegal_punishment_factors.pdf. See also Paul H. Robinson and Sarah M. Robinsin, Shadow Vigilantes: How Distrust in the Justice System Breeds a New Kind of Lawlessness (2018).

75. Moshe Halbertal, At the Threshold of Forgiveness: A Study of Law and Narrative in the Talmud, Jewish Review of Books (Fall 2011), https://jewishreviewofbooks.com/articles/74/at-the-threshold-of-forgiveness-a-study-of-law-and-narrative-in-the-talmud/.

76. See Sorry Works! Making Disclosure a Reality for Healthcare Organizations, http://www.sorryworks.net/apology-laws-cms-143.

77. Charles R. Swindoll, Simple Faith 258 (2003) (describing Inspector Javert as a "consummate legalist").

78. Matthew 6:9–13: "Our Father who art in heaven, hallowed be thy name. Thy kingdom come. Thy will be done, on earth as it is in heaven. Give us this day our daily bread; and forgive us our trespasses, as we forgive those who trespass against us; and lead us not into temptation, but deliver us from evil." See also Luke 11:2–4: "Father, hallowed be your name. Your kingdom come. Give us each day our daily bread; and forgive us our sins, for we ourselves forgive everyone who is indebted to us; and lead us not into temptation."

79. For thoughtful explorations of the risks of forced forgiveness, see Adam Grant, Give and Take (2013); Carol Greenhouse, Praying for Justice (1989), and Deborah Shurman-Kauflin, Why You Don't Always Have to Forgive, Psychology Today, Aug. 21, 2012, https://www.psychologytoday.com/blog/disturbed/201208/why-you-dont-always-have-forgive.

80. Charleston Church Shooting: Angry, Forgiving Families Confront Dylann Roof at Sentencing Hearing, Chicago Tribune (Jan. 11, 2017), http://www.chicagotribune.com/news/nationworld/ct-dylann-roof-death-sentence-20170111-story.html; Mark Berman, "I forgive you": Relatives of Charleston Church Shooting Victims Address Dylann Roof, Wash. Post (June 19, 2015), https://www.washingtonpost.com/news/post-nation/wp/2015/06/19/i-forgive-you-relatives-of-charleston-church-victims-address-dylann-roof/?utm_term=.695553b987d5; Nikita Stewart and Richard Pérez-Peña, In Charleston, Raw Emotion at Hearing for Suspect in Church Shooting, N.Y. Times, June 19, 2015, https://www.nytimes.com/2015/06/20/us/charleston-shooting-dylann-storm-roof.html.

81. Charleston Church Shooting, supra.

82. Quoted in Stacey Patton, Black America Should Stop Forgiving White Racists, Wash. Post (June 22, 2015), https://www.washingtonpost.com/posteverything/wp/2015/06/22/black-america-should-stop-forgiving-white-racists/?utm_term=.28f3245cacf1.

83. Robert Barron, Forgiving Dylann Roof, First Things (Mar. 2017), https://www.firstthings.com/article/2017/03/forgiving-dylann-roof.

84. Brandon Tensley, With Dylann Roof, Sentenced to Death, Black People Are Expected to Forgive, Pacific Standard (Jan. 11, 2017), https://psmag.com/news/with-dylann-roof-sentenced-to-death-black-people-are-expected-to-forgive.

85. Myisha Cherry, Can You Find It in Your Heart to Forgive: Race, Request, and Repair, presented at Harvard (Sept. 13, 2017), http://hutchinscenter.fas.harvard.edu/fall-colloquium-myisha-cherry-.

86. Patton, supra. See also Julia Craven, It's Not Black Folks' Burden to Forgive Racist Killers, Huff. Post (July 1, 2015), https://www.huffingtonpost.com/2015/07/01/forgiveness-charleston-shooting_n_7690772.html; Kiese Laymon, Black Churches Taught Us to Forgive White People: We Learned to Shame Ourselves, Guardian (June 23, 2015), https://www

.theguardian.com/commentisfree/2015/jun/23/black-churchesforgive
-white-people-shame.

87. Women Are Better at Forgiving, AAS EurekAlert (Feb. 18, 2011), describing Carmen Maganto and Maite Garaigordobil, Evaluación del perdón: Diferencias generacionales y diferencias de sexo, 42 Revista Latinoamericana de Psicología 391–403 (2010); Kara Post Kennedy, Where Is the Gender Divide When It Comes to Forgiveness? Do We Understand the Fine Line Between Forgiveness and Enabling?, Good Men Project (Apr. 30, 2017), https:// goodmenproject.com/featured-content/the-gender-bias-of-forgiveness-kpk -jrmk/; and Leah Whittington, Renaissance Suppliants: Poetry, Antiquity, Reconciliation 178–79, 196 (2016).

88. See Cordelia Fine, Delusions of Gender: How Our Minds, Society, and Neurosexism Create Difference (2011); Psyched, Why Women Are Tired: The Price of Unpaid Emotional Labor, Huff. Post (April 6, 2016), https:// www.huffingtonpost.com/psyched-in-san-francisco/why-women-are-tired -the-p_b_9619732.html. On emotional labor and gender, see Suzannah Weiss, 50 Ways People Expect Constant Emotional Labor from Women and Femmes, Everyday Feminism (Aug. 15, 2016), https://everydayfeminism .com/2016/08/women-femmes-emotional-labor/. Attending to power relations between men and women in reconciliation efforts arising from authoritarian settings and situations of armed conflict is particularly challenging and crucial if the gendered aspects of forgiveness are not to be manipulated. See Fanie du Toit, When Political Transitions Work 219–220 (2018).

89. Mitchel P. Roth, An Eye for an Eye? A Global History of Crime and Punishment (2015); Peter Townsend, An Eye for an Eye? The Morality of Punishment, Jubilee Centre, http://www.jubilee-centre.org/an-eye-for-an-eye-the -morality-of-punishment/.

90. Timothy V. Kaufman-Osborn, Proportionality Review and the Death Penalty, 29 Just. System J. 257 (2013), https://www.tandfonline.com/doi/abs/10 .1080/0098261X.2008.10767892.

91. David Mitchell, Families of Murder Victims Rally Against the Death Penalty, KWGN TV (Jan. 8, 2014), http://kwgn.com/2014/01/08/families -of-murder-victims-rally-against-death-penalty/; Rachel King, Don't Kill in Our Names: Families of Murder Victims Speak Out Against the Death Penalty (2003).

92. Stephenie Duvien, Battered Women and the Full Benefit of Self-Defense Laws, 12 Berkeley J. Gender L. & Just. 103, 106 (1997).

93. Nicola Lacey and Hanna Pickard, To Blame or to Forgive?: Reconciling Punishment and Forgiveness in Criminal Justice, 35 Oxford J. Legal Stud. 655 (2015), https://www.ncbi.nlm.nih.gov/pmc/articles/PMC4768713/.

94. William J. Stuntz, The Collapse of American Criminal Justice (2011); and William J. Stuntz, The Pathological Politics of Criminal Law, 100 Mich. L. Rev. 505 (2001).

95. Carol Steiker, Murphy on Mercy: A Prudential Reconsideration, 27 Crim. Just. Ethics 45, 48–50 (2008); Carol S. Steiker, Criminalization and the Criminal Process: Prudential Mercy as a Limit on Penal Sanctions in an Era of Mass Incarceration, in R. A. Duff, Lindsay Farmer, S. E. Marshall, Massimo Renzo, and Victor Tadros, eds., The Boundaries of Criminal Law (2010).

96. Aleksandra Wagner, Introduction: "I Was Born in an Unforgiving Country," in Aleksandra Wagner and Carin Kuoni, eds., Considering Forgiveness 13, 14 (2009).

97. Carol J. Cramer, The Politics of Resentment: Rural Consciousness in Wisconsin and the Rise of Scott Walker 5, 6, 23, 223 (2016).

98. Van der Merwe and Chapman, supra; Mahmood Mamdani, The Truth According to the TRC, in Ifi Amadiume and Abdullahi A. An-Naim, eds., The Politics of Memory: Truth, Healing and Social Justice 176–83 (2000); Mahmood Mamdani, A Diminished Truth, in Wilmot James and Linda van der Vijver, eds., After the TRC: Reflections on Truth and Reconciliation 58–61 (2001); and Claire Moon, Narrating Political Reconciliation: Truth and Reconciliation in South Africa, 15 Soc. & Legal Stud. 257–75 (2006).

99. See Jill Lepore, I.O.U.: How We Used to Treat Debtors, New Yorker (Apr. 13, 2009), https://www.newyorker.com/magazine/2009/04/13/i-o-u.

100. Paul Butler, Chokehold: Policing Black Men (2017); and Paul Butler, The System Must Counteract Prosecutors' Natural Sympathies for Cops, N.Y. Times (Apr. 28, 2015), https://www.nytimes.com/roomfordebate/2014/12/04/do-cases-like-eric-garners-require-a-special-prosecutor/the-system-must-counteract-prosecutors-natural-sympathies-for-cops.

101. Susan Jacoby, Wild Justice: The Evolution of Revenge (1983). The desire for revenge seems associated with deterring individuals from harming again. See Michael E. McCullough, Eric. J. Pedersen, Benjamin A. Tabak, and Evan C. Carter, Conciliatory Gestures Promote Forgiveness and Reduce Anger in Humans, 111 P. Nat'l. Acad. Sci. USA (July 14, 2014), http://www.pnas.org/content/111/30/11211.full.

102. For a thoughtful debate, see Murphy and Hampton, supra.

103. Reinhold Neibuhr, The Irony of American History 63 (1952–2008) ("No virtuous act is quite as virtuous from the standpoint of our friend or foe as it is from our standpoint. Therefore we must be saved by the final form of love, which is forgiveness.")

104. Whitehead and Lab, supra, at 355–56. Restorative justice initiatives expand beyond juvenile justice to involve religious and other organizations. See Center for Restorative Justice, http://www.suffolk.edu/college/centers/14521.php; Community Justice Initiatives Association, http://www.cjibc.org/restorative_justice.

105. See Lenore Weitzman, The Divorce Revolution: The Unexpected Social and Economic Consequences for Women and Children in America 16–17 (1985).

106. Victim Impact Statements, Forensic Psychology (n.d.), https://psychology

.iresearchnet.com/forensic-psychology/trial-consulting/victim-impact
-statements/.

107. Susan A. Bandes, What Are Victim Impact Statements For?, Atlantic (July 23, 2016), https://www.theatlantic.com/politics/archive/2016/07/what-are -victim-impact-statements-for/492443/.

108. See Stewart Macaulay, Non-Contractual Relationships in Business: A Preliminary Study, 28 Am. Soc. Rev. 55 (1963); Ian MacNeil, The Many Futures of Contract, 47 S. Cal. L. Rev. 691 (1974).

109. See Lee Taft, The Lawyer as Victim: The Psychic Cost of Legal Error on Practitioners (2017); Douglas R. Richmond and John C. Bonnie, My Bad: Creating a Culture of Owning Up to Lawyer Missteps and Resisting the Temptation to Bury Professional Error, presentation to the Annual Conference of the Litigation Section of the American Bar Association, New Orleans, Apr. 16, 2015, http://www.americanbar.org/content/dam/aba/administrative/litigation/ materials/2015-sac/written_materials/18_1_my_bad_creating_a_culture_ of_owning_up_to_lawyer_missteps.authcheckdam.pdf. Taft connects the rates of lawyers' substance abuse to such limitations. See Taft, supra (citing Joseph Wielebinski, Culture Shock: A Groundbreaking Empirical Study Confirms that Lawyers Face Unprecedented Substance Abuse and Mental Health Challenges, Tex. Bar J. [Mar. 2016], https://www.texasbar.com/AM/ Template.cfm?Section=Table_of_contents&Template=/CM/ContentDisplay .cfm&ContentID=32751.) For further discussion, see Lee Taft, When More Than Sorry Matters, 13 Pepp. Disp. Resol. L. J. 181, 185 n. 21 (2013).

110. Allais, supra, at 33.

111. It is important to acknowledge that even jurisdictions with the "no-drop" rule (requiring prosecution even if the victim desires otherwise) can be undermined if the victim refuses to participate.

112. "Judge Rosemarie Aquilina, sentencing Larry Nassar for criminal sexual conduct, decided to let any women who said they'd been assaulted by the former USA Gymnastics team doctor face him in court and describe how his actions had affected them. The Confrontation Clause in the Sixth Amendment grants all Americans the right to face their accusers in court; Aquilina upended this, allowing all of Nassar's accusers to give victim-impact statements, telling him, and the world, what he had done." Sophie Gilbert, The Transformative Justice of Judge Aquilina, Atlantic (Jan. 25, 2018), https://www.theatlantic .com/entertainment/archive/2018/01/judge-rosemarie-aquilina-larry -nassar/551462/. The trial of Adolf Eichmann in Israel for crimes arising from the German Final Solution during World War II allowed 120 victims to testify and in retrospect helped change the status of victims in international criminal trials. See The Eichmann Trial Fifty Years On, 29 German History 265 (June 2011) (questions and responses by editors Leora Bilsky, Donald Bloxham, Lawrence Douglas, Annette Weinke, and Devin Pendas), https://academic .oup.com/gh/article/29/2/265/705308.

113. Jill Radsken, Nassar (*sic*) Accuser Opts for Justice, Forgiveness, Harv. Gazette (Apr. 6, 2018), https://news.harvard.edu/gazette/story/2018/04/faith-helped -former-gymnast-surmount-abuse-she-tells-harvard-audience/.

114. Simon Wiesenthal, The Sunflower: On the Possibilities and Limits of Forgiveness (rev. ed. 1998).

115. Colombia Pardons First FARC Troops Under Amnesty Law, Telesur (Feb. 28, 2017), https://www.telesurtv.net/english/news/Colombia-Pardons-First -FARC-Troops-Under-Amnesty-Law-20170228-0002.html.

116. See Solomon Schimmel, Wounds Not Healed by Time: The Power of Repentance and Forgiveness 45 (2002); and Linda Mills, Violent Partners: A Breakthrough Plan for Ending the Cycle of Abuse (2009).

117. And if so, should the forgiveness extend to tax treatment—for loan forgiveness is a taxable event—or to future credit scores?

118. This is the position pressed by Jeffrie Murphy in Murphy and Hampton, supra. See Derrida, supra (exploring irreconcilable poles of unconditional forgiveness and condititional forgiveness).

119. See Martha Minow and Elizabeth V. Spelman, In Context, 63 S. Cal. L. Rev. 1597 (1997).

120. Thomas Schröpfer, Material Design: Informing Architecture by Materiality 68 (2011); Jan Kośny and David W. Yarbrough, Thermal Bridges in Building Structures, in Raj P. Chhabra, ed., CRC Handbook of Thermal Engineering (2d. ed. 2017).

Chapter 1: Forgiving Youth

1. David Alan Harris, When Child Soldiers Reconcile: Accountability, Restorative Justice, and the Renewal of Empathy, 2 J. Hum. Rts. Prac. 332 (2010), doi.org/10.1093/jhuman/huq015.

2. Theresa S. Betancourt, The Social Ecology of Resilience in War-Affected Youth: A Longitudinal Study from Sierra Leone, in Michael Ungar, ed., The Social Ecology of Resilience: A Handbook of Theory and Practice, 347, 351–52 (2012).

3. Id.

4. See "Assessing Agency and Responsibility," pages 45–53 of this book.

5. See generally Gary Bass, Stay the Hand of Vengeance: The Politics of War Crimes Tribunals (2000); Lynn Hunt, Inventing Human Rights: A History (2007); Samuel Moyn, The Last Utopia: Human Rights in History 44–83 (2010); and Nadia Bernaz and Remy Prouveze, International and Domestic Prosecutions, in M. Cherif Bassiouni, ed., The Pursuit of International Criminal Justice: A World Study on Conflicts, Victimization, and Post-Conflict Justice 269–398 (2010).

6. William A. Schabas, An Introduction to the International Criminal Court 1 (2001); and René Blattmann and Kïrsten Bowman, Achievements and Problems of the International Criminal Court: A View from Within, 6 J. Int'l Crim. Just. 711 (2008).

7. "The international criminal law has distanced itself from prosecuting children and left this option to national legislatures, in which the age threshold for criminal responsibility goes from as young as six years old." Darija Markovic, Child Soldiers: Victims or War Criminals?: Criminal Responsibility and Prosecution of Child Soldiers Under International Criminal Law, Dec. 14, 2015, http://www.ra-un.org/uploads/4/7/5/4/47544571/paper__2_.pdf, citing "Special Protections: Progress and Disparity," UNICEF website, http://www.unicef.org/pon97/p56a.htm.

8. The World Health Organization defines *adolescent* as a person between the ages of ten and nineteen. World Health Organization, Adolescent Development, http://www.who.int/maternal_child_adolescent/topics/adolescence/dev/en/. In 1940, recognizing that young people could pose threats during wartime, Britain ordered the internment or deportation of all male refugees from enemy countries as young as sixteen, including Jewish refugees sent there for their safety. WWII People's War, BBC (2003–5), http://www.bbc.co.uk/history/ww2peopleswar/timeline/factfiles/nonflash/a6651858.shtml.

9. On coercion, including drugging, see Magali Chelpi-den Hamer, Youngest Recruits: Pre-War, War and Post-War Experiences in Western Côte d'Ivoire (2010). Hamer stresses that different individuals show different motivations and that coercion operates for many. Other scholars, emphasizing coercion and drugging, embrace the image of the child soldier as victim. See, e.g., Susan Tiefenbrun, Child Soldiers, Slavery and the Trafficking of Children, 31 Fordham Int'l L. J. 415 (2008); Sara A. Ward, Criminalizing the Victim: Why the Legal Community Must Fight to Ensure that Child Soldier Victims Are Not Prosecuted as War Criminals, 25 Georgetown J. Legal Ethics 821 (2012); and Kathryn White, A Chance for Redemption: Revising the "Persecutor Bar" and "Material Support Bar" in the Case of Child Soldiers, 43 Vand. J. Transnat'l L. 191 (2010). Francisco Gutiérrez Sanin argues that the FARC in Colombia developed platoon solidarity and socializes recruits effectively enough to receive a steady stream of applicants. Francisco Gutiérrez Sanin, Organizing Minors: The Case of Colombia, in Scott Gates and Simon Reich, eds., Child Soldiers in the Age of Fractured States 121, 132–33 (2010).

On the impact of new lightweight guns, crucial work was done by Graça Machel, a political leader and humanitarian from Mozambique. Her landmark 1996 report detailed the connection between escalating numbers of child soldiers and the spread of light and inexpensive weapons that small children can easily learn to operate. Graça Machel, Impact of Armed Conflict on Children: Report of the Expert of the Secretary-General, submitted pursuant to General Assembly resolution 48/157 (Aug. 26, 1996), https://www.securitycouncilreport.org/atf/cf/%7b65BFCF9B-6D27-4E9C-8CD3-CF6E4FF96FF9%7d/CAC%20A51%20306.pdf; and UN News Centre, Strong Link Between Child Soldiers and Small Arms Trade, UN Experts Say (July 15, 2008), http://www.un.org/apps/news/story.asp?NewsID=27382#

.U-pCA6PO9gY. See Margaret Angucia, Broken Citizenship: Formerly Abducted Children and Their Social Reintegration in Northern Uganda, Ph.D. thesis, Rijksuniversiteit Gronigen, 2010, http://www.researchgate.net/ publication/50985029_Broken_Citizenship._Formerly_abducted_children_ and_their_social_reintegration_in_northern_Uganda; and Roméo Dallaire, They Fight Like Soldiers, They Die Like Children: The Global Quest to Eradicate the Use of Child Soldiers 120–21 (2010).

10. Amnesty International, Hidden Scandal, Secret Shame: Torture and Ill-Treatment of Children (2000), https://www.amnesty.org/en/documents/ act76/005/2000/en/.

11. Sarah Kenyon Lischer, War, Displacement, and the Recruitment of Child Soldiers in the Democratic Republic of Congo, in Gates and Reich, supra, at 143, 151.

12. Machel, supra; and UN News Centre, supra.

13. The ICC came into being in 2002 after ratification by an initial sixty states— the minimum specified by the Rome Statute. Brazil currently plans to withdraw, which will reduce the number to 122.

14. "Conscripting or enlisting children under the age of fifteen years into the national armed forces or using them to participate actively in hostilities." Rome Statute, Article 8 (2)(b) (xxvi), http://www.icc-cpi.int/NR/rdonlyres/ ADD16852-AEE9–4757-ABE7–9CDC7CF02886/283503/RomeStatutEngl .pdf (defining war crimes). This provision drew on the 1989 Convention on the Rights of the Child and on Additional Protocol 1 of the Geneva Conventions; see Schabas, supra, at 50–51. The Optional Protocol, adopted by the General Assembly in 2000 and entered into force in 2002, increased the relevant age to eighteen. Optional Protocol to the Convention on the Rights of the Child on the Involvement of Children in Armed Conflict, A/RES/54/263 (2000); Schabas, supra, at 51; and UNICEF, Coalition to Stop the Use of Child Soldiers, Guide to the Optional Protocol on the Involvement of Children in Armed Conflict (2003), http://www.unicef.org/publications/files/ option_protocol_conflict.pdf.

15. International human rights conferences in 1997 (Cape Town) and in 2007 (Paris) articulated norms endorsed by nearly one hundred nations against the recruitment of children by armed groups and for the protection and demobilization of such individuals. See Paris Principles, Principles and Guidelines on Children Associated with Armed Forces or Armed Groups (Feb. 2007), https://www .unicef.org/protection/files/Paris_Principles_EN.pdf; Cape Town Principles and Best Practices (April 1997), https://www.unicef.org/emerg/files/Cape _Town_Principles(1).pdf. By 2010, ninety-five countries endorsed the principles calling for the end of the use of individuals under seventeen in war. Office of the Special Representative of the Secretary-General for Children and Armed Conflict, New Countries Endorse the Paris Commitments to End the Use of Child Combatants (Sept. 28, 2010), https://childrenandarmedconflict

.un.org/press-release/28Sep10/. Compliance is another matter. Many of the countries signing on to the Paris Commitments are nonetheless also on the UN blacklist for recruiting child soldiers. Gates and Reich, supra, at 3, 4.

16. Save the Children, Forgotten Casualties of War: Girls in Armed Conflict (2005).

17. Graça Machel, foreword, in Sharanjeet Parmar, Mindy Jane Roseman, Saudamini Siegrist, and Theo Sowa, eds., Children and Transitional Justice: Truth-Telling, Accountability and Reconciliation ix, xii (2010).

18. Angucia, supra, at 123–25.

19. Dallaire, supra at 149; and Human Rights Watch, "Maybe We Live and Maybe We Die": Recruitment and Use of Children by Armed Groups in Syria 3 (June 23, 2014), http://www.hrw.org/print/reports/2014/06/23/maybe-we-live-and-maybe-we-die-0. The Rome Statute authorizing the ICC specifically punishes individuals who conscript or enlist children under fifteen or use them in hostilities including for support functions. Id., at 23.

20. Wairagala Wakabi, Lubanga Given 14-Year Jail Sentence, AllAfrica (July 10, 2012), https://allafrica.com/stories/201207101242.html; and Human Rights Watch, Courting History: The Landmark International Criminal Court's First Years (July 12, 2008), http://www.hrw.org/reports/2008/07/10/courting-history. The Special Court for Sierra Leone had a prior prosecution for recruitment of minors to be soldiers that resulted in an acquittal.

21. Office of the Special Representative of the [UN] Secretary-General for Children and Armed Conflict, Child Recruitment and Use (n.d.), https://childrenandarmedconflict.un.org/six-grave-violations/child-soldiers/.

22. Under the 1998 Rome Statute, it is a war crime for any national army or other armed group to conscript or enlist children under age fifteen, or to use these children actively to participate in hostilities. Rome Statute of the International Criminal Court, Article 8(2)(b)(xxvi), July 17, 1998, 2187 U.N.T.S. 90. Article 8(2)(b)(xxvi), Article 8(2)(e)(vii) ("any person who was under the age of 18 at the time of the alleged commission of a crime"). A similar provision appears in the Statute of the Special Court for Sierra Leone, art. 4(c), Jan.16, 2002, 2178 U.N.T.S. 145.

23. Rome Statute of the International Criminal Court, Article 26, July 17, 1998, 2187 U.N.T.S. 90. This jurisdictional provision leaves choices about the age of criminal responsibility to national law. Penal Reform International, The Minimum Age of Criminal Responsibility (Justice for Children Briefing No. 4) (Feb. 2013), https://www.penalreform.org/wp-content/uploads/2013/05/justice-for-children-briefing-4-v6-web_0.pdf.

24. Peter W. Singer, Facing Saddam's Child Soldiers, Brookings (Jan. 14, 2003), http://www.brookings.edu/research/papers/2003/01/14iraq-singer. Some academic estimates identify 300,000 children as part of armed forces—governmental and nongovernmental—in recent years, although others dis-

pute this figure. The actual number is probably impossible to confirm. One observer identified 30,000 children who have been abducted and turned into soldiers in Uganda by Joseph Kony alone. Jo Becker, Child Soldiers: A Worldwide Scourge, Human Rights Watch (Mar. 23, 2012), http://www.hrw.org/news/2012/03/23/child-soldiers-worldwide-scourge.

25. Becker, supra (noting uses of child soldiers in fourteen countries, including Colombia, Myanmar, and Afghanistan). The U.S. State Department identified seven countries using child soldiers. See also Jo Becker, U.S. Must Enforce Ban on Child Soldiers, Human Rights Watch (June 28, 2012), http://www.hrw.org/news/2012/06/28/us-must-enforce-ban-child-soldiers.

26. See generally Coalition to Stop the Use of Child Soldiers, Child Soldiers Global Report (2008).

27. Michael Wessells, Child Soldiers, Peace Education, and Postconflict Reconstruction for Peace, 44 Theor. Pract. 364 (2005).

28. Id., at 363.

29. Gates and Reich, supra, at 12.

30. Sima Atri and Salvator Cusimano, Perceptions of Children Involved in War and Transitional Justice in Northern Uganda 6 (2012), http://munkschool.utoronto.ca/wp-content/uploads/2012/07/Atri-Cusimano_UgandaChildSoldiers_2012.pdf.

31. Dallaire, supra, at 118.

32. Gates and Reich, supra, at 3, 7.

33. Arne Chorn-Pond recalls that in Cambodia, during the Khmer Rouge regime, he and other children had to repress their emotions and take up a gun or be killed. He was handed a gun when he was twelve: "children who refused were shot in the head. . . . The Khmer Rouge would shoot us from behind if, against orders, we tried to leave the battleground. Arne Chorn-Pond, in Frederick Franck, Janis Roze, and Richard Connolly, eds., What Does it Mean to Be Human? 196 (2001).

34. Graça Machel, The Impact of War on Children: A Review of Progress Since the 1996 United Nations Report on the Impact of Armed Conflict on Children (2001). Even when children's own perspective is included and lends an understanding of their own sense of agency, their involvement in war roles terminates the lives they otherwise would have led. See Opiyo Oloya, Child to Soldier: Stories from Joseph Kony's Lord's Resistance Army 6, 13, 18–25 (2013).

35. Péter Klemensits and Ráchel Czirják, Child Soldiers in Genocidal Regimes: The Cases of the Khmer Rouge and the Hutu Power, 15 AARMS 215–22 (2016), https://www.uni-nke.hu/document/uni-nke-hu/aarms-2016-3-01-klemensits-czirjak.original.pdf.

36. Oloya, supra, at 61.

37. Erin K. Baines, The Haunting of Alice: Local Approaches to Justice and Reconciliation in Northern Uganda, 1 Int'l J. of Transitional Justice 170–71, 180

(2007). At least in some conflicts, many and perhaps most child soldiers are not coerced to participate. David M. Rosen, International Humanitarian Law and the Globalization of Childhood, 109 Am. Anthropol. 296 (2007).

38. Baines, supra.

39. See Robyn Linde, The Globalization of Childhood: The International Diffusion of Norms and Law Against the Child Death Penalty (2016). For further exploration of debates over the legal status of childhood, see Virginia Morrow, Understanding Children and Childhood, Centre for Children and Young People, Background Briefing Series No. 1 (2011), https://epubs.scu.edu.au/cgi/viewcontent.cgi?article=1027&context=ccyp_pubs.

40. Oloya, supra, at 25.

41. UN Convention on the Rights of the Child, Article 1. Ratified by 196 nations (although some include reservations), this document is now endorsed by all nations except the United States. The convention itself does not set a minimum age of criminal responsibility, although comment 10, paragraph 32, recommends establishing the age of twelve: "It can be concluded that a minimum age of criminal responsibility below the age of 12 years is considered by the Committee not to be internationally acceptable. States parties are encouraged to increase their lower MACR to the age of 12 years as the absolute minimum age and to continue to increase it to a higher age level." Children's rights in juvenile justice, General Comment No. 10, Convention on the Rights of the Child (2007), http://www2.ohchr.org/english/bodies/crc/docs/CRC.C.GC.10.pdf. In light of the convention, Ireland raised its age of criminal responsibility from seven to twelve. Children's Rights Alliance, From Rhetoric to Rights: Second Shadow Report to the United National Committee on the Rights of the Child (2006) (Republic of Ireland), para. 514, p. 73. France makes criminal liability depend not on age but on capacity for discernment. Children's Rights: France, http://www.loc.gov/law/help/child-rights/france.php.

42. UN Convention on the Rights of the Child, Article 38 (1989). The Optional Protocol to the convention, embraced by many state parties, raises the age to eighteen at which the participation nations should try to ensure youth stay out of hostilities and also directs no compulsory recruitment into the armed forces for individuals under eighteen. Optional Protocol to the Convention on the Rights of the Child on the Involvement of Children in Armed Conflict, A/RES/54/263 (2000) (Article 1, Article 2).

43. Two of the last three countries outside the convention—Somalia and Sudan—have recently ratified it. The United States has signed the treaty but not ratified it, citing concerns about national sovereignty and parental rights. A past objection that defended use of the death penalty for minors became moot when the U.S. Supreme Court ruled the death penalty unconstitutional when applied to individuals under eighteen. Roper v. Simmons, 543 U.S. 551 (2005). Some argue ratification would make no difference in terms of actual compliance because the U.S. Constitution already provides comparable pro-

tections. The United States is engaged in a case-by-case review of the use of life-without-parole punishment for offenses committed by minors. No other nation currently authorizes this punishment for minors. See Connie de la Vega, Amanda Solter, Soo-Ryun Kwon, and Dana Marie Isaac, Cruel and Unusual: U.S. Sentencing Practices in a Global Context, University of San Francisco 61 (2012), http://www.usfca.edu/law/docs/criminalsentencing. See also James Garbarino, Miller's Children: Why Giving Teenage Killers a Second Chance Matters for All of Us 6–8 (2018).

44. U.S. federal law establishes that individuals can vote at age eighteen but cannot legally drink alcohol or enter into a binding contract until age twenty-one. The fifty states, the District of Columbia, and the territories set varying ages of criminal responsibility, as low as six in North Carolina. While some states have a minimum age of criminal responsibility, in thirty-five American states, children of any age can be tried and convicted for crimes. The Minimum Age of Criminal Responsibility Continues to Divide Opinion, Economist (Mar. 15, 2017), https://www.economist.com/blogs/graphicdetail/2017/03/daily -chart-7. States across the nation commonly try juveniles as adults based on the seriousness of the offenses. See Judicial "Waiver" (Transfer to Adult Court), http://criminal.findlaw.com/juvenile-justice/juvenile-waiver-transfer-to -adult-court.html; Campaign for Youth Justice, Fact Sheet, http://www .act4jj.org/media/factsheets/factsheet_20.pdf; Akash Kumar, Age of Criminal Responsibility, 3 Int'l J. Soc. Sci. and Humanities Res. ISSN 2348–3164 (online) 115–21 (Jul.–Sept. 2015), http://www.researchpublish.com/journal/ IJSSHR/Issue-3-July-2015-September-2015/30. Taking steps closer to the global standard, the Supreme Court has banned the death penalty and life without parole sentences for nonhomicide offenses when the individuals are convicted of crimes committed while minors. Graham v. Florida, 560 U.S. 48 (2010); and Roger v. Simmons, 543 U.S. 551 (2005) (banning death penalty applied to individuals for crimes committed under the age of eighteen). The Court has also rejected mandatory sentences of life without parole for individuals convicted of crimes committed under the age of eighteen, but it allows its use based on individualized assessments. Miller v. Alabama, 567 U.S. 460 (2012). Individual states have been reviewing their laws in light of these decisions, and some call for federal legislation opening for review after ten years any sentences of life without parole for individuals convicted of crimes committed under the age of eighteen. See Mandatory Life Without Parole for Juveniles: A State-By-State Look at Sentencing, Associated Press (Aug. 1, 2017), http:// www.masslive.com/news/index.ssf/2017/08/a_look_at_mandatory_life_ witho.html.

45. Jeff Tietz, The Unending Torture of Omar Khadr, Rolling Stone (Aug. 24, 2006), http://www.rollingstone.come/politics/news-the-unending-torture-of -omar-khadr-20060824. See Michelle Shephard, Omar Khadr Fact Check Paints a Clearer Picture of the Case and the Incident Underlying It, Star (July 10, 2010),

https://www.thestar.com/news/world/2017/07/10/omar-khadr-fact-check
-paints-a-clearer-picture-of-the-case-and-the-incident-underlying-it.html.

46. Outgoing SRSG Radhika Coomaraswamy Calls for Omar Khadr's Repatriation
    to Canada, Children and Armed Conflict, http://childrenandarmedconflict
    .un.org/press-releases/outgoing-srsg-radhika-coomaraswamy-calls-for-omar
    -khadrs-repatriation-to-canada/.

47. Compare Jonathan Kay, Omar Khadr Deserves His Settlement and His Apol-
    ogy from the Canadian Government: Brainwashed Child Soldiers Aren't
    Responsible for Their Actions, CBC News (July 5, 2017), http://www.cbc
    .ca/news/opinion/omar-khadr-settlement-1.4189890, with Aaron Wherry,
    What 3 Legal Minds Think About the Omar Khadr Settlement, CBC News
    (July 12, 2017), http://www.cbc.ca/news/politics/omar-khadr-legal-analysis
    -aaron-wherry-1.4199409 (discussing views of law professor Craig Forcese).

48. Boumedienne v. Bush, 553 U.S. 723 (2008). The U.S. Supreme Court has
    had its own debates over whether an adolescent has the maturity and culpa-
    bility to face the death penalty and to make health care decisions. Compare
    Roper v. Simmons, 543 U.S. 551, 568–73 (2005) with id., at 617 (Scalia, J.,
    dissenting); and Kathryn Kickey, Minors' Rights in Medical Decisionmak-
    ing, 9 Healthcare Law, Ethics, & Regulation 100 (2007), http://www.bhslr
    .edu/!userfiles/pdfs/course-materials/Minors%20Rights%20Decision%20
    Making.pdf.

49. Khadr, tried before a military commission, pleaded guilty to five war crimes:
    (1) murder in violation of the law of war; (2) attempted murder in violation of
    the law of war; (3) conspiracy; (4) providing material support for terrorism; and
    (5) spying. Omar Khadr Returns to Canada, CBC News, Sept. 29, 2012, http://
    www.cbc.ca/news/canada/story/2012/09/29/omar-khadr-repatriation.html.

50. Jeanne Meserve, Youngest Guantanamo Detainee Pleads Guilty, CNN,
    http://www.cnn.com/2010/US/10/25/khadr.plea/index.html.

51. Sheema Khan, Omar Khadr's Return Will Test Canada's Commitment, Globe
    and Mail, Sept. 30, 2012, https://www.theglobeandmail.com/opinion/
    omar-khadrs-return-will-test-canadas-commitment-to-war-children/
    article4577917/.

52. Omar Khadr to Stay Out on Bail After Federal Government Drops Appeal;
    Liberal Government Says It Is Reviewing Its "Litigation Strategy," CBC News
    (Feb. 18, 2016), http://www.cbc.ca/news/politics/omar-khadr-bail-fight-1
    .3454278. See Omar Khadr Returns to Canada, supra. See also Kent Roach,
    The Supreme Court at the Bar of Politics: The Afghan Detainee and Omar
    Khadr Cases, 28 Nat'l J. Const. L. (Canada) 115 (2010). See also Omar Khadr
    Fact Check, supra.

53. Rebecca Joseph, Justin Trudeau Says Anger Over Omar Khadr Case Will
    Ensure It Never Happens Again, Global News (Sept. 27, 2017), https://
    globalnews.ca/news/3773166/justin-trudeau-says-anger-over-omar-khadr
    -case-will-ensure-it-never-happens-again/; Omar Khadr: Canada Pays ex-

Guantanamo Detainee $8.1m, Al Jazeera (July 7, 2017), http://www.aljazeera
.com/news/2017/07/omar-khadr-canada-pays-guantanamo-detainee-81m
-170707085329897.html; and Wherry, supra.

54. Wherry, supra (citing Angus Reid Institute survey). For an argument that the
United States undermined Omar Khadr's legal rights under international law
due to his age at the time of the offenses, see M. Mehdi Ali, Omar Khadr's
Legal Odyssey: The Erasure of Child Soldier as a Legal Category, 46 Ga. J.
Int'l & Comp. L. 347 (2018). Ali argues that Khadr's recruitment violated the
Optional Protocol to the Convention on the Rights of the Child, and multiple
Security Council resolutions opposing the use of child soldiers—all of which
have the backing of the United States. Id., at 354–58.

55. See Patrick Griffin, Sean Addie, Benjamin Adams, and Kathy Firestine, Trying Juveniles as Adults: An Analysis of State Transfer Laws and Reporting,
Juvenile Offenders and Victims: National Report Series Bulletin (Sept. 2011),
https://www.ncjrs.gov/pdffiles1/ojjdp/232434.pdf.

56. Nadia Grant, Duress as a Defence for Former child Soldiers?: Dominic
Ongwen and the International Criminal Court, International Crimes Database
Brief No. 21 (2016), http://www.internationalcrimesdatabase.org/upload/
documents/20161209T155029-ICD%20Brief%20Nadia%20Grant%202.pdf.

57. See Nicola Lacey and Hanna Pickard, To Blame or to Forgive? Reconciling
Punishment and Forgiveness in Criminal Justice, 35 Oxford J. Legal Stud.
665 (2015).

58. Id. Girl soldiers are often raped or made to serve as "wives" of rebels; they
may experience severe physical damage following sexual violation and child-
birth, but many describe rejection by their own communities as a more sear-
ing harm. Amnesty International, Democratic Republic of Congo (DRC):
Child Soldiers Abandoned (Oct. 11, 2006), https://www.amnesty.org/
download/Documents/72000/afr620192006en.pdf; and Romaire, supra,
174–78. International law has recognized rape as a war crime. United
Nations, International Criminal Tribunal for the Former Yugoslavia, http://
www.icty.org/en/features/crimes-sexual-violence/landmark-cases; Report
of the Secretary-General on Children and Armed Conflict, A/62/6009-
S/2007/757 para. 42 (Dec. 21, 2007) (evidence that Gen. Laurent Khundra's
fighters in the DRC deliberately used rape as a weapon of war).

59. Theresa S. Betancourt, Ivelina Borisova, et al., Research Review: Psychosocial Adjustment and Mental Health in Former Child Soldiers—A Systematic
Review of the Literature and Recommendations for Future Research, 54 J.
Child Psychol. Psychiatry 17, 28, 30 (2013). Some boys as well are abused
sexually and face trauma as a result. Romaire, supra, at 133. Not all girls who
are kidnapped or join rebel or guerrilla forces are raped or engage in sexual
relationships. Experts call for more attention to the varied circumstances and
experiences of these young people in efforts to assist their transitions back to
mainstream society. Chris Coulter, Female Fighters in the Sierra Leone War:

Challenging the Assumptions?, 88 Feminist Rev. 54 (2008); and Yvonne E. Kearns, The Voices of Girl Child Soldiers 6–7, 15–17 (2002), http://www .quno.org/newyork/Resources/QUNOchildsoldiers.pdf.

60. Betancourt and Borisova, supra, 28–30. See also Elisabeth Schauer and Thomas Elbert, The Psychological Impact of Child Soldiering, in Erin Martz, ed., Trauma Rehabilitation after War and Conflicts 311, 330, 341 (2010) (traumatic experiences build upon each other and cumulatively increase risks of post-traumatic stress). At the same time, exclusive focus on the sexual violence neglects the totality of their experiences. Machel, foreword, supra, at xiii; Fiona Ross, Bearing Witness: Women and the Truth Commission in South Africa 89 (2003); and Fionnuala Ní Aoláin, Exploring a Feminist Theory of Harm in the Context of Conflicted and Post-Conflict Societies, 35 Queen's L.J. 219, 240 (2009).

61. In the Democratic Republic of Congo and Uganda, local prosecutors have charged returning child soldiers with crimes carrying the death penalty, despite criticism from international groups. Matthew Happold, The Age of Responsibility in International Law, in Karin Arts and Vesselin Popovski, International Criminal Accountability and the Rights of Children (2006), https://papers.ssrn.com/sol3/papers.cfm?abstract_id=934567; Dallaire, supra, at 125, 179–80. Even where the nation's law would not permit severe punishment of someone who had been a child during the alleged violence, community attitudes and traditional practices may press for culpability and sanctions. At the same time, a formal law permitting prosecution of those under eighteen may conflict with popular views. And the same individual might be treated as legally accountable in one country but be immune from prosecution in a neighboring country, due to different views about the minimum age for criminal responsibility. Matthew Happold, Child Soldiers in International Law (2005); and The Minimum Age of Criminal Responsibility Continues to Divide Opinion, Economist (March 15, 2017), https://www .economist.com/blogs/graphicdetail/2017/03/daily-chart-7.

62. Special Rapporteur Radhika Coomaraswamy has argued, "If minor children who have committed serious war crimes are not prosecuted, this could be an incentive for their commanders to delegate to them the dirtiest orders, aiming at impunity. For this reason the ICC and SCSL focus strongly on those persons most responsible for human rights and IHL violations and apply the concept of command responsibility to political and military leaders." Radhika Coomaraswamy, quoted in Should Child Soldiers Be Prosecuted for Their Crimes? IRIN (Oct. 6, 2011), http://www.irinnews.org/analysis/2011/10/06/should -child-soldiers-be-prosecuted-their-crimes.

63. Many families and communities resist reintegrating former child soldiers because, in the words of one international aid worker, "They're afraid that their behavior won't have changed or that they'll be rejected and stigmatized by the community because of the violent acts they've committed in the

past. International Committee of the Red Cross, Democratic Republic of the Congo: 152 Demobilized Children Reunited with Families (Jan. 9, 2015), https://www.icrc.org/en/document/democratic-republic-congo-152-former -child-soldiers-reunited-families (quoting Marie-Geneviève Nightingale, head of ICRC child protection work in Eastern Democratic Republic of the Congo). These are particular problems for girls and women who return to communities that regard sexual conduct outside marriage as more unforgiveable than violent behavior. See Angucia, supra, 164–67; Beth Verhey, Reaching the Girls 3 (2004); and Save the Children, Forgotten Casualties of War: Girls in Armed Conflict 20–21 (2005).

64. See, e.g., Betancourt, Borisova, et al., supra, at 1.

65. See Atri and Cusimano, supra, 9. On child soldiers as victims, see Cécile Aptel, International Criminal Justice and Child Protection, in Parmar, Roseman, Siegrist, and Sowa, supra, at 67, 107; Jo Boyden, Moral Development of Soldiers: What Do Adults Have to Fear?, 9 Peace & Conflict: J. Peace Psychol. 343, 355 (2003), https://www.tandfonline.com/doi/abs/10.1207/s15327949pac0904_6. In contrast, at least according to studies in Rwanda and in Sierra Leone, community members stress child soldiers' responsibility for their actions. See Steven Freeland, Mere Children or Weapons of War—Child Soldiers and International Law, 29 U. of La Verne L. Rev. 19 (2012) (citing Save the Children Federation study). Wessells, supra, at 363, 367. Similarly, see Mark A. Drumbl, Reimagining Child Soldiers in International Law and Policy (2012) (describing a spectrum of "circumscribed action"); Alcinda Honwana, Negotiating Postwar Identities: Child Soldiers in Mozambique and Anglo, in George Clement Bond and Nigel C. Gibson, eds., Contested Terrains and Constructed Categories: Contemporary Africa in Focus 277–98 (2002); Id., n. 42; Rosen, supra; and Christine Ryan, The Children of War: Child Soldiers as Victims and Participants in the Sudan Civil War (2012) (describing how many of the surveyed youth felt they had become an adult by the age of 15 given their abilities to distinguish right and wrong and to make decisions for themselves). See also Jeff McMahan, An Ethical Perspective on Child Soldiers, in Scott Gates and Simon Reich, eds., Child Soldiers in the Age of Fractured States 27, 33 (2010) ("Even if they are cognitively and emotionally immature, and even if they have been brutalized and brainwashed, [child soldiers] are still, it might be argued, sufficiently morally responsible to be able to recognize that indiscriminate killing is wrong.) People understandably may have ambivalence about the blameworthiness of returning child soldiers. Atri and Cusimano, at 41–42.

66. There has been some criticism of Eggers to the effect that, by writing the book as a fictional autobiography, he "expropriated [Deng's] identity." Valentino Achak Deng and Dave Eggers discussed their work process and how the book reflected the voice of Achak in an interview that now appears on the website for the foundation Achak runs, funded in part by proceeds from the book.

They met through the Lost Boys Foundation and became friends. "[W]e really hadn't decided whether I was just helping Valentino write his own book, or if I was writing a book about him," reported Eggers, and Achak commented, "I thought I might want to write my own book, but I learned that I was not ready to do this. I was still taking classes in basic writing at Georgia Perimeter College." Dave Eggers explained, "For a long while there, we continued doing interviews, and I gathered the material. But all along, I really didn't know exactly what form it would finally take—whether it would be first person or third, whether it would be fiction or nonfiction. After about eighteen months of struggle with it, we settled on a fictionalized autobiography, in Valentino's voice." Eggers noted, "Valentino's voice is so distinct and unforgettable that any other authorial voice would pale by comparison. Very early on, when the book was in a more straightforward authorial voice, I missed the voice I was hearing on the tapes. So writing in Val's voice solved both problems: I could disappear completely, and the reader would have the benefit of his very distinct voice." The Valentino Achak Deng Foundation, Interview with Valentino Achak Deng and Dave Eggers, http://www.valentinoachakdeng.org/interview.php

67. In the preface to the novel, Valentino Achak explains, "Over the course of many years, Dave and I have collaborated to tell my story. . . . I told [him] what I knew and what I could remember, and from that material he created this work of art." Valentino Achak Deng, preface, in Dave Eggers, What Is the What: The Autobiography of Valentino Achak Deng 5 (2006). For a collection of oral histories of the Lost Boys of Sudan, see Alphonsion Deng, et al., They Poured Fire on Us from the Sky (2005).

68. Eggers, supra, at 49–50; and Angucia, supra, at 126–28, 133.

69. Eggers, supra, at 50.

70. Pamela D. Couture, Victims, Perpetrators, or Moral Agents: Children and Youth Survivors of the War in the Democratic Republic of Congo, 2 J. Childhood & Relig. 1, 13–14 (2011).

71. Alpaslan Ozerdem and Sukyana Podder, eds., Child Soldiers: From Recruitment to Reintegration (2011); Analysis: Girl Child Soldiers Face New Battles in Civilian Life, IRIN (Feb. 2013), http://www.irinnews.org/printreport .aspc?reportid=97463. Angela Veale also found a sense of empowerment for female combatants, many of whom started as child soldiers, in Ethiopia but not in other African conflicts. Angela Veale, From Child Soldier to Ex-Fighter: Female Fighters, Demobilisation and Reintegration in Ethiopia (2003). Describing teens who voluntarily joined rebels and reflecting motives ranging from defense of their communities to desires for a military career, Christine Ryan stresses how incorrectly, nongovernmental organization workers tried to conceive of the youth as lacking in agency and completely victimized. Ryan, supra. The problem of international human rights discourse obscuring the agency of children in wartime is cited by other researchers as well. See, e.g., David M. Rosen, Armies of the Young: Child Soldiers in War and Terrorism (2005).

72. See Corinna Csaky, No One to Turn To: The Under-Reporting of Child Sexual Exploitation and Abuse by Aid Workers and Peacekeepers 5, 20 (2008); and Machel, supra (2001), at 31.

73. Susan McKay and Dyan Mazurana, Where Are the Girls?: Girls in Fighting Forces in Northern Uganda, Sierra Leone, and Mozambique: Their Lives During and After the War (2004).

74. Christine Knudsen, Demobilization and Reintegration During an Ongoing Conflict, 37 Cornell Int'l L. J. 487, 499 (2012).

75. Hamer, supra.

76. Myriam Denov and Richard Maclure, Child Soldiers in Sierra Leone: Experiences, Implications, and Strategies for Community Reintegration (2005); and Myriam Denov and Richard Maclure, Engaging the Voices of Girls in the Aftermath of Sierra Leone's Conflict: Experiences and Perspectives in a Culture of Violence, 48 Anthropologica 73 (2006).

77. William P. Murphy, Military Patrimonialism and Child Soldier Clientalism in the Liberian and Sierra Leonean Civil Wars, 46 Afr. Stud. Rev. 61, 62 (2012). See Cecilia Wainryb, "And So They Ordered Me to Kill a Person": Conceptualizing the Impacts of Child Soldiering on the Development of Moral Agency, 54 Hum. Dev. 273, 283 (2011); and Theresa S. Betancourt, Developmental Perspectives on Moral Agency in Former Child Soldiers: Commentary on Wainryb, 54 Hum. Dev. 307 (2011) (endorsing Wainryb's analysis).

78. P. W. Singer, Children at War (2006).

79. In Dave Eggers, What Is the What (2006), the boy Achak recounts the story he heard from Deng, another boy who tried to escape the Sudan People's Liberation Army by climbing into a truck filled with deserters: "I sat in the truck with all the rebels. It was very scary at first because they all had guns. They were very tired and they looked mean and like they hated me. But I stayed quiet and because I was quiet, they liked me. I rode with them to another village and they let me stay with them. I was a rebel, Achak! I lived at their camp for weeks staying with a man named Malek Kuach Malek. He was a commander of the SPLA. He was very important. . . . He became my father. He said I would be a soldier soon, that he was going to train me. I became his assistant. I fetched water for him and cleaned his sunglasses and turned his radio on and off. . . . I thought I would just be his son forever, Achak. I was happy to live with him as long as I could" (116–17). But soon the government army arrived, the rebels scattered, explosions occurred, and Deng never saw Malek again.

80. Oloya, supra, 138–40.

81. Angucia, supra, at 119–20.

82. See Rebecca Florey, The Reality of Colombia's Child Soldiers, Colombia Reports (Feb. 17, 2015), http://colombiareports.com/reality-colombias -child-soldiers/ (reporting study by Dr. Natalia Springer in 2012 suggesting that 81 percent of children studied "volunteer" due to economic or social

pressures or because they believe the group will offer an income, food, or security).

83. Adults who claim coercion or lack of autonomy may be reflecting societal tumult, mental illness, or brainwashing. See William Graebner, Patty's Got a Gun: Patricia Hearst in 1970s America (1980); and Patricia Campbell Hearst, Patty Hearst: Her Story (1988).

84. Susan Shepler, The Rise of the Child: Global Discourses of Youth and Reintegrating Child Soldiers in Sierra Leone, 4 J. Hum. Rts. 197 (2012).

85. Mats Utas, Victimcy, Girlfriending, Soldiering: Tactic Agency in a Young Woman's Social Navigation of the Liberian War Zone, 78 Anthropological Q. 403, 414–15, 426 (2005). Placed in an arranged marriage at sixteen, the young woman ran away and started dating military men. After one was murdered, she (by then nineteen) formed a relationship with the commando sent to interrogate her.

86. Id. See also Betancourt (2011), supra, at 307.

87. See Ping Fu, Bend, Not Break: A Life in Two Worlds (2012) (the memoir of a former child soldier in China who became CEO in the United States); and Theresa S. Betancourt, The Social Ecology of Resilience in War-Affected Youth: A Longitudinal Study from Sierra Leone, in Michael Ungar, ed., The Social Ecology of Resilience: A Handbook of Theory and Practice 347 (2012).

88. Kearns, supra.

89. Rosen (2005), supra.

90. Wainryb, supra.

91. See "Assessing Agency and Responsibility," pages 45–53 of this book.

92. Ozerdem and Podder, supra; Rosen (2005), supra; and Ryan, supra.

93. Ryan, supra (discussing Southern Sudan). For discussions of reintegration efforts—which often involve integration into a new community, see James B. Pugel, Disaggregating the Causal Factors Unique to Child Soldiering: The Case of Liberia, in Scott Gates and Simon Reich, eds., Child Soldiers in the Age of Fractured States 173–74 (2010) (discussing Liberia); Laura Stovel, "There's No Bad Bush to Throw Away a Bad Child"; "Tradition"-Inspired Reintegration in Post-War Sierra Leone, 46 J. Mod. Afr. Stud. 305 (2008) (Sierra Leone). Participation in cleansing ceremonies can assist girls returning from serving as sex slaves or "wives" of combatants, yet some communities involve only male returnees in such rituals. See Lindsay Stark, Cleansing the Wounds of War: An Examination of Traditional Healing, Psychosocial Health, and Reintegration in Sierra Leone, 4 Intervention 206 (2006); and Vivu Savrou, Breaking the Silence: Girls Abducted During the Armed Conflict in Angola (2004).

94. Children and Armed Conflict in the Democratic Republic of the Congo: Report of the Secretary-General, May 2018, http://www.un.org/ga/search/view_doc.asp?symbol=S/2018/502&Lang=E&Area=UNDOC.

95. Michael Wessells, The Reintegration of Formerly Recruited Girls: A Resil-

ience Approach, in Daniel Thomas Cook and John Wall, eds., Children and Conflict: Cross-Disciplinary Investigations 189 (2011).

96. Child Soldiers International, Democratic Republic of Congo: Make Home Again (2017), https://www.child-soldiers.org/democratic-republic-of-congo (quoting sixteen-year-old Neema in the Democratic Republic of the Congo).

97. See Michael Wessells, Girls in Armed Force and Groups in Angola: Implications for Ethical Research and Reintegration, in Gates and Reich, supra, at 183, 194–95.

98. Shepler, supra.

99. Michael Wessells, Psychosocial Issues in Reintegrating Child Soldiers, 37 Cornell Int'l L. J. 513 (2004)

100. Id., at 523; and Rosen (2007), supra. A successful strategy is to direct goods to schools that integrate former child soldiers into regular classrooms so that benefits flow to the community. Dallaire, supra, at 174.

101. K. Amone-P'Olak, N. Garnefski, and V. Kraaj, The Impact of War Experiences and Physical Abuse on Formerly Abducted Boys in Northern Uganda, S. Afr. Psychiatr. Rev. 80–81 (2007).

102. Angela Veale and Aki Stavrou, Former Lord's Resistance Army Child Soldier Abductees: Explorations of Identity in Reintegration and Reconciliation, 13 J. Peace Psychol. 273 (2007).

103. Grace Akello, Annemiek Richters, and Ria Reis, Reintegration of Former Child Soldiers in Northern Uganda: Coming to Terms with Children's Agency and Accountability, 4 Intervention 229 (2006); Tim Allen, Trial Justice: The International Criminal Court and the Lord's Resistance Army 114 (2006); and Honwana, supra.

104. Peter Aldhous, Brutalised Child Soldiers Can Return to Normalcy, 10 New Scientist 6–7 (2008) (citing the work of Neil Boothby on Mozambique).

105. Id.

106. Drumbl, supra.

107. Baines, supra, at 103–4 (discussing Achioli traditions).

108. Id., at 114.

109. Theresa S. Bentacourt, Jessica Agnew-Blais, Stephen E. Gilman, David R. Williams, and B. Heidi Ellis, Past Horrors, Present Struggle: The Role of Stigma in the Association Between War Experiences and Psychosocial Adjustment Among Former Child Soldiers in Sierra Leone, 70 Soc. Sci. & Med. 17, 18–19, 24 (2010). This study indicates that stigma upon returning home affects the consequences of former child soldiers' involving in wounding or killing others; stigma also plays a role in depression following rape of girls, but experiencing rape "appears to exert independent effects on anxiety, hostility and prosocial behavior over time" (24).

110. Thanks to Netta Barak Cohen for this formulation.

111. UNICEF, Paris Principles (2007), http://www.unicef.org/emerg/files/ParisPrinciples310107English.pdf.

112. Theresa S. Betancourt, Ryan McBain, Elizabeth A. Newnham, Adeyinka M. Akinsulure-Smith, Robert T. Brennan, John R. Weisz, and Nathan B. Hansen, A Behavioral Intervention for War-Affected Youth in Sierra Leone: A Randomized Controlled Trial, 53 J. Am. Acad. Child & Adolesc. Psychiatry 1288 (2014) (finding significant effects on the emotional regulation, attitudes, behaviors, and functioning and school engagement of youth in war-affected regions with group intervention, using cognitive-behavioral therapy, group interpersonal therapy, and trauma-focused assistance). See also Todd F. Holzman and Terry Holzman, Healing the Invisible Wounds: Persistence of Traumatic Stress Among Former Child Soldiers in Uganda, Reflections from Work in 2 African Journal of Traumatic Stress 79–84 (2011) (Teachers and others report that "prayer, traditional cleansing ceremonies, acceptance by their communities, sharing stories, consistently enforced behavior rules, and athletic activities have helped to ease" the children's acute pain "but nothing erases it entirely"). See Child Soldiers Program, FROUganda, http://frouganda.org/child-soliders-and-abductees/; Community Engagement for Universal Access, International HIV-AIDS Alliance, http://frouganda.org/wp-content/uploads/2018/03/Community_Engagement_for_ARV_treatment.pdf; Anywar Ricky Richard: Healing the Wounds of War, World of Children, October 10, 2012, https://worldofchildren.org/anywar-ricky-richard-world-of-children/.

113. Harvard Humanitarian Initiative, "We Came Back with Empty Hands": Understanding the Disarmament, Demobilization and Reintegration of Children Formerly Associated with Armed Groups in the DRC (2013), https://hhi.harvard.edu/publications/we-came-back-empty-hands-understanding-disarmament-demobilization-and-reintegration.

114. Atri and Cusimano, supra, at 45, 46, 49.

115. Id., at 55.

116. See Brandon A. Kohrt, Mark J. D. Jordans, and Christopher A. Morley, Four Principles of Mental Health Research and Psychosocial Intervention for Child Soldiers: Lessons Learned in Nepal, 7 International Psychiatry 57 (2010); and Aoife R. Singh and Ashok N. Singh, The Mental Health Consequences of Being a Child Soldier—An International Perspective, 7 Int'l Psychiatry 55 (2010).

117. Myriam Denov, Coping with the Trauma of War: Former Child Soldiers in Post-Conflict Sierra Leone, 553 Int'l. Social Work 791, 798 (2010).

118. Dallaire, supra, at 152 (quoting Emmanuel Jal's song "Baakiwara").

119. Byron Williston, The Importance of Self-Forgiveness, 48 Am. Philos. Q. 67 (2012) (discussing how wrongdoers must forgive themselves in order to merit forgiveness). Thoughtful reflections on self-forgiveness are developed in Solomon Schimmel, Wounds Not Healed by Time: The Power of Repentance and Forgiveness 123 (2002): "A central idea in self-forgiveness is that the offender learns to differentiate between the specific offense(s) he committed and his

overall estimate of his worth as a human being. This is similar to what happens in interpersonal forgiveness in Enright's model. The victim allows his appreciation of the intrinsic human worth of the offender, and his right to love and compassion, to overcome his hostility toward him for the specific unjust acts he committed. So too in self-forgiveness, you don't judge yourself solely, or primarily, on the basis of your specific sins, crimes, or offenses. You acknowledge the wrongs that you did and hold yourself responsible for them and their consequences, but you also look upon yourself with love and compassion, which dissipates your guilt, your shame, and your anger at yourself." See Robert D. Enright and the Human Development Study Group, Counseling Within the Forgiveness Triad: On Forgiving, Receiving Forgiveness, and Self-Forgiveness, 40 Counseling & Values 107 (1996).

120. Verhey, supra; and Schauer and Elbert, supra, at 341.

121. Save the Children, Forgotten Casualties of War: Girls in Armed Conflict (2005).

122. Joanna Shapland, Forgiveness and Restorative Justice: Is It Necessary? Is It Helpful?, 5 Oxford J. Law & Relig. 94 (2016), https://doi.org/10.1093/ojlr/rwv038; and Ted Wachtel, Restorative Justice Is Not Forgiveness, Huff. Post (Jan. 30, 2013), https://huffingtonpost.com/ted-watchtel/restorative-justice-is-no_b_256753.html. For a thoughtful critique of restorative justice in light of the demands it places on victims, see Analise Acron, Compulsory Compassion: A Critique of Restorative Justice 24–25, 142–59, 161–62 (2004).

123. See Theresa S. Betancourt and A. Ettien, Transitional Justice and Youth Formerly Associated with Armed Forces and Armed Groups: Acceptance, Marginalization and Psychosocial Adjustment, UNICEF and Innocenti Research Centre Working Paper (2010); and Emily Vargas-Baron, National Policies to Prevent Recruitment of Child Soldiers, in Gates and Reich, supra, at 203, 220–21.

Ishmael Beah, author of the 2007 memoir A Long Way Gone, has commented in an interview: "In my opinion, Sierra Leone and these reintegration programs failed miserably because a lot of things were not put into account. When you reintegrate with society, they have to provide a peaceful environment where you're not pulled back again; they have to find families that really care and want to take you in. You're going to have to include community as part of this process. Also, if you give them vocational training, they feel like they can use that to find a livelihood, but a lot of things have to happen for it to succeed. There's quite a number of people who survived, but compared to the number of people that were subjected to this it's very little. Very few people were able to completely step away." See Ishmael Beah Was Never Very Far Away, PowellsBooks (Feb. 21, 2007), http://www.powells.com/blog/interviews/ishmael-beah-was-never-very-far-away-by-dave/.

124. Pew Charitable Trusts, State of Recidivism (2011), http://www.pewtrusts.org/~/media/legacy/uploadedfiles/pcs_assets/2011/pewstateofrecidivismpdf.pdf.

125. Center on Juvenile and Criminal Justice, Juvenile Justice History, http:// www.cjcj.org/Education1/Juvenile-Justice-History.html.

126. Id.

127. Jane Addams Hull House Association, Jane Addams and Child Protection, https://janeaddamshullhouse.org/history/jane-addams-and-child-protection/. For an exploration of the promise and limits of this effort, see Martha Minow, Making All the Difference: Inclusion, Exclusion, and American Law (1990) (chap. 8).

128. See David M. Levy, Beginnings of the Child Guidance Movement, 38 Am. J. Orthopsychiatr. 799 (1968). For a philosophical treatment of the capacities of "juveniles" compared with children, and the contrast between a status as a person and as a future adult, see Tom D. Campbell, The Rights of the Minor: As Person, as Child, as Juvenile, as Future Adult, 6 Int'l. J. Law & Fam. 1, 19, 22 (1992).

129. Aaron Kupchik, Judging Juveniles: Prosecuting Adolescents in Adult and Juvenile Courts (2006). Building on psychological research and empirical evidence, recent reformers revive juvenile justice ideals after part of the United States developed laws shifting juveniles to adult court and prisons. Thomas Grisso and Robert G. Schwartz, eds., Youth on Trial: A Developmental Perspective on Juvenile Justice (2000).

130. Juvenile justice courts and detention centers often depart from the ideal, however, and increasingly, reformers urge efforts to divert juveniles from detention in order to avoid abuse and bad influences in prison. See Models for Change, Diversion Guidebook (2011), http://www.modelsforchange.net/ publications/301; and Laurence Steinberg, Age of Opportunity: Lessons from the New Science of Adolescence (2015).

131. Convention on the Rights of the Child (1989), Section 1 (37)(a) (calling for periodic review of incarcerated children); Committee on the Rights of the Child, General Comment No. 10; and Children's Rights in Juvenile Justice (2007), Paragraph 77, available in Magne Frostad, Child Soldiers: Recruitment, Use and Punishment, 1 Int'l Fam. L., Pol'y & Prac. 87 (2013).

132. Anthony M. Platt, The Child Savers: The Invention of Delinquency (40th anniversary ed. 2009). In the United States, institutions reflecting racial prejudices seem to have marked many black and Hispanic boys for paths to prison rather than to constructive support. See Ann Arnett Ferguson, Bad Boys: Public Schools in the Making of Black Masculinity (2001); and Victor Rios, Punished: Policing the Lives of Black and Latino Boys (2011).

133. See Thomas J. Bernard and Megan C. Kurlychek, The Cycle of Juvenile Justice 213215 (2d ed. 2010).

134. Id., at 26235.

135. M. S. Umbreit, R. B. Coates, and B. Kalanj, Victim Meets Offender: The Impact of Restorative Justice and Mediation (1994) (quantitative and qualitative evaluation showing successful effects of mediation on juveniles' likelihood of

following through on restitution); and Howard Zehr, The Little Book of Restorative Justice (rev. ed. 2015) (classic handbook about restorative justice methods).

136. See Barbara Crossette, Sierra Leone to Try Juveniles Separately in UN Tribunal Plan, N.Y. Times (Oct. 10, 2006), http://www.nytimes.com/2000/10/06/world/sierra-leone-to-try-juveniles-separately-in-un-tribunal-plan.html. Academics supported the proposal. See, e.g., Diane Marie Amann, Calling Children to Account: The Proposal for Juvenile Chamber in the Special Court for Sierra Leone, 29 Pepp. L. Rev. 167 (2001); Joshua A. Romero, The Special Court for Sierra Leone and the Juvenile Soldier Dilemma, 2 Nw. J. Int'l Hum. Rts. 8 (2004), http://www.law.northwestern.edu/journals/jihr/v2/8/; and Tiefenbrun, supra.

137. Aptel, supra, at 104–5 (quoting Report of the Secretary-General on the Establishment of a Special Court for Sierra Leone, UN Doc S/2000/915, Oct. 4, 2000, Paragraph 35). The statute authorizing prosecution of minors also emphasized the importance of not jeopardizing rehabilitation programs for juveniles and pointed to the possibility of "an alternative truth and reconciliation mechanism." Statute of the Special Court for Sierra Leone, Article 15, Paragraph 5, Jan. 16, 2002.

138. See Statute of the Special Court for Sierra Leone, Articles 7(2), 15(5), 19(1), http://www.rscsl.org/Documents/scsl-statute.pdf.

139. Compare Ilene Cohen, The Protection of Children and the Quest for Truth and Justice in Sierra Leone, 55 J. Int'l Aff. 1 (2001), with Monique Ramgoolie, Prosecution of Sierra Leone's Child Soldiers: What Message Is the UN Trying to Send? J. Public & Int'l Aff. (2001), https://jpia.princeton.edu/sites/jpia/files/2001–8.pdf.

140. Special Court for Sierra Leone, Press Release, Nov. 2, 2002, quoted in Aptel, supra, at 104 (statement of David Crane indicating he would not prosecute children). The special Panels for Serious Crimes in East Timor, a hybrid between international and domestic legal systems, was authorized to pursue persons over twelve, but they chose not to invoke that authorization in only one case. Reconciliation activities involving families and community members provide a model for similar symbolic and practical mechanisms for reintegration. See Dionísio Babo-Soares, Nahe biti: The Philosophy and Process of Grassroots Reconciliation (and Justice) in East Timor, 5 Asia Pac. J. Anthropol. 15 (2004), http://www.tandfonline.com/doi/full/10.1080/1444221042000201715?src=recsys; Spencer Zifcak, The Asia Foundation—Restorative Justice in East Timor: An Evaluation of the Community Reconciliation Process of the CAVR, http://pdf.usaid.gov/pdf_docs/Pnado632.pdf. Representing some accommodations in light of the defendant's age, the proceedings were closed to the public, the judges did not wear robes, the individual was permitted to halt the proceedings to ask questions or to rest, and the individual's name was replaced with an "X" in all court records. But questions have been raised about the nature of the police interrogation, the use of a four-month pretrial deten-

tion with no review, and others elements of the case, leading up to a guilty plea to manslaughter after the individual was prosecuted for crimes against humanity occurring when he was fourteen. Aptel, supra, at 102–3.

141. Elisabeth Schauer and Thomas Elbert, The Psychological Impact of Child Soldiering, in Erin Martz, ed., Trauma Rehabilitation After War and Conflict 311, 344–45 (2010).

142. Irene Cohn, The Protection of Children in Peacemaking and Peacekeeping Processes, 12 Harv. Hum. Rts. J. 129 (1999).

143. See Save the Children, Unspeakable Crimes Against Children: Sexual Violence in Conflict (2013) (stressing that attention to structural problems leading to the recruitment of child soldiers is more critical than efforts to hold individuals accountable); and Corinna Csaky, No One to Turn To: The Under-Reporting of Child Sexual Exploitation and Abuse by Aid Workers and Peacekeepers (2008) (arguing that short-term transitional justice processes neither invest in mental health and infrastructure nor prevent future recruitment and exploitation of children).

144. Even an adult criminal system could allow the former child soldier the defense of duress or a mitigated sentence if the atrocities were perpetrated under coercion, and it would also take into account the special vulnerabilities of former child soldiers. Amnesty International, Child Soldiers: Criminals or Victims? (2000), https://www.amnesty.org/en/documents/ior50/002/2000/en/.

145. Amnesty International (2000), supra.

146. Mohamed Pa-Momo Fofanah, Juvenile Justice and Children in Armed Conflict: Facing the Fact and Forging the Future via the Sierra Leone Test (2004) (LL.M. thesis, Harvard Law School).

147. In Re Gault, 387 U.S. 1 (1967).

148. Fofanah, supra. See also Happold (2006), supra.

149. Michael Custer, Punishing Child Soldiers: The Special Court for Sierra Leone and the Lessons to be Learned from the United States' Juvenile Justice System, 19 Temple Int'l & Comp. L.J. 499 (2005).

150. Dallaire, supra, at 171; and Betancourt and Ettien, supra. See Emily Delap, No Place Like Home? Children's Experiences of Reintegration in the Kailahun District of Sierra Leone (2004) (urging that disarmament, demobilization, and reintegration programs assist all child soldiers, whether or not they physically fought, in order to avoid resentment between those helped and those not helped).

151. See "Analogies Between Youth Gangs and Child Soldiers," pages 65–68 of this book.

152. Stovel, supra, at 312.

153. Stephanie Lee Goins, The Place of Forgiveness in the Reintegration of Former Child Soldiers in Sierra Leone, 27 Transformation 133 (2010).

154. Quoted in Stovel, supra, at 312.

155. Mark Austin Walters, Hate Crime and Restorative Justice: Exploring Causes,

Repairing Harms (2014) (empirical study of restorative justice efforts to address hate crimes in England). Restorative justice efforts around the world include traditional conflict resolution institutions and new programs, influenced by psychology and mediation. See Restorative Justice Online, Restorative Justice Around the World, http://www.restorativejustice.org/university-classroom/02world.

156. Philip Cook and Cheryl Heykoop, in Children and Transitional Justice, in Parmar, Roseman, Siegrist, and Sowa, supra, at 159. See generally Nicholas A. Jones and Rob Nestor, Sentencing Circles in Canada and the Gacaca in Rwanda: A Comparative Analysis, 21 Int'l. Crim. Just. Rev. (2011), http://journals.sagepub.com/doi/pdf/10.1177/1057567711399433.

157. Parmar, Roseman, Siegrist, and Sowa, supra; and Jessica Senehi and Sean Byrn, in Siobhan McEvoy-Levy, ed., Troublemakers or Peacemakers?: Youth and Post-Accord Peace Building (2006).

158. Alexander Laban Hinton, Transitional Justice: Global Mechanisms and Local Realities After Genocide and Mass Violence 6 (2010).

159. Human Rights Watch, Lasting Wounds: Consequences of Genocide and War for Rwanda's Children (2003), https://www.hrw.org/report/2003/04/03/lasting-wounds/consequences-genocide-and-war-rwandas-children. Rwanda treated children fourteen to eighteen as criminally responsible but eligible for leniency in penalties. Id. at n.120.

160. Véronica Beatriz Piñero, The Challenges of Reconstruction and Reconciliation Following an Armed Conflict: The Implementations for Child Soldiers as Perpetrators, 1 Eyes on the ICC (2004); Michael Wessells, Child Soldiers: From Violence to Prevention (2006); and Wainryb, supra.

161. See Drumbl, supra. Some who favor use of truth and reconciliation processes find this an alternative for some with juvenile justice an alternative for others. See, e.g., Amann, supra; Godfrey M. Musila, Challenges in Establishing the Accountability of Child Soldiers for Human Rights Violations: Restorative Justice as an Option, 5 Afr. Hum. Rts. L. J. 321 (2005); Piñero, supra, at 30; and David M. Rosen, Who Is a Child? The Legal Conundrum of Child Soldiers, 25 Conn. J. Int'l L. 81 (2009).

162. Fania E. Davis, Restorative Justice, Social Movements, and the Law, Harvard Law School Forum (Mar. 21, 2018). See Restorative Justice for Oakland Youth, http://rjoyoakland.org/restorative-justice/; Sonia Jain, Henrissa Bassey, Martha A. Brown, and Preety Kalra, Restorative Justice in Oakland Schools: Implementation and Impacts (2014), https://www.ousd.org/cms/lib/CA01001176/Centricity/Domain/134/OUSD-RJ%20Report%20revised%20Final.pdf.

163. See Cécile Aptel and Virginie Ladisch, Through a New Lens: A Child-Sensitive Approach to Transitional Justice 12 (2011); and Saudamini Siegrist, Child Rights and Transitional Justice, in Parmar, Roseman, Siegrist, and Sowa, supra, at 1, 14. John Braithwaite argues for "reintegrative shaming" to

advance social inclusion and healing through rituals of repentance and forgiveness. John Braithwaite, Crime, Shame and Reintegration 150–57 (1989).

164. Jessica Senehi and Sean Byrne, From Violence Toward Peace: The Role of
Storytelling for Youth Healing and Political Empowerment After Social Conflict, in Siobhan McEvoy-Levy, ed., Troublemakers or Peacemakers? Youth
and Post-Accord Peace Building (2006) (the RIREC Project on Post Accord
Peace Building).

165. UNICEF and Innocenti Research Centre, Children and Truth Commissions
10 (2010).

166. Statute of the Special Court for Sierra Leone, Article 15, Paragraph 5, Jan.
16, 2002.

167. UNICEF and Innocenti Research Centre, supra, at 11; Alison Smith, Basic
Assumptions of Transitional Justice and Children, in Parmar, Roseman,
Siegrist, and Sowa, supra, at 31, 41.

168. Philip Cook and Cheryl Heykopp, Child Participation in the Sierra Leonean
Truth and Reconciliation Commission, in Parmar, Roseman, Siegrist and
Sowa, supra, at 159, 183.

169. UNICEF and Innocenti Research Centre, supra, at 11; Theo Sowa, Children
and the Liberian Truth and Reconciliation Commission, in Parmar, Roseman,
Siegrist, and Sowa, supra, at 193.

170. Hema Chatlani, Uganda: A Nation in Crisis, 37 Cal. West. Int'l L. J. 277
(2007). See also UNICEF and Innocenti Research Centre, supra, at 8 (children are "to describe their roles in violations committed and to be heard and
supported by their communities").

171. See Mark. A. Drumbl, Child Soldiers: Agency, Enlistment, and the Collectiv-
ization of Innocence, in Alette Smeulers, ed., Collective Violence and International Criminal Justice: An Interdisciplinary Approach 207 (2010).

172. See Chapter 1, discussing South African TRC.

173. Rosalind Shaw, Rethinking Truth and Reconciliation Commissions: Lessons
from Sierra Leone (2005); and Rosalind Shaw, Memory Frictions: Localizing
the Truth and Reconciliation Commission in Sierra Leone, 1 Int'l. J. Transitional Just.183 (2007).

174. See Stovel, supra, 305, 312.

175. Atri and Cusimano, supra, at 65.

176. Id., at 61, 65 (describing northern Uganda).

177. Id., at 65.

178. Angucia, supra, at 177–79, 182–83. Despite tension between traditional rituals and Christian beliefs, some people sought both in reintegration efforts in
northern Uganda. Id., at 180. A critic of any accountability effort applied to
child soldiers warns that even nonjudicial truth and reconciliation commissions or local cleansing practices may interfere with rehabilitation by inducing
shame or trauma for child soldiers. Sonja C. Grover, Child Soldier Victims
of Genocidal Forceful Transfer (2012) (chap. 5). See also Michael Wessells,

Supporting the Mental Health and Psychosocial Well-Being of Former Child Soldiers, 48 J. Am. Acad. Child Psy. 587 (2009) (community ritual responding to views of past violence as an injury to the community); Melanie Lidman, Heart of Forgiveness: Ugandan Women Once Child Soldiers Now Lead Peace, Global Sisters Report (Dec. 21, 2017), https://www.globalsistersreport.org/news/equality/heart-forgiveness-ugandan-women-once-child-soldiers-now-lead-peace-51061.

179. Oloya, supra, at 166–76; and Atri and Cusimano, supra, at 56–59.

180. Joseph Yav Katshung, Mato Oput Versus the International Criminal Court (ICC) in Uganda, Pambazuka News (Sept. 28, 2006), https://www.pambazuka.org/governance/mato-oput-versus-international-criminal-court-icc-uganda; and Patrick Tom, The Acholi Traditional Approach to Justice and the War in Northern Uganda, Beyond Intractability (Oct. 2006), https://www.beyondintractability.org/casestudy/tom-acholi.

181. Lindsay Stark, Cleansing the Wounds of War: An Examination of Traditional Healing, Psychosocial Health and Reintegration in Sierra Leone, 7 Intervention 206 (2006); and Carol B. Thompson, Beyond Civil Society: Child Soldiers as Citizens in Mozambique, 80 Rev. Afr. Polit. Econ. 191 (1999). For a general endorsement of traditional cleansing and healing rituals for child soldiers, see Honwana, supra. Revisions of old traditions would be needed to overcome exclusion or judgmental approaches to returning girls and women. Prudence Acirokop, The Potential and Limits of Matu Oput as a Tool for Reconciliation and Justice, in Parmar, Roseman, Siegrist, and Sowa, supra, at 267; Kristopher Carlson and Dyan Mazurana, Accountability for Sexual and Gender-Based Crimes by the Lord's Resistance Army, in Parmar, Roseman, Siegrist, and Sowa, supra, at 235; and Dallaire, supra, at 175–82.

182. Thompson, supra.

183. An award-winning documentary offers a different kind of truth telling about an individual who became a commander in the Revolutionary United Front in the years after his abduction by the group in its fight against the government of Sierra Leone. Rebecca Richmond Cohen, War Don Don (2010), http://www.wardondonfilm.com/. On dilemmas in prosecuting and defending Issa Hassan Sesay, see Hague Justice Portal, Issa Hassan Sesay, http://haguejusticeportal.net/index.php?id=8320 (criminal trial by the Special Court for Sierra Leone).

184. Harris, supra (describing author's use of dance/movement therapy with ex-combatant teenagers in Sierra Leone, to dramatize their time with the rebel army, express suppressed rage, and practice reconnecting with others).

185. International groups engaged in drug and arms dealing specifically recruit young people to advance their own ends. See Amado Philip de Andrés, West Africa Under Attack: Drugs, Organized Crime, and Terrorism as the New Threats to Global Security, UNISCI Discussion Papers No. 16 (Jan. 2008), https://www.ucm.es/data/cont/media/www/pag-72513/UNISCI%20

DP%2016%20-%20Andres.pdf; Patrick Sawyer, Young Guns for Hire: Gangs Recruiting Children for Contract Killings, Telegraph (May 29, 2011), http://www.telegraph.co.uk/news/uknews/crime/8544029/Young-guns-for-hire-gangs-recruiting-children-for-contract-killings.html; Frances Robles, Fleeing Gang, Children Head for the US Border, N.Y. Times (July 9, 2014), http://www.nytimes.come/2014/07/10/world/americas/fleeing-gangs-head-to-us-border.html; Annabel Symington, Pakistan's Criminal and Terrorist Gangs Have New Recruits: Street Kids, Global Post (Mar. 3, 2014), https://www.pri.org/stories/2014-03-03/pakistans-criminal-and-terrorist-gangs-have-new-recruits-street-kids; and Jim Heiser, Mexican Cartels Are Recruiting American Children, New American (Oct. 9, 2011), http://www.thenewamerican.com/usnews/crime/item/7547-mexican-cartels-are-recruiting-american-children.

186. Danielle Allen, Cuz: The Life and Times of Michael A. 99, 150–51, 216 (2017).

187. U.S. Department of Justice, Office of Juvenile Justice and Delinquency Prevention, Juveniles in Corrections (2016), https://www.ojjdp.gov/ojstatbb/corrections/qa08201.asp?qaDate=2016 (as of October 26, 2016, 45,567 juvenile offenders were held in residential placement facilities).

188. Derek W. Black, Ending Zero Tolerance: The Crisis of Absolute School Discipline (2016).

189. Editors of Rethinking Schools, Restorative Justice: What It Is and What It Is Not, 29 Rethinking Schools (Fall 2014), https://www.rethinkingschools.org/articles/restorative-justice. See ACLU, Locating the School-to-Prison Pipeline, https://www.aclu.org/files/images/asset_upload_file966_35553.pdf (discussing the policies and practices that affect the movement of youth out of classrooms and into juvenile and criminal justice systems); and Dan J. Losen, Discipline Policies, Successful Schools, and Racial Justice (2011), http://nepc.colorado.edu/publication/discipline-policies.

190. Belinda Hopkins, Restorative Justice in Schools, 17 Support for Learning 144 (2002), https://onlinelibrary.wiley.com/doi/abs/10.1111/1467-9604.00254; Susan Dominus, An Effective but Exhausting Alternative to High School Suspensions, N.Y. Times (September 7, 2016), https://www.nytimes.com/2016/09/11/magazine/an-effective-ut-exhausting-alternative-to-high-school-suspensions.html?_r=0; and Fania Davis, "Restorative Justice" Program Has Become a Vital Tool for Public, East Bay Times (Dec. 9, 2014), https://www.eastbaytimes.com/2014/12/09/guest-commentary-restorative-justice-program-has-become-a-vital-tool-for-public/.

191. See Special Representative of the Secretary General on Violence Against Children, Report on Restorative Justice for Children (2013), http://srg.violenceagainstchildren.org/sites/default/files/publications_final/srgvac_restorative_justice_for_children_report.pdf; International Juvenile Justice Observatory, http://www.oijj.org/en/busqueda/docs?title='restorative; and Janice Wearmouth, Rawiri Mckinney, and Ted Glynn, Restorative Justice in

Schools: A New Zealand Example, 49 Educational Research 37 (Mar. 2007), http://sharepoint.tcrsb.ca/ycmhs/webpage/RA/Relevant%20Literature/Restorative%20Justice%20New%20Zealand.pdf.

192. Petula Dvorak, For One of Sudan's "Lost Boys" and Teens in D.C. Jail, a Shared Struggle, Wash. Post (Oct. 8, 2010), http://www.washingtonpost.com/wp-dyn/content/article/2010/10/07/AR2010100707012.html.

193. Juliana Ratner to author, Jan. 21, 2015. Before attending Harvard Law School, Ratner worked with the youth in the D.C. jail.

194. Ishamail Al-Sankoh, Why the Youths of Sierra Leone Agree with Kofi Annan, Awareness Times, Freetown, Sierra Leone, July 7, 2006, http://news.sl/drwebsite/exec/view.cgi?archive=3&num=2976.

195. Wessells (2006), supra.

196. Dominique DuBois Gilliard, Rethinking Incarceration: Advocating for Justice That Restores 21–27 (2018). "While the United States constitutes only 5 percent of the world's population, we have 25% of its incarcerated populace" (27).

197. For a stunning story of one individual's encounter with the system, see Jennifer Gonnerman, Before the Law, New Yorker (Oct. 6, 2014), https://www.newyorker.com/magazine/2014/10/06/before-the-law.

198. Miller v. Alabama, 567 U.S. 460 (2012), Montgomery v. Louisiana, 577 U.S., 136 S.Ct. 718 (2016). Challenging Juvenile Life Without Parole: How Has Human Rights Made a Difference?, Columbia Law School Human Rights Institute (June 2014), http://www.law.columbia.edu/sites/default/files/microsites/human-rights-institute/files/jlwop_case_study_hri_0.pdf.

199. Compare Tatum v. Arizona, 580 U.S., 137 S.Ct. 11 (2016) (Sotomayor, J. concurring), with Tatum v. Arizona, 580 U.S., 113 S.Ct. 137 (2016) (Alito, J., joined by Thomas, J., dissenting from the decision to grant, vacate, and remand).

200. Human Rights Project for Girls, Center on Poverty and Inequality, and Ms. Foundation for Women, The Sexual Abuse to Prison Pipeline: The Girls' Story (2015), http://rights4girls.org/wp-content/uploads/r4g/2015/02/2015_COP_sexual-abuse_layout_web-1.pdf.

201. Anastasia Maloney, Ex-Child Soldiers in Colombia Face Their Tormentors, Christian Science Monitor (Feb. 23, 2015), http://www.csmonitor.com/World/Making-a-difference/Change-Agent/2015/0223/Ex-child-soldiers-in-Colombia-face-their-tormentors-video.

202. Id.

203. Id. (quoting Maria Eugenia Morales, a senior official at the government's victims' unit).

204. Richard Pascale, Jerry Sternin, and Monique Sternin, The Power of Positive Deviance: How Unlikely Innovators Solve the World's Toughest Problems (2010) (chap. 6, describing efforts to learn from previously outcast girls and former soldiers who had been shunned in Uganda). A program connecting former child soldiers with relatives and potential mentors abroad may

strengthen the resilience of these young people. Eric Schmidt and Jared Cohen, The New Digital Age: Reshaping the Future of People, Nations, and Businesses 246 (2013).

205. Ishmael Beah Was Never Very Far Away, PowellsBooks, Feb. 21, 2007, http://www.powells.com/blog/interviews/ishmael-beah-was-never-very-far -away-by-dave/.

Chapter 2: Forgiving Debt

1. Rabbi Jonathan Sacks, Has Europe Lost Its Soul to the Markets?, Times (Dec. 12, 2011), http://rabbisacks.org/the-times-has-europe-lost-its-soul -to-the-markets/.

2. Some propose to forgive loans for those who enter public service; see Robert Applebaum, The Proposal: Forgive Student Loan Debt, Jan. 29, 2009, http://www.forgivestudentloandebt.com/content/proposal. Others seek loan forgiveness for specified periods following graduation; see Cuomo Floats Student Loan Forgiveness Program and Sexual Assault Policies, Daily Star, Jan. 19, 2015, http://www.thedailystar.com/news/ local_news/cuomo-floats-student-loan-forgiveness-program-and-sexual -assault-policies/article_8d314ffb-c616-5c57-ad0a-290bf3356b65.html. Sen. Elizabeth Warren has advocated allowing students to refinance their loans at rates available to big banks: Elizabeth Warren's Student Loan Bill Is Worth Talking About, Boston Globe, June 10, 2014, http://www .bostonglobe.com/opinion/editorials/2014/06/10/elizabeth-warren -student-loan-bill-worth-talking-about/k0T8p8NFSd6cdXrEG3DuIO/ story.html.

3. Cameron Huddleston, The Biggest Source of Debt for Americans in Every State, GoBankingRates (Oct. 10, 2016), https://www.gobankingrates.com/net -worth/biggest-source-debt-americans-state/ (reporting on fifty-state survey).

4. OECD, OECD Sovereign Borrowing Outlook 2018: Borrowing Outlook for OECD Countries, https://www.oecd.org/finance/Sovereign-Borrowing -Outlook-in-OECD-Countries-2018.pdf; and Sovereign Debt, Why It's Important, and Rankings, Balance (2018), https://www.thebalance.com/ sovereign-debt-definition-importance-and-rankings-3306353.

5. Alexandra Bastien, Ending the Debt Trap: Strategies to Stop the Abuse of Court-Imposed Fines and Fees, PolicyLink (Mar. 2017), https://www .policylink.org/sites/default/files/ending-the-debt-trap-03-28-17.pdf.

6. Solomon Schimmel, Wounds Not Healed by Time: The Power of Repentance and Forgiveness 78 (2002) (in the Lord's Prayer, Matthew 6:12, Jesus says, "Forgive us our debts, as we have forgiven our debtors"). Margaret Atwood notes that the word for *debt* was the same as the Aramaic word for *sin* used by Jesus. Margaret Atwood, Payback: Debt and the Shadow Side of Wealth 45 (2008). She suggests that over time debt lost its association with sin, but moral judgments of debtors have restored the association with it (41).

7. Shawn Garrison, Texas Law Indicative of Counterproductive Child Support System, DadsDivorce (Oct. 2016), https://dadsdivorce.com/articles/texas -law-indicative-counterproductive-child-support-system.

8. Bruce Mann, Republic of Debtors: Bankruptcy in the Age of American Independence (2003); and Sanjay G. Reddy, International Debt: The Constructive Implications of Some Moral Mathematics, 21 Ethics & Int'l Aff. 81 (2007).

9. David Graeber, Debt: The First 5,000 Years (2011).

10. Leviticus 25–26 (calling for release of those enslaved because of debts, a Sabbath *rest* for land and people, *redistribution* of lands lost because of debt, and a *reordering* of prices for land and labor in the seventh year of a seven-year cycle). See also Luke 4:16–30, 7:36–50, 11:2–4, 16:1–13; and Matthew 6:9– 15, 18:21–35. Leviticus 25 never explicitly mentions debt, but the Jubilee is all about debt cancellation, restored community, and freedom from debt bondage. The Jubilee cycle of release builds on the Sabbath year debt release- and-rest cycle outlined in Deuteronomy 15 and Exodus 21:2 and 23:10–11, expanding from an every-seventh-year rest and release to a super-release in the fiftieth year. It was no accident that rebels against colonial authority chose a line from Leviticus 25:10: "Proclaim liberty throughout all the land, unto all the inhabitants thereof . . ." as the inscription for their liberty bell.

11. Josine Blok and Julia Krul, Debt and Its Aftermath: The Near Eastern Background to Solon's Seisachtheia, 86 Hesperia 607 (Oct.–Dec. 2017); Rossiter Johnson, Charles Horne, and John Rudd, eds., The Great Events by Famous Historians, vol. 1 (rpt. 2005); George Grote, Solon's Early Greek Legislation B.C. 594 (1905); and Solon Secundus, A Letter to Professor R. Containing a Scheme for a Seisachtheia or Modern Solonian Debt Relief Law (1863). See also William Harms, Linking Ancient Peoples, 15 U. Chicago Chronicle (1996), http://chronicle.uchicago.edu/960201/hittites.shtml (discussing Hittite text that explores the idea of debt release, and deity Tessub ordering his followers to release the people of Ebla from their debt).

12. Blok and Krul, supra, at 612.

13. Could/Should Jubilee Debt Cancellations be Reintroduced Today?, Michael Hudson (Jan. 17, 2018), http://michael-hudson.com/2018/01/could-should -jubilee-debt-cancellations-be-reintroduced-today/.

14. See "Criminal Law and Debt," pages 108–10 of this book.

15. Roland Obenchain, Roman Law of Bankruptcy, 3 Notre Dame L. Rev. 169a (1928), https://scholarship.law.nd.edu/cgi/viewcontent.cgi?article=4440& context=ndlr; Stasy Velyvis and Vilija Mikuckiene, Origin of Bankruptcy Procedure in Roman Law, 3 Jurisprudencia 285 (2009), https://www.mruni .eu/upload/iblock/b17/velyvis_mikuckiene.pdf.

16. Leviticus 25–26; Luke 4:16–30; Matthew 18:22–35; Jason J. Kilborn, Foundations of Forgiveness in Islamic Bankruptcy Law: Sources, Methodology, Diversity, 85 Am. Bank. L. J. 323 (2011). On the foundation ideas of debt in Western morality, see Gary Shapiro, Debts Due and Overdue: Beginnings of

Philosophy in Nietzsche, Heidegger, and Anaximander, in Richard Schacht, ed., Nietzsche, Genealogy, Morality: Essays on Nietzsche's Genealogy of Morals 358 (1994); Shalini Satkunanandan, Morality's Debt Perspective, in Shalini Satkunanandan, Extraordinary Responsibility: Politics Beyond the Moral Calculus (2015).

17. In Merchant of Venice, Act I, Scene 4, Portia argues:

> The quality of mercy is not strained
> it droppeth as the gentle rain from heaven
> Upon the place beneath
> It is twice blessed.
> It blesseth him that gives and him that takes.

18. Alice N. Benston, Portia, the Law, and the Tripartite Structure of the Merchant of Venice, 30 Shakespeare Quarterly 367, 369 (1979), https://www.jstor.org/stable/pdf/2869472.pdf?refreqid=excelsior%3Ac96e5201b94c86 5e5e8e85223e9ee0ee.

19. See Emma Rothschild, Economic Sentiments: Adam Smith, Condorcet, and the Enlightenment 1 (2001).

20. Thomas M. LeCarner, Of Dollars and Sense: Economies of Forgiveness in Antebellum American Law, Literature, and Culture (2014), English Graduate Theses & Dissertations 66, https://scholar.colorado.edu/cgi/viewcontent.cgi?article=1066&context=engl_gradetds; Emma Mason, Introduction: Exploring Forgiveness in Nineteenth-Century Poetry, 11 Literature Compass (Feb. 4, 2014), https://doi.org/10.1111/lic3.12123; Richard Hughes Gibson, Forgiveness in Victorian Literature: Grammar, Narrative, and Community (2015). For an exploration of the place of debt in several centuries of Western literature, see Colin Burrow, The Borrowers, Guardian (Dec. 6, 2008), https://www.theguardian.com/books/2008/dec/06/debt.

21. Atwood, supra, at 59.

22. Thomas Jefferson to James Madison, Paris (Sep. 6, 1789), in Letters of Thomas Jefferson, 1743–1826, http://www.let.rug.nl/usa/presidents/thomas-jefferson/letters-of-thomas-jefferson/jefl81.php. Indebtedness during his lifetime surely contributed to the situation, as did his decision to free his slaves (some of whom were his relatives) upon his death. The image of a clean slate began when pubs recorded the running tabs of regular customers on a blackboard; the slate was clean when the debts were all paid up or forgiven. See Atwood, supra, at 80.

23. Herbert E. Sloan, Principle and Interest: Thomas Jefferson and the Problem of Debt (1995).

24. U.S. Constitution, Fourteenth Amendment, Section 4.

25. The first bankruptcy law, enacted in 1800, covered only involuntary bankruptcy by traders; expansions to voluntary bankruptcy and more people occurred in 1841, 1867, 1898, and 1938. Further reforms altered the structure of the bankruptcy courts and other elements of the process.

26. See Franklin Noll, Repudiation!: The Crisis of United States Civil War Debt, 1865–1870, Financial History (Spring 2013), http://www.franklinnoll.com/Repudiation.pdf.

27. See Katherine Porter, ed., Broke: How Debt Bankrupts the Middle Class (2012); Teresa A. Sullivan, Elizabeth Warren, and Jay Westbrook, The Fragile Middle Class: Americans in Debt (2001); and Teresa A. Sullivan, Jay Lawrence Westbrook, and Elizabeth Warren, As We Forgive Our Debtors: Bankruptcy and Consumer Credit in America (1989). See also Joseph E. Stiglitz, The Price of Inequality: How Today's Divided Society Endangers Our Future (2013).

28. NOLO, Filing a Chapter 7 Bankruptcy: The Basic Steps, https://www.nolo.com/legal-encyclopedia/chapter-7-bankruptcy-29454.html. In the United States, individuals and business entities may choose between filing under Chapter 7, which cancels debts and liquidates property to repay creditors; and Chapters 11, 12, or 13, which establish a multiyear plan for repaying creditors and allow the individuals to keep some large assets as long as they make scheduled payments. See U.S. Courts, Liquidation Under the Bankruptcy Code, http://www.uscourts.gov/FederalCourts/Bankruptcy/BankruptcyBasics/Chapter7.aspx, http://www.uscourts.gov/FederalCourts/Bankruptcy/BankruptcyBasics/Chapter11.aspx, http://www.uscourts.gov/FederalCourts/Bankruptcy/BankruptcyBasics/Chapter12.aspx, http://www.uscourts.gov/FederalCourts/Bankruptcy/BankruptcyBasics/Chapter13.aspx.

29. NOLO, Steps in a Typical Chapter 13 Bankruptcy Case, https://www.nolo.com/legal-encyclopedia/steps-chapter-13-bankruptcy-case.html.

30. Troy Segal, Corporate Bankruptcy: An Overview (Dec. 21, 2017), https://www.investopedia.com/articles/01/120501.asp.

31. United States v. Kras, 409 U.S. 434 (1973) (holding that an indigent person barred by filing fees from filing for bankruptcy has other options, such as renegotiating with creditors).

32. See 11 U.S.C. 725; 11 U.S.C. Chapter 13; see Carron Armstrong, When to Consider Filing Under Chapter 13 Instead of Under Chapter 7, Balance (Feb. 14, 2017), https://www.thebalance.com/filing-for-chapter-13-instead-of-chapter-7–316364.

33. Rafael Efrat, The Evolution of Bankruptcy Stigma, 7 Theoretical Inquiries in Law 365 (2006), http://www.csun.edu/~re38791/pdfs/Evolution%20of%20Bankruptcy%20Stigma%20Article.pdf (discussing seventeenth- and eighteenth-century European practices).

34. Shakespeare, Merchant of Venice, Act 3, Scene 1.

35. See Efrat, supra, at 376–80 (citing reports and studies); id., at 385–92 (reporting original empirical research).

36. Frank Pipitone, Is Bankruptcy Wrong? Adjusting Your Moral Compass, Pipitone Law (Mar. 6, 2012), http://fpbankruptcylaw.com/253/is-bankruptcy-wrong-adjusting-your-moral-compass/.

37. See Bruce H. Mann, Republic of Debtors: Bankruptcy in the Age of American Independence (2002); David Skeel, Debt's Dominion: A History of Bankruptcy Laws in America (2003).

38. See., e.g., Scott Reynolds Nelson, A Nation of Deadbeats: An Uncommon History of America's Financial Disasters (2012); Recent Changes to Bankruptcy Law Hurting Consumers, Say Experts (press release on 2007 congressional hearing), Linda Sánchez, May 1, 2007, https://lindasanchez.house.gov/media-center/press-releases/recent-changes-bankruptcy-law-hurting-consumers-say-experts; Roxanne DeLaurell and Robert Rouse, The Bankruptcy Reform Act of 2005: A New Landscape, CPA Journal Online (Nov. 2006), http://www.nysscpa.org/cpajournal/2--6/1106/essentials/p36.htm. See also Jacob S. Hacker, The Great Risk Shift: The New Economic Insecurity and the Decline of the American Dream (2008). For an apparently humorous call for a return of debtors prison, see Michelle Crouch, Bring Back the Debtors Prison: Take Me, I'm Yours!, Billfold, http://thebillfold.com/2013/06/bring-back-the-debtors-prison-take-me-im-yours.

39. Jonathan C. Lipson, Debt and Democracy: Toward a Constitutional Theory of Bankruptcy, 83 Notre Dame L. Rev. 605, 613, 628, 633, 635, 685–687 (2007).

40. See Takehiro Sugiyama, Yusuke Tsugawa, Chi-Hong Tseng, Yasuki Kobayashi, and Martin F. Shapiro, Different Time Trends of Caloric and Fat Intake Between Statin Users and Nonusers Among US Adults: Gluttony in the Time of Statins?, 174 JAMA Intern. Med.1038 (2014).

41. See Oren Bar-Gill, Seduction by Contract: Law, Economics, and Psychology in Consumer Markets (2012); Only a Fraction of Those in Need File for Relief, USA Today, June 9, 2010, http://usatoday30.usatoday.com/money/economy/2010--06--09-bankruptcy09_CV_N.htm; Michelle White, Bankruptcy Reform and Credit Cards, 21 J. Econ. Perspect. 175–200 (2007).

42. See Jeremy M. Simon, Expect Credit Card Offers After Bankruptcy, Credit Cards.com (Aug. 30, 2007), http://www.creditcards.com/credit-card-news/credit-card-offers-after-bankruptcy.php; Lynette Kahlfani-Cox, Life After Bankruptcy: Five Steps to Rebuilding your Credit, Finances, and Emotions (June 3, 2011), http://www.dailyfinance.com/2011/06/03/life-after-bankruptcy-5-steps-to-rebuilding-your-credit-financ/; and Uni Bul, Why Banks Want to Give You Credit Cards After Bankruptcy, http://blog.unibulmerchantservices.com/why-banks-want-to-give-you-credit-cards-after-bankruptcy/.

43. See Richard Bitner, Confessions of a Subprime Lender: An Insider's Tale of Greed, Fraud, and Ignorance (2008); Paul Muolo and Mathew Padilla, Chain of Blame: How Wall Street Caused the Mortgage and Credit Crisis (2008); and Joseph William Singer, No Freedom Without Regulation (2015).

44. "Much of the excess debt was incurred through irresponsible mortgage refinancing, which peaked in 2006 at $322 billion, representing 2.4 percent of G.D.P. The reckless use of houses as A.T.M.'s was a major factor in decapital-

izing and destabilizing the American economy. Forgiving such debts will teach the wrong lesson: borrow in haste, repent never." Martin Hutchinson and Robert Cyran, "The Downside to a Debt Jubilee," N.Y. Times, Oct. 4, 2011, https://www.nytimes.com/2011/10/05/business/the-downside-to-a-debt-jubilee-breakingviews.html.

45. Ian Mount, Adviser to Businesses Laments Changes to Bankruptcy Law, N.Y. Times, Feb. 29, 2012, http://www.nytimes.com/2012/03/01/business/smallbusiness/bankruptcy-becomes-unaffordable-for-small-businesses.html?_r=0.

46. Christopher Farrell, Bankruptcy Reform Bites Back, Business Week, Nov. 28, 2007, http://www.businessweek.com/stories/2007–10–28/bankruptcy-reform-bites-back.

47. Susan Johnston, Five Bankruptcy Myths Debunked, May 14, 2012, http://money.usnews.com/money/personal-finance.articles/2012/05/14/5-bankruptcy-myths-debunked?page=2.

48. See Michelle J. White, Sovereigns in Distress: Do They Need Bankruptcy?, 1 Brookings Pap. Eco. Ac. 287 (2002).

49. Jessica Silber-Greenberg, New York Prosecutors Charge Payday Lenders with Usury, N.Y. Times, Aug. 12, 2014, http://dealbook.nytimes.com/2014/08/11/new-york-prosecutors-charge-payday-lenders-with-usury/.

50. Edward L. Glaeser and Jose Schinkman, Neither a Borrower Nor a Lender Be: An Economic Analysis of Interest Restrictions and Usury Laws, 41 J. Law & Econ. 1 (1998).

51. Viral V. Acharya and Krishnamurthy Subramanian, Bankruptcy Codes and Innovation, 22 Rev. Finan. Stud. 4949 (2009), https://doi.org/10.1093/rfs/hhp019.

52. See Atwood, supra, at 79–80.

53. Acharya and Subramanian, supra (referring to proposal by Australian economist Steven Keen).

54. For a discussion of what levels of debt are excessive, see Stephen G. Cecchetti, M.S. Mohanty, and Fabrizio Zampolli, The Real Effects of Debt, BIS (Sept. 2011), http://www.bis.org/publ/work352.htm (a study of debt in eighteen OECD countries from 1980 to 2010 found that debt becomes a drag on growth when governmental debt is around 85 percent of GDP, when corporate debt goes beyond 90 percent of GDP, and when household debt hits around 85 percent of GDP, although the impact is imprecisely estimated).

55. Stephen Castle, That Debt from 1720? Britain's Payment Is Coming, N.Y. Times (Dec. 28, 2014), https://www.nytimes.com/2014/12/28/world/that-debt-from-1720-britains-payment-is-coming.html. The government of Great Britain created a joint-stock company in 1711 as a public-private partnership to consolidate and reduce the cost of national debt. It was also given exclusive power to trade with South America and nearby islands (called "South Sea" in England at the time). The company's stock rose as it tackled government debt

but collapsed after it became clear that there would be no substantial trading profits from the territories, which were then controlled by Spain.

56. Lessons from Argentina's Bond Battle (editorial), N.Y. Times, July 7, 2014, http://www.nytimes.com/2014.07/05/opinion/05sat2.html.

57. Initial terms of a sovereign debt instrument could offer help for negotiated restructuring by including clauses to allow restructuring of the debts if a majority or two-thirds of all investors agree to it. Id. But such clauses can themselves be challenged in court. Ellen Brown, Cry for Argentina: Fiscal Mismanagement, Odious Debt or Pillage?, Inter Press Service News Agency, Aug. 14, 2014, http://www.ipsnews.net/2014/08/cry-for-argentina-fiscal-mismanagement-odious-debt-or-pillage/.

58. Carmen M. Reinhart and Kenneth Rogoff, This Time is Different: Eight Centuries of Financial Folly (2011).

59. William Easterly, The Elusive Quest for Growth (2001).

60. Odette Lineau, Rethinking Sovereign Debt: Politics, Reputation, and Legitimacy in Modern Finance 98 (2014).

61. Aristotle, Politics, bk. III.

62. Alexander Nahum Sack, Les effets des transformations des états sur leurs dettes publique et autres obligations financières (1927) (translated by author).

63. Norway began a program of sovereign debt forgiveness in 1999 and shared a detailed plan for using debt relief as a strategy for combating poverty. Norway, Ministry of Foreign Affairs, A Plan of Action, Debt Relief for Development (2004),http://www.regjeringen.no/upload/kilde/ud/rap/2004/0225/ddd/pdfv/217380-debtplan.pdf. See Anna Gelpern, Odious, Not Debt, 70 Law & Contemp. Probs. 110, 108 (2007) (emphasizing that Norway's decision was unilateral and not obligatory); Robert Howse, The Concept of Odious Debt in Public International Law, U.N. Conference on Trade and Development Discussion Paper 16 (July 2007), http://econpapers.repec.org/paper/uncdispap/185.htm (discussing Norway's debt cancellation in relation to the Ship Export Campaign of 1977–80).

64. Graeme Smith, A New Euro Crisis Strategy: Deny the Debt, Globe and Mail, https://www.theglobeandmail.com/news/world/a-new-euro-crisis-strategy-deny-the-debt/article4183949/.

65. Its advocates tend to identify five elements that can be summarized this way: (1) Do the leaders declining repayment of the debt represent a new and responsible sovereign regime, replacing a prior oppressive one? (2) Was the debt undertaken by a prior leader or government, acting at the time as sovereign of the nation? (3) Did the debt fail to reflect the general consent of the nation at the time it was undertaken? (4) Were the funds borrowed or obtained and then spent for ends contrary to the interests of the nation? (5) Were creditors who made the loan aware or should they have been aware that the debt failed to reflect general public consent and were the funds used for ends contrary to the interests of the nation? See Mitu Gulati, Sarah Ludington, and Alfred L. Brophy, Applied Legal

History: Demystifying the Doctrine of Odious Debts, 11 Theoretical Inquiries in Law 247, 248–49 (2010); and Howse, supra, at 2.

66. James L. Foorman and Michael E. Jehle, Effects of State and Government Succession on Commercial Bank Loans to Foreign Sovereign Borrowers, 1982 U. Ill. L. Rev. 9 (1982). Advocates of a doctrine of odious debt would create an exception to the usual rule that treats a nation's debts as continuous even after a regime change, and hence criticize an emerging theory attaching liability to the match of burdens and benefits, because its uncertainty would disrupt banking practices. Id., at 13.

67. For an argument with this assertion, see Alexander W. Cappelen, Rune Hansen Hagen, and Bertil Tungodden, National Responsibility and the Just Distribution of Debt Relief, 21 Ethics & Int'l. Aff. 69 (2007).

68. Gulati, Luddington, and Brophy, supra, at 247, 250, 253 (not clear in U.S. practice that the regime has to be despotic for its debts to be odious); Lee C. Buchheit, Mitu Gulati, and Robert B. Thompson, The Dilemma of Odious Debts, 56 Duke L. J. 1201, 1228–30 (2007) (discussing difficulties in judgments about what is odious, the whole regime vs. a particular use, and over what time frame).

69. Buchheit, Gulati, and Thompson, supra, at 1201, 1228–30; Daniel K. Tarullo, Odious Debt in Retrospect, 70 Law & Contemp. Probs. 263–74 (2007) (noting difficulties in distinguishing harm from how the funds are used from harm from the fact of unsustainable debt). See David C. Gray, Devilry, Complicity, and Greed: Transitional Justice and Odious Debt, 70 Law & Contemp. Probs. 137, 139 (2007); and Yvonne Wong, Sovereign Finance and the Poverty of Nations: Odious Debt in International Law 121 (2012).

70. Patrick Bolton and David Skeel, Odious Debts or Odious Regimes?, 70 Law & Contemp. Probs. 83, 99 (2007). See also Michael Kremer and Seema Jayachandran, Odious Debt, IMF Working Paper (2002), https://www.imf.org/external/np/res/seminars/2002/poverty/mksj.pdf; Seema Jayachandran and Michael Kremer, Odious Debt, Brookings (2005), https://www.brookings.edu/research/odious-debt/.

71. Tom Ginsburg and Thomas S. Ulen, Odious Debt, Odious Credit, Economic Development, and Democratization, 70 Law & Contemp. Probs. 115, 130 (2007) (arguing that China would block such a role for the United Nations). Prior efforts to devise an international mechanism to restructure have not worked. Brown, supra.

72. Ginsburg and Ulen, supra, at 125.

73. Tai-Heng Cheng, Renegotiating the Odious Debt Doctrine, 70 Law & Contemp. Probs. 7, 51 (2007).

74. Gelpern, supra, 81, 103. For a prediction that loan forgiveness would adversely affect creditors and reduce funds available for sovereign loans, see Andre Schleifer, Will the Sovereign Debt Market Survive?, NBER Working Paper No. 9493, February 2003, http://www.nber.org/papers/w9493.pdf.

75. Howse, supra, at 21.
76. See Allison M. Jaggar, A Feminist Critique of the Alleged Southern Debt, 17 Hypatia 119, 134 (2002).
77. Id.
78. Gray, supra, 137, 142–45, 155–58; Robert Howse and Ruti Teitel, Debt, Dictatorship, and Democratization, Project Syndicate, http://www.project-syndicate.org/commentary/debt--dictatorship--and-democratization; Howse (2007), supra, at 16.
79. Saddled with Apartheid Debts, Probe International (May 22, 1997), https://journal.probeinternational.org/1997/05/22/saddled-with-apartheid-debts/ (quoting Archbishop Ndugane).
80. Federal Reserve Bank of St. Louis, Central Government Debt as a Percentage of Gross National Product, https://fred.stlouisfed.org/series/DEBTTLZAA188A; Trading Economics, South Africa Government Debt (Aug. 2018), https://tradingeconomics.com/south-africa/government-debt.
81. See Wong, supra, at 31–39.
82. Id., at 136–68. Procedures for renegotiating debt terms with banks also could be developed, rather than simply relying on markets for distressed sovereign debt. See A. Mechele Dickerson, Insolvency Principles and the Odious Debt Doctrine: The Missing Link in the Debate, 75 Law & Contemp. Probs. 53 (2007); and Gelpern, supra, at 103. See Adam Feibelman, Equitable Subordination, Fraudulent Transfer, and Sovereign Debt, 70 Law & Contemp. Probs. 171 (2007) (noting option of sovereign bankruptcy); White (2002), supra, at 287. Revisions of tax rules and rules affecting bank balance sheets would also be needed to reduce the disincentives for lenders to forgive debt and then face a tax liability as well as disincentives to hold onto unpaid sovereign debt and face a down-grading under the Basel Accords and comparable standards.
83. Wong, supra, at 141–44, 149–51.
84. Ashfaq Khalfan, Jeff King, and Bryan Thomas, Advancing the Odious Debt Doctrine 43–44 (2003), http://cisdl.org/public/docs/pdf/Odious_Debt_Study.pdf.
85. Feibelman, supra, at 171, 172, 189–90. Feibelman also suggests borrowing the bankruptcy concept of equitable subordination that allows a court to subordinate a claim when a creditor harmed the debtor or other creditors (174).
86. Wong, supra, at 136–68.
87. Great Britain apparently plans to take advantage of record low interest rates and inflation in paying off debt incurred through government bonds after the 1720 South Sea Bubble. Stephen Castle, That Debt from 1720? Britain's Payment is Coming, N.Y. Times (Dec. 28, 2014), p. 12.
88. See Dickerson, supra, at 53; Robert K. Rasmussen, Integrating a Theory of the State into Sovereign Debt Restructuring, 53 Emory L. J. 119 (2004).
89. See Dickerson, supra, at 53; Gelpern, supra, at 103; Feibelman, supra, at 171; White (2002), supra, at 287.

90. Adrian Salbuchi, How to Solve Argentina's Recurrent Foreign Debt Crises: Proposal for a Long-Term Solution, Global Research (Nov. 7, 2006), http://www.globalresearch.ca/how-to-solve-argentina-s-recurrent-foreign-debt-crises/3750 (calling for recognition as odious the debt created by "an illegal and de facto military-civilian regime. [with] close ties with, and the respect of, powerful international private banking interests . . . implement[ing] a series of highly destructive, speculative, illegitimate—even illegal—economic and financial policies and legislation, which increased Public Debt almost eightfold to 46 billion dollars in a few short years"); Brown, supra (describing how U.S. federal courts supported bondholders holding out for 100 percent repayment and blocking a negotiated debt restructuring in which most creditors accepted payment at a 70 percent loss); Floyd Norris, Ruling on Argentina Gives Investors an Upper Hand, N.Y. Times June 19, 2004, http://www.nytimes.com/2014/06/20/business/economy/ruling-on-argentina-gives-investors-an-upper-hand.html (discussing Republic of Argentina v. NML Capital, Ltd., U.S. 134 S.Ct. 2250 [2014]).

91. Pierre Pénet, Rethinking Odious Debt, Committee for the Abolition of Illegitimate Debt (Apr. 6, 2018), http://www.cadtm.org/Rethinking-Odious-Debt (arguing for extension of odious debt to democratic nations in instances of predatory lending).

92. The biblical calls for a Jubilee (Exodus 21:1–11; Deuteronomy 15:1–18; Leviticus 25) imagined a sabbatical for land and people every seven years. On the seventh seventh year—the Jubilee year—when slaves would be freed, debts would be forgiven, and land would be returned. Further discussions of the Jubilee appear in the writings of Hebrew Prophets Nehemiah 5:1–13, Jeremiah 3:4–22, and Isaiah 61:1–2, and in the New Testament, Luke 4:16–30. The Jubilee 2000 movement combines biblical and human rights arguments to challenge third world debt and loaning practices. The Jubilee Story, Jubilee USA, https://www.jubileeusa.org/the_jubilee_story.

93. Aimee Pichee, Could Illinois Be the First State to File for Bankruptcy?, CBS Moneywatch (June 16, 2017), https://www.cbsnews.com/news/could-illinois-be-the-first-state-to-file-for-bankruptcy/.

94. Michal Kranz, Here's How Puerto Rico Got Into So Much Debt, Business Insider (Oct. 9, 2017), http:// http://www.businessinsider.com/puerto-rico-debt-2017–10.

95. Franklin California Tax-Free Trust v. Puerto Rico, 85 F. Supp. 3d 577 (D.P.R. 2015). The decision was affirmed by the court of appeals and left standing by the Supreme Court. Franklin California Tax-Free Trust v. Puerto Rico, 805 F.3d 322 (1st Cir. 2015); "Puerto Rico v. Franklin California Tax-Free Trust," SCOTUSblog (Feb. 28, 2017).

96. Mary Williams Walsh, Puerto Rico's Debt Crisis Addressed in Bi-Partisan Bill, N.Y. Times (May 19, 2016), https://www.nytimes.com/2016/05/20/business/puerto-rico-debt-bankruptcy.html?mtrref=www.nytimes.com&

gwh=C9D20D0850221C91DAAEEEF755A21BF2&gwt=pay; Steven Mufson, Puerto Rico Offers Fiscal Plan Settling Debt for Pennies on the Dollar, Wash. Post (Jan. 25, 2018), https://www.washingtonpost.com/business/economy/puerto-rico-offers-fiscal-plan-settling-debt-for-pennies-on-the-dollar/2018/01/25/04f3adca-01e0–11e8–8acf-ad2991367d9d_story.html?utm_term=.d77349402e0e.

97. Patricia Mazzei, What Puerto Rico Is, and Is Not, Getting in Disaster Relief, N.Y. Times (Feb. 8, 2018), https://www.nytimes.com/2018/02/08/us/puerto-rico-disaster-relief.html?mtrref=www.google.com&gwh=ABEEE10 5CC22D46E7105F980FCDE9E4B&gwt=pay; and Adriana Garriga-López, Here's What Has to Happen for Puerto Rico to Recover after Maria, Fortune (Sept. 25, 2017), http://fortune.com/2017/09/25/puerto-rico-hurricane-maria-relief-debt-crisis/.

98. Mary Williams Walsh and Alan Rappeport, White House Walks Back Trump's Vow to Clear Puerto Rico's Debt, N.Y. Times (Oct. 4, 2017), https://www.nytimes.com/2017/10/04/business/dealbook/trump-puerto-rico-debt.html.

99. Steven Mufson, In Puerto Rico, A Skirmish over How Much Debt the Bankrupt Island Can Handle, Wash. Post (Feb. 16, 2018), https://www.washingtonpost.com/business/economy/in-puerto-rico-a-skirmish-over-how-much-debt-the-bankrupt-island-can-handle/2018/02/16/3870e8b6–127a-11e8–9570–29c9830535e5_story.html?utm_term=.5f42ee23295a; Mary Williams Walsh, Puerto Rico Declares a Form of Bankruptcy, N.Y. Times (May 3, 2017), https://www.nytimes.com/2017/05/03/business/dealbook/puerto-rico-debt.html?mtrref=www.google.com&gwh=B50C14E B67F892B5A1E6F9B56804A597&gwt=pay.

100. Nathan Bomey, Brent Snavely, and Alisa Priddle, Detroit Becomes Largest U.S. City to Enter Bankruptcy, USA Today (Dec. 3, 2013), https://www.usatoday.com/story/news/nation/2013/12/03/detroit-bankruptcy-eligibility/3849833/.

101. Nathan Bomey, Detroit Resurrected: To Bankruptcy and Back (2016); Anna Clark, Five Revelations About Detroit's Bankruptcy Story, Next City (Apr. 20, 2016), https://nextcity.org/daily/entry/detroit-resurrected-book-nathan-boomey-bankruptcy.

102. Julie Bosman and Monica Davey, Anger in Michigan over Appointing Emergency Managers, N.Y. Times (Jan. 22, 2016), http://www.nytimes.com/2016/01/23/us/anger-in-michigan-over-appointing-emergency-managers.html.

103. Detroit Mayor Proposes "Last" Budget Under State Oversight, Reuters (Feb. 23, 2018), http://www.reuters.com/article/us-detroit-budget/detroit-mayor-proposes-last-budget-under-state-oversight-idUSKCN1G72R4.

104. Bomey, Snavely, and Priddle, supra (quoting Brimer).

105. Id. (quoting Bing).

106. Amanda Albright, Any Deeply Indebted City Might Want the Bailout Hartford Got, Bloomberg (Mar. 28 2018), http://www.bloomberg.com/news/articles/2018–03–28/any-deeply-indebted-city-might-want-the-bailout-hartford-got; and Jenna Carlesso, Bronin Presses for State Contract Ahead of April Debt Payment, Hartford Courant (Mar. 21, 2018), http://www.courant.com/community/hartford/hc-news-hartford-debt-agreement-20180321-story.html.

107. Albright, supra.

108. Id.

109. Merrit Kennedy, Two Former Flint Emergency Managers, 2 Others Face Felony Charges over Water Crisis, NPR (Dec. 20, 2016), https://www.npr.org/sections/thetwo-way/2016/12/20/506314203/2-former-flint-emergency-managers-face-felony-charges-over-water-crisis.

110. Clayton P. Gillette and David A. Skeel, Jr., Governance Reform and the Judicial Role in Municipal Bankruptcy, 125 Yale L. J. 1150 (2016).

111. Id., at 1154.

112. Deborah Thorne, Pamela Foohey, Robert M. Lawless, and Katherine M. Porter, Graying of U.S. Bankruptcy: Fallout from Life in a Risk Society (Aug. 5, 2018), https://papers.ssrn.com/sol3/papers.cfm?abstract_id=32265740.

113. Tara Siegel Bernard, "Too Little Too Late": Bankrupcy Booms Among Older Americans, N.Y.Times (Aug. 6, 2018), https://www.nytimes.com/2018/08/05/business/bankruptcy-older-americans.html?smprod=nytcore-ipad&smid=nytcore (describing findings in Thorne, Foohey, Lawless and Porter, supra).

114. David Haynes, What Are the Consequences of Bankruptcy, Balance (April 11, 2018), https://www.thebalance.com/consequences-of-bankruptcy-316128; and Personal Bankruptcy: What You Should Know, ABC News (Nov. 12, 2008), http://www.nbcnews.com/id/27684203/ns/business-personal_finance/t/personal-bankruptcy-what-you-should-know/#.W2mqPzknaM8.

115. U.S. Department of Education, Federal Student Aid (n.d.), http://studentaid.ed.gov/repay-loans/forgiveness-cancellation#teacher-loan; and Justin Harelik, Debts That Can't Be Wiped Out in Bankruptcy, Bankrate, Jan. 31, 2012, http://www.bankrate.com/finance/debt/debts-wiped-bankruptcy.aspx. See Megan McCardle, Debt Jubilee? Start with Student Loans, Atlantic (Oct. 6, 2011), http://www.theatlantic.com/business/archive/2011/10/debt-jubilee-start-with-student-loans/246307/; and U.S. Department of Education, Default Rates Continue Rise, https://www.ed.gov/news/press-releases/default-rates-continue-rise-federal-student-loans.

116. Shahien Nasiripour, Student Debt is a Major Reason Millennials Aren't Buying Homes, Bloomberg News (July 17, 2017), https://www.bloomberg.com/news/articles/2017–07–17/student-debt-is-hurting-millennial-homeownership.

117. Josh Mitchell and Katy Stech Ferek, White House Explores Easing Student-Loan Burden, Wall St. J. (Feb. 21, 2018).

118. See Rod Dreher, Student Loans and Moral Hazard, American Conservative, Oct. 31, 2011, http://www.theamericanconservative.com/dreher/student-loans-and-moral-hazard/ ("Aside from the power of negative example, shouldn't there be banking reform laws in place that restrict the ability of banks to loan money to students who are getting degrees in fields in which there is a reduced likelihood that they'll be able to pay the loans back? Or is that going too far, given that it can be difficult to predict which professional fields are likely to be solid in the future? Is it kind, or even wise, to have a system that allows teenagers to dig themselves into such a deep financial hole?"); Student Loan Debt: To Pay or Not to Pay?, PBS NewsHour, May 31, 2012, https://www.pbs.org/newshour/show/student-loan-debt-to-pay-or-not-to-pay ("They made a contractual commitment in a very different economy. And you can say, well, it's their tough luck, they should've known it all wasn't going to last. But their elders and betters and wisers told them to do this"); Mitchell and Ferek, supra; Five Reasons People of Faith Should Care about Student Loan Debt, Center for American Progress, June 27, 2013, http://www.americanprogress.org/issues/religion/news/2013/06/27/68238/5-reasons-people-of-faith-should-care-about-student-loan-debt.

119. See Jane C. Timm, Students Seek Loan Forgiveness in Overwhelming Numbers (Apr. 22, 2014), http://www.msnbc.com/morning-joe/students-seek-debt-forgiveness-costs-surge ("Enrollment in federal student loan debt forgiveness programs skyrocketed nearly 40% in the last six months, the U.S. Education Department told The Wall Street Journal, as education costs rise"). U.S. Department of Education, Education Department Launches "Pay As You Earn" Student Loan Repayment Plan (Dec. 21, 2012), http://www.ed.gov/news/press-releases/education-department-launches-pay-you-earn-student-loan-repayment-plan; and Stacy Teicher Khadaroo, Student Loan Forgiveness: Five Ways Obama Wants to Ease Student Debt, Christian Science Monitor, Oct. 26, 2011, http://www.csmonitor.com/USA/2011/1026/Student-loan-forgiveness-5-ways-Obama-wants-to-ease-student-debt/Pay-as-you-earn. For descriptions of the program since President Trump was elected, see Paula Pant, REpaye: Everything You Need to Know About the Revised Pay As You Earn Program, Student Loan Hero (June, 2, 2018), https://studentloanhero.com/featured/repaye-revised-pay-as-you-earn-program-guide/; Christy Rakoczy, Complete Guide to the Pay As You Earn (PAYE) Repayment Program, Student Loan Hero (March 15, 2018), https://studentloanhero.com/student-loans/student-loan-repayment/pay-as-you-earn-guide/.

120. Robert Farington, Trump Student Loan Provisions Changes and Proposals, College Investor (Mar. 19, 2018), https://thecollegeinvestor.com/21636/trump-student-loan-forgiveness/#tab-con-6; and Steve Rosen, Bankruptcy Must Be Last Resort for Student Borrowers, Chicago Tribune (Apr. 16, 2018),

https://bit.ly/2BBhcG8. See also Stacy Cowley, Borrowers Face Hazy Path as Program to Forgive Student Loans Stalls Under Betsy DeVos, N.Y. Times (Nov. 11, 2018), https://www.nytimes.com/2018/11/11/business/student -loans-betsy-devos.html.

121. Victoria McGrane, Trump Policy Halts Loan Relief for Thousands of Students, Boston Globe (Oct. 2, 2017), https://www.bostonglobe.com/ news/nation/2017/10/01/trump-policy-hurts-student-borrowers/ fq9bkhlWh176FTjxwZlNPJ/story.html; Toby Merrill, Federal Financing of Predatory Higher Education, Harv. L. Rev. Blog (Nov. 6, 2017), https://blog .harvardlawreview.org/federal-financing-of-predatory-higher-education/.

122. Erica L. Green, DeVos Proposes to Curtail Debt Relief for Defrauded Students, N.Y. Times (July 25, 2018), https://www.nytimes.com/2018/07/25/us/politics/ betsy-devos-debt-relief-for-profit-colleges.html?smprod=nytcorereversal (describing federal reversal of full debt relief for defrauded students and proposal to eliminate all relief for the students, while shielding the for-profit colleges from accountability for misrepresentations); and Jillian Berman, ITT Is Second Major For-Profit College to Declare Bankruptcy Since Last Year, Market Watch (Sept. 16, 2016), https://www.marketwatch.com/story/itt-is-second-major-for-profit -college-to-declare-bankruptcy-since-last-year-2016-09-16.

123. Stacy Cowley and Jessica Silber-Greenberg, As Paperwork Goes Missing, Private Student Loan Debts May Be Wiped Away, N.Y. Times (July 18, 2017), https://www.nytimes.com/2017/07/17/business/dealbook/student-loan-debt -collection.html; and Miranda Marquit,"Don't Celebrate Yet: Here's Why That $5 Billion in Student Loan Debt Won't Be Forgiven," Student Loan Hero, https:// studentloanhero.com/featured/private-student-loan-debt-wiped-away/.

124. Latoya Urby, Tactics to Deal with Medical Debt, Balance (Mar. 26, 2018), https://www.thebalance.com/tactics-to-deal-with-medical-debt-960859; Susan Hogan, Patti Petitte, and Meredith Royster, NBC Makes Donation to Buy and Forgive $1.5 Million in Medical Debt, NBC Washington (Mar. 14, 2018), https://www.nbcwashington.com/news/local/NBC-Donation-Forgive -Medical-Debt-475691983.html. For a critique of these estimates' reliance on bankruptcy filings, see Megan McCardle, The Truth About Medical Bankruptcies, Wash. Post (March 26, 2018), https://www.washingtonpost.com/blogs/ post-partisan/wp/2018/03/26/the-truth-about-medical-bankruptcies/?no redirect=on&utm_term=.76ff16153c9e (relying on a study that uses medical records to track how many hospitalized people file for bankruptcy and found that only 4 percent of bankruptcies stem from medical costs). Yet many people with serious medical problems are not hospitalized, and income loss due to medical problems may well lead to debt approximating this larger estimate. Id.

125. Michelle Andrews, Medical Debt Is Top Reason Consumers Hear from Collection Agencies, NPR (Jan. 24, 2017), https://www.npr.org/sections/health -shots/2017/01/24/511269991/medical-debt-is-top-reason-consumers-hear -from-collection-agencies.

126. Id. ("The study found that the percentage of families that had problems paying medical bills declined from 22 percent in 2013 to 17.3 percent in 2015. Being uninsured, having a low income and enrolling in a high-deductible plan each increased the odds of having trouble paying medical bills, the study found.")

127. IRS, Home Foreclosure and Debt Cancellation, https://www.irs.gov/ newsroom/home-foreclosure-and-debt-cancellation; The White House, Fact Sheet: The Mortgage Forgiveness Debt Relief Act, http://georgewbush -whitehouse.archives.gov/news/releases/2007/12/20071220–6.html.

128. Anna Cuevas, Mortgage Debt Relief Act Receives Much-Needed Extension, Huff. Post, http://www.huffingtonpost.com/anna-cuevas/mortgage-debt -relief-act_b_2427431.html.

129. Victoria Pynchon, Rolling Jubilee: A Bailout of the People, By the People, Forbes (Feb. 19, 2013), http://www.forbes.com/sites/shenegotiates/2013/02/19/ rolling-jubilee-a-bailout-of-the-people-by-the-people/; Rolling Jubilee, http:// rollingjubilee.org/. See Occupy Student Debt Campaign, Our Principles, http://www.occupystudentdebtcampaign.org/our-principles (seeking forgive- ness of student debt in the spirit of Leviticus 25).

130. See Rolling Jubilee, supra; Pynchon, supra.

131. Jillian Berman, Why Are These Students Refusing to Pay Back Their Loans?, Wall St. J. (June 14, 2009), http://www.marketwatch.com/story/why-these -students-are-refusing-to-pay-back-their-loans-2016–09–14.

132. Hogan, Petitte and Royster, supra (describing Craig Antico).

133. Toby Nitti, John Oliver Buys and Forgives $15 Million in Medical Debt: But Is the Forgiveness Taxable?, Forbes (June 6, 2016), https://www.forbes.com/ sites/anthonynitti/2016/06/06/john-oliver-buys-and-forgives-15-million-in -medical-debt-but-is-the-forgiveness-taxable/#38c15c84b4f0.

134. Alexandra Bastien, Ending the Debt Trap: Strategies to Stop the Abuse of Court-Imposed Fines and Fees, PolicyLink (2017), https://www.policylink .org/sites/default/files/ending-the-debt-trap-03–28–17.pdf; Lauren-Brooke Eisen, Charging Inmates Perpetuates Mass Incarceration, Brennan Center for Justice (2015), https://www.brennancenter.org/sites/default/files/blog/ Charging_Inmates_Mass_Incarceration.pdf; Alexandra Natapoff, Misde- meanor Decriminalization, 68 Vand. L. Rev. 2079 (2015); National Center for State Courts, Actions Taken by State Courts on Fines Fees and Bail Practices, https://www.ncsc.org/~/media/microsites/files/trends%202017/work-of -task-force-fines-fees-trends-2017.ashx; Criminal Justice Policy Program, Confronting Criminal Justice Debt: A Guide for Policy Reform, Harvard Law School (2016), http://cjpp.law.harvard.edu/assets/Confronting-Crim -Justice-Debt-Guide-to-Policy-Reform-FINAL.pdf.

135. Bastien, supra, at 2.

136. Id., at 3. For a thoughtful history of the recent developments, see Christopher Hampson, The New American Debtors Prisons, 44 Am. J. Crim. L. 1 (2016).

137. Karin D. Martin, Sandra Susan Smith, and Wendy Still, Shackled to Debt: Criminal Justice Financial Obligations and the Barriers to Re-Entry They Create, New Thinking in Community Corrections (2017), https://www.hks.harvard.edu/sites/default/files/centers/wiener/programs/pcj/files/shackled_to_debt.pdf.

138. Id. For a rich collection of judicial opinions, research studies, and other writings on the topic, see Yale Law School Arthur Liman Center, Who Pays?: Fines, Fees, Bail, and the Cost Of Courts (2018), https://law.yale.edu/system/files/area/center/liman/document/liman_colloquium_book_04.20.18.pdf.

139. Bastien, supra, at 4.

140. Id., at 7; Council of Economic Advisers, Issue Brief, Fines, Fees, and Bail (2015), https://www.americanbar.org/content/dam/aba/images/abanews/ODonnell_v_HarrisCounty_amicus.pdf.

141. Bastien, supra, at 7 (quoting Karakatsanis). Karakatsanis has successfully challenged such practices under the federal due process and equal protection clauses. See Shaila Dawan, Court by Court, Lawyers Fight Practices that Fall Heavily on the Poor, N.Y. Times (Oct. 23, 2015), https://www.nytimes.com/2015/10/24/us/court-by-court-lawyers-fight-practices-that-punish-the-poor.html?mtrref=www.google.com&gwh=A29AC5EE375DA55747B087413E103D6B&gwt=pay; and Civil Rights Corps, http://www.civilrightscorps.org/. See Curtis Killman, Plaintiffs Suing Every Oklahoma Sheriff File Injunction to Avoid Arrests on Old Court Debts, Tulsa World (Feb. 2, 2018), http://www.tulsaworld.com/news/courts/plaintiffs-suing-every-oklahoma-sheriff-file-injunction-to-avoid-arrests/article_65a83edd-a08f-5e24-abf1-bab12f49636d.html. See generally The Liman Center Reports: 2018, Who Pays? Fines, Fees, Bail, and the Cost of Courts.

142. Criminal Justice Policy Program at Harvard Law School, Confronting Criminal Justice Debt: A Guide for Policy Reform (2016), http://cjpp.law.harvard.edu/assets/Confronting-Crim-Justice-Debt-Guide-to-Policy-Reform-FINAL.pdf.

143. Bastien, supra, at 8.

144. Id., at 9.

145. Id., at 10–11. Federal legislation, if enforced, would help. See Fair Debt Collection Practices Act, 15 U.S.C. sec.1692–1692p (2010) (banning unfair measures and self-help remedies for creditors). So would state and federal reforms addressing underlying practices trapping low-income people in confusing and burdensome debt created by government. See State Bans on Debtors' Prisons and Criminal Justice Debt, 129 Harv. L. Rev. 1024 (2016); Hampson, supra; Noah Zatz, What's Wrong with Work or Jail?, L.A. Times (April 8, 2016), http://www.latimes.com/opinion/op-ed/la-oe-0408-zatz-debt-peonage-20160408-story.html#.

Chapter 3: Amnesties and Pardons

1. Scott Shane, For Ford, Pardon Decision Was Always Clear-Cut, N.Y. Times (Dec. 29, 2006), https://www.nytimes.com/2006/12/29/washington/29pardon.html.

2. Adriaan Lanni, Transitional Justice in Ancient Athens: A Case Study, 32 U. Pa. J. Int'l L. 551, 551–52, 566 (2010).

3. Id., at 552, 564.

4. Id., at 552, 569, 581–83.

5. Id., at 553–54, 570–71, 586.

6. Id., at 566.

7. Id., at 582.

8. Id., at 583.

9. Id., at 589–90, 593–94.

10. See Louis Maillinder, Amnesty, Human Rights and Political Transitions: Bridging the Peace and Justice Divide 404 (2008). See also David Ignatius, Punishment or Pardon: Opposition Bid to Stop Syria's Slide into Anarchy, Australian (Jan. 5, 2013), https://www.theaustralian.com.au/in-depth/middle-east-in-turmoil/punishment-or-pardon-opposition-bid-to-stop-syrias-slide-to-anarchy/news-story/bdedd6a4048b13d353ce9b688efd56c3 (discussing proposal for amnesties).

11. BBC News, "World Prison Populations," http://news.bbc.co.uk/2/shared/spl/hi/uk/06/prisons/html/nn2page1.stm; Michele Ye Hee Lee, Yes, U.S. Locks People Up at a Higher Rate than Any Other Country, Wash. Post (July 7, 2017), https://www.washingtonpost.com/news/fact-checker/wp/2015/07/07/yes-u-s-locks-people-up-at-a-higher-rate-than-any-other-country/; TyjenTsaiand Paola Scommegna, U.S. Has World's Highest Incarceration Rate, Population Reference Bureau (2012), http://www.prb.org/Publications/Articles/2012/us-incarceration.aspx; and Peter Wagner, Leah Sakala, and Josh Begley, States of Incarceration, Prison Policy (2016), https://www.prisonpolicy.org/global/.

12. The amnesty, adopted following much-criticized punishments of dissent, excluded people charged with serious crimes such as murder, terrorism, and religious extremism. Radio Free Europe, Tajik Parliament Adopts Law on Mass Amnesty (Aug. 24, 2016), https://www.rferl.org/a/tajikistan-mass-amnesty/27943239.html.

13. King of Cambodia Grants Amnesty to Prison Inmates, L.A. Times (Oct. 19, 1996), http://articles.latimes.com/1996–10–19/news/mn-55632_1_khmer-rouge-guerrillas; and Seth Mydans, An Amnesty in Cambodia, N.Y. Times (Sept. 18, 1996), http://www.nytimes.com/1996/09/18/world/an-amnesty-in-cambodia.html.

14. Amanda Sakuma, Ronald Reagan Amnesty Haunts Immigration Action, MSNBC (Aug. 3, 2014), http://www.msnbc.com/msnbc/reagan-amnesty-haunts-immigration-action.

15. Id.

16. Nassim Benchaabane, St. Louis to Offer Four-Day Amnesty for Outstanding Warrants, St. Louis Dispatch (Jan. 23, 2018) (amnesty program that

excluded offenses including driving under the influence of alcohol, leaving the scene of an accident, and prostitution), http://www.stltoday.com/news/local/crime-and-courts/st-louis-to-offer-four-day-amnesty-for-outstanding-warrants/article_7d9847ef-52db-527e-8ceb-86bfa638c2e9.html. Many legislatures adopt tax amnesties, waiving fines and interest on unpaid taxes if the taxes themselves are paid during specified periods of forgiveness. See, e.g., Spotlight on Maryland Taxes, Tax Amnesty: Frequently Asked Questions (2015), http://taxes.marylandtaxes.gov/Individual_Taxes/Individual_Tax_Compliance/Tax_Amnesty/Tax_Amnesty_FAQs.shtml#5.

17. Sheheryar Kaoosji, Bankruptcies and Amnesty Fuel More Changes to the LA/LB Port Trucking Industry, Port Innovations (May 26, 2016), http://portinnovations.com/bankruptcies-and-amnesty-fuel-more-changes-to-the-lalb-port-trucking-industry/.

18. Federalist No. 74 (Mar. 25, 1788), http://avalon.law.yale.edu/18th_centursy/fed74.asp.

19. Kathleen Dean Moore, Pardons: Justice, Mercy, and the Public Interest 51 (1989).

20. Burdick v. United States, 236 U.S. 79, 94–95 (1915).

21. Tarek Amara, Tunisia Parliament Approves Controversial Amnesty for Ben Ali-era Corruption, Reuters (Sept. 13, 2017), https://www.reuters.com/article/us-tunisia-politics-corruption/tunisia-parliament-approves-controversial-amnesty-for-ben-ali-era-corruption-idUSKCN1BO218.

22. William D. Cohan, How Wall Street's Bankers Stayed Out of Jail, Atlantic (Sept. 2015), https://www.theatlantic.com/magazine/archive/2015/09/how-wall-streets-bankers-stayed-out-of-jail/399368/; Glenn Greenwald, The Real Story of How "Untouchable" Wall Street Execs Avoided Prosecution, Guardian (Jan. 23, 2013), http://www.businessinsider.com/why-wall-street-execs-werent-prosecuted-2013-1. In 1999 Attorney General Eric Holder wrote a memorandum warning of collateral consequences, such as collapse of the corporations, if prosecutions proceeded. Cohan, supra. More than a thousand bankers were jailed following prosecutions arising from the savings and loan disaster of the 1980s. Id. One executive from Credit Suisse was prosecuted and convicted for concealing actual finances, but no top decision-makers faced personal legal consequences for decisions that produced global financial suffering. Jesse Eisinger, Why Only One Top Banker Went to Jail for the Financial Crisis, N.Y. Times (April 30, 2014), https://www.nytimes.com/2014/05/04/magazine/only-one-top-banker-jail-financial-crisis.html.

23. Agnew pleaded no contest to a charge of federal income tax evasion, and in exchange, the prosecutors dropped the charges of political corruption. The court fined him $10,000 and sentenced him to three years of probation; the Maryland court of appeals took away his license to practice law. Vice President Agnew Resigns, This Day in History, Oct. 10. 1973, http://www.history.com/this-day-in-history/vice-president-agnew-resigns.

24. Faith Karimi, Watergate Scandal: A Look Back at Crisis that Changed US Politics, CNN, May 17, 2017, https://www.cnn.com/2017/05/17/politics/watergate-scandal-look-back/index.html.

25. U.S. Constitution, Article I, Section 2. Because of federalism, however, the president does not have pardon power over state crimes or state civil claims.

26. The House could have continued an inquiry after Nixon left office, although then it would not have been an impeachment proceeding. Mark J. Rozell, President Ford's Pardon of Richard M. Nixon: Constitutional and Political Considerations, 24 Presidential Stud. Q. 121–37 (1994), https://www.jstor.org/stable/pdf/27551198.pdf?refreqid=excelsior%3A21441a870f0ca00c4df0f002a35dc025.

27. Ex parte Garland, 71 U.S. 4 Wall. 333 (1866); and Burdick v. United States, 236 U.S. 79 (1915).

28. See John Herbers, Ford Gives Pardon to Nixon, Who Regrets "My Mistakes," N.Y. Times (Sept. 8, 1974), http://www.nytimes.com/learning/general/onthisday/big/0908.html. The use of presidential pardons reflects public attitudes about crime, and U.S. presidents have given fewer pardons during times when public attitudes and policies value being "tough on crime." Moore, supra, at vii.

29. The official pardon included this statement: "the tranquility to which this nation has been restored by the events of recent weeks could be irreparably lost by the prospects of bringing to trial a former President of the United States. The prospects of such trial will cause prolonged and divisive debate over the propriety of exposing to further punishment and degradation a man who has already paid the unprecedented penalty of relinquishing the highest elective office of the United States." Proclamation 4311—Granting Pardon to Richard Nixon (Sept. 8, 1974), https://www.presidency.ucsb.edu/documents/proclamation-4311-granting-pardon-richard-nixon; Herbers, supra.

30. Herbers, supra; Kayla Epstein, Trump Is Considering Presidential Pardons. Ford Never Recovered from the One He Gave Nixon, Wash. Post (July 22, 2017), https://www.washingtonpost.com/news/retropolis/wp/2017/07/22/trump-is-considering-presidential-pardons-ford-never-recovered-from-the-one-he-gave-nixon/?utm_term=.d3204b5eec6e.

31. Rozell, supra.

32. Herbers, supra.

33. Id. (quoting Woodward).

34. National Constitution Center, The Nixon Pardon in Constitutional Retrospect (Sept. 8, 2017), https://constitutioncenter.org/blog/the-nixon-pardon-in-retrospect-40-years-later (quoting Gallup polls).

35. Lee Lescaze, President Pardons Viet Draft Evaders, Wash. Post (Jan. 22, 1977), https://www.washingtonpost.com/archive/politics/1977/01/22/president-pardons-viet-draft-evaders/dfa064a5-83fc-4efb-a904-d72b390a909e/?utm_term=.c4f615ae5d64. On President Ford's action,

see Marjorie Hunter, Ford Offers Amnesty Program Requiring Two Years Public Work, N.Y. Times (Sept. 16, 1974), http://www.nytimes.com/learning/general/onthisday/big/0916.html.

36. Andrew Glass, President Carter Pardons Draft Dodgers, Jan. 21, 1977, Politico (Jan. 21, 2018), https://www.politico.com/story/2018/01/21/president-carter-pardons-draft-dodgers-jan-21–1977–346493 .

37. Ford Foundation, Vietnam: Veterans, Deserters, and Draft Evaders: A Summer Study (Sept. 1974), https://www.fordlibrarymuseum.gov/library/document/0067/1562799.pdf.

38. Id., at II-2. See id., at II-18 (citing Gallup and Harris polls).

39. Historically, European kings used conditional pardons or amnesties at times to ease labor shortages in the colonies; offenders could obtain pardons if they agreed to work for a specified time in the colonies. Moore, supra, at 19.

40. Ford Foundation, supra, at II-16. On prior U.S. amnesties related to violations of military conscription, see Lieutenant Colonel Wilfred L. Ebel, The Amnesty Issue: A Historical Perspective, IV J. Am. War College 67 (1974), http://www.dtic.mil/get-tr-doc/pdf?AD=ADA531961.

41. Ford Foundation, supra, at II-17.

42. See Geoffrey Chaucer, The Canterbury Tales, ed. Jill Mann (2005); Linda Georgianna, Anticlericism in Boccacio and Chaucer, in Leonard Michael Koff and Brenda Dean, eds., The Decameron and the Canterbury Tales: New Essays on an Old Question 148, 167 (2000).

43. Chaucer, Pardoner's Tale, in Canterbury Tales, supra; George Lyman Kittridge, Chaucer's Pardoner, Atlantic Monthly (1893) (translated into modern English), http://sites.fas.harvard.edu/~chaucer/canttales/pardt/kitt-par.html.

44. See Jim Jones, Background to "Against the Sale of Indulgences" by Martin Luther (2012), http://courses.wcupa.edu/jones/his101/web/37luther.htm; and Randy Peterson, Selling Forgiveness: How Money Sparked the Protestant Revolution, 14 Christianity Today (1987), http://www.christianitytoday.com/history/issues/issue-14/selling-forgiveness-how-money-sparked-protestant.html. In 1567 the Council of Trent forbade any exchange of money for indulgences—temporal relief from penance. Indulgences, in The Catholic Encyclopedia, http://www.newadvent.org/cathen/07783a.htm.

45. Michael Gryboski, 12 Memorable Quotes from Martin Luther's 95 Theses, Christian Post, Oct. 29, 2017, https://www.christianpost.com/news/memorable-quotes-martin-luther-95-theses-204435/.

46. Moore, supra, at 10.

47. Oklahoma Historical Society, John Calloway Walton, http://www.okhistory.org/publications/enc/entry.php?entry=WA014.

48. Ken Whitehouse, Where Are They Now?: Impeachment, Tennessee Style, Nashville Post (June 5, 2012), https://www.nashvillepost.com/home/article/20464607/where-are-they-now-impeachment-tennessee-style.

49. See Michael Walzer, Spheres of Justice (1984); and Rebecca C. H. Brown,

Social Values and the Corruption Argument Against Financial Incentives for Healthy Behavior, J. Med. Ethics (2016), http://jme.bmj.com/content/early/2016/10/13/medethics-2016–103372.

50. Peru: The Troubling Pardon of Alberto Fujimori, Economist (Jan. 4, 2018), https://www.economist.com/news/leaders/21733999-presidential-powers -should-not-be-used-undermine-rule-law-troubling-pardon.

51. Id.

52. Id. See Peru's Presidential Hostage, Economist (Jan. 4, 2018), https://www .economist.com/the-americas/2018/01/04/perus-presidential-hostage.

53. Biddle v. Perovich, 274 U.S. 480, 486 (1927) (president's pardon power includes power to commute a death sentence to life imprisonment, even without the prisoner's consent).

54. Eric Lichtblau and Davan Maharaj, Clinton Pardon of Rich a Saga of Power, Money, Chicago Tribune (Feb. 18, 2001), http://www.chicagotribune.com/sns-clinton-pardons-analysis-story.html. An indeterminate case may be President George H. W. Bush's end-of-term pardon of former Reagan-era officials affiliated with the Iran-Contra scandal. Bush claimed the public good was his motivation, but 49 percent of those surveyed in a Gallup poll at the time believed that he sought to "protect himself from legal difficulties or embarrassment result from his own role in Iran-Contra." See Larry Hugick, Iran Contra Pardons Opposed, Gallup Poll Monthly (Dec. 21–22, 1992); William C. Banks and Alejandro D. Carrió, Presidential Systems in Stress: Emergency Powers in Argentina and the United States, 15 Mich. J. Int'l. L. 1 (1993) (citing Gallup poll).

55. Editorial, Indefensible Pardon, N.Y. Times (Jan. 2, 2001), http://www .nytimes.com/2001/01/24/opinion/an-indefensible-pardon.html.

56. E.J. Dionne, Bill Clinton's Last Outrage; The President's Defenders Feel Betrayed by His Pardon of Marc Rich, Brookings (Feb. 6, 2001), https://www.brookings.edu/opinions/bill-clintons-last-outrage-the-presidents -defenders-feel-betrayed-by-his-pardon-of-marc-rich/.

57. Indefensible Pardon, supra.

58. Margaret Love, who once served as the pardon attorney at the Department of Justice, along with other scholars argues that administrative review has recently become part of law enforcement, with each petition for clemency treated as a potential challenge to law enforcement policies and prosecutors' authority. Margaret Colgate Love, Justice Department Administration of the President's Pardon Power: A Case Study in Institutional Conflict of Interest, 47 U. Toledo L. Rev. 89, 99, 103–7 (2015). See Rachel E. Barkow and Mark Osler, Restructuring Clemency: The Cost of Ignoring Clemency and a Plan for Renewal, 82 U. Chi. L. Rev. 1, 13–15, 18–19 (2015); Rachel E. Barkow, Clemency and Presidential Administration of Criminal Law, 90 N.Y.U. L. Rev. 802 (2015); Paul Rosenzweig, Report: The Constitution—A Federalist Conception of the Pardon Power, Heritage Foundation 6 (Dec. 4, 2012),

http://www.heritage.org/the-constitution/report/federalist-conception-the
-pardon-power; and Evan P. Schultz, Does the Fox Control Pardons in the
Henhouse?, 13 Fed. Sentencing Rep. 177, 178 (2001).

59. Love, supra, 97–98, 104. See also Moore, supra, at 82 (tracing the "atrophy of
the pardon power").

60. Barkow, supra, 850–55 (citing Federalist No. 74).

61. Federalist No. 74, in Charles R. Kesler and Clinton Rossiter, eds., The Federalist Papers 445, 446 (2003).

62. Different institutional designs intended to advance independence and freedom
from corruption reflect contrasting worries about what threatens independence. See Adrian Vermeule, Bureaucracy and Distrust: Landis, Jaffe, and
Kagan on the Administrative State, 130 Harv. L. Rev. 2473 (2017) (threats
to independence may come from elected officials of any branch; from interest groups, parochial legislators, and entrenched agency staff, or from the
presidency).

63. The notion may have important limits. See Adrian Vermeuele, Contra Nemo
Judex in Causa Sua: The Limits of Impartiality, 122 Yale L. J. 314 (2012),
https://www.yalelawjournal.org/essay/contra-nemo-iudex-in-sua-causa-the
-limits-of-impartiality.

64. Schick v. Reed, 419 U.S. 256 (1974).

65. The so-called Emoluments Clause reads: "No Title of Nobility shall be granted
by the United States: And no Person holding any Office of Profit or Trust
under them, shall, without the Consent of the Congress, accept of any present, Emolument, Office, or Title, of any kind whatever, from any King,
Prince, or foreign State," U.S. Constitution, Article 1, Section 9, Clause 8.

66. On self-pardons, see Max Kutner, No President Has Pardoned Himself, But
Governors and a Drunk Mayor Have, Newsweek (July 24, 2017), http://www
.newsweek.com/trump-granting-himself-pardon-governors-641150.

67. See Sean Iling, President Trump Is Considering Pardoning Himself. I Asked 15
Experts If That's Legal, Vox (July 21, 2017), https://www.vox.com/policy-and
-politics/2017/7/21/16007934/donald-trump-mueller-russia-investigation
-pardon-impeachment; Brian Kalt, Can Trump Pardon Himself?, Foreign
Policy (May 19, 2017), http://foreignpolicy.com/2017/05/19/what-would
-happen-if-trump-pardoned-himself-mueller-russia-investigation/; and Nina
Totenberg, Could Trump Pardon Himself? Probably Not, NPR (July 29,
2017), https://www.npr.org/2017/07/29/539856280/could-trump-pardon
-himself-probably-not.

68. Jed Handelsman Shugerman, Trump Can't Escape the States, Slate (July 21,
2017), http://www.slate.com/articles/news_and_politics/jurisprudence/2017/
07/no_matter_who_he_fires_or_pardons_trump_won_t_be_able_to_
escape_state_attorneys.html.

69. On June 4, 2018, President Trump tweeted that he has an "absolute right"
to pardon himself; several hours later his press secretary acknowledged that

the president is not above the law. Tara Golshan, Sarah Sanders Reluctantly Says President Trump Is Not above the Law, Vox (June 4, 2018), https://www.vox.com/2018/6/4/17426546/sarah-sanders-white-house-press-briefing-trump-pardon.

70. Austin Sarat, At the Boundaries of Law: Executive Clemency, Sovereign Prerogative, and the Dilemma of American Legality, 57 Am. Q. 611, 614 (2005).

71. President of the Republic of South Africa and Another v. Hugo (CCT11/96) [1997] ZACC 4; 1997 (6) BCLR 708; 1997 (4) SA 1 (Apr. 18, 1997), http://www.saflii.org/za/cases/ZACC/1997/4.html (interpreting the South African interim constitution that subjected all exercises of governmental power to the equality provisions of that constitution).

72. Pierre de Vos, Amnesty for President Zuma? No, It Is Not Legally Possible, Daily Maverick (South Africa) (July 24, 2017), https://www.dailymaverick.co.za/opinionista/2017-07-24-amnesty-for-president-zuma-no-it-is-not-legally-possible/#.WqHXEbNG2M8 ("it is well-established that no one can serve as a judge in his or her own cause. This principle is captured by the Latin maxim: *nemo iudex in sua causa*").

73. Id.

74. Moore, supra, at 90–92. A survey of the pardon power across the world shows reliance on elections—not a very precise tool—to hold to account executives wielding the power to pardon. Leslie Sebba, 68 J. Criminal Law and Criminology 83, 120 (1977).

75. See Chapters 2 and 3 for discussions of moral hazard.

76. Mark Thoma, Explainer: What is "Moral Hazard"?, CBS Moneywatch (Nov. 22, 2013), https://www.cbsnews.com/news/explainer-moral-hazard/.

77. John Binder, Poll: Plurality of Americans Believe Amnesty Encourages More Illegal Immigration, Breitbart (Dec. 14, 2017), http://www.breitbart.com/big-government/2017/12/14/poll-majority-of-americans-continue-to-believe-amnesty-encourages-more-illegal-immigration/ (citing Rasmussen poll).

78. Louise Maillander, Can Amnesties and International Justice Be Reconciled?, 1 Int'l J. Transitional Justice 208, 210, 215 (July 2007), https://doi.org/10.1093/ijtj/ijm020, at 406; Allie Malloy, Obama Grants Clemency to 231 Individuals, CNN (Dec. 19, 2016), https://www.cnn.com/2016/12/19/politics/obama-clemency/index.html.

79. Maillander, supra, n. 78; and David Ignatius, Punishment or Pardon: Opposition Bid to Stop Syria's Slide into Anarchy, Australian (Jan. 5, 2013), https://www.theaustralian.com.au/in-depth/middle-east-in-turmoil/punishment-or-pardon-opposition-bid-to-stop-syrias-slide-to-anarchy/news-story/bded6a4048b13d353ce9b688efd56c3 (discussing proposal for amnesties).

80. Lorelei Laird, Clemency Project: Sentencing Reform and Criminal Defense Groups Launch State-Level Clemency Project 6 (Aug. 25, 2017), http://www.abajournal.com/news/article/sentencing_reform_and_criminal_defense_groups_launch_state_level_clemency (ABA Blueprint).

81. Id.; see Moore, supra, at 5 (reprieves "postpone execution of the sentence for a specified period of time").

82. Laird, supra; Moore, supra, at 5.

83. See Margaret Colgate Love, Jenny Roberts, and Cecilia Klingele, Collateral Consequences of Criminal Convictions: Law, Policy, and Practice (2013).

84. Deva Pager, Marked: Race, Crime, and Finding Work in an Era of Mass Incarceration 58–85, 100–16 (2007); Bruce Western, Homeward: Life in the Year After Prison 83–120, 156–73 (2018).

85. Dafna Linzer and Jennifer LaFleur, ProPublica Review of Pardons in Past Decade Shows Process Heavily Favored Whites, Wash. Post (Dec. 3, 2011), https://www.washingtonpost.com/investigations/propublica-review-of-pardons-in-past-decade-shows-process-heavily-favored-whites/2011/11/23/gIQAElnVQO_story.html?utm_term=.e5a64daac657.

86. Id. Sari Horwitz, Obama Grants Final 330 Commutations to Nonviolent Drug Offenders, Wash. Post (Jan. 19, 2017), https://www.washingtonpost.com/world/national-security/obama-grants-final-330-commutations-to-nonviolent-drug-offenders/2017/01/19/41506468-de5d-11e6–918c-99ede3c8cafa_story.html?utm_term=.d56600edf2c7.

87. Laird, supra, at 7–19; Malloy, supra ("Obama has previously said he hopes to bring the existing sentences of inmates more in line with current laws, which have been relaxed after an era of strict mandatory minimums mostly related to non-violent drug crimes"). The initiative ended with President Trump's arrival in office.

88. See Department of Justice Pardon, Clemency Initiative, http://www.justice.gov/pardon/clemency-initiative.

89. Laird, supra, at 11, 34.

90. Neil Eggleston, President Obama Grants 153 Commutations and 78 Pardons to Individuals Deserving of a Second Chance, White House (Dec. 19, 2016), https://obamawhitehouse.archives.gov/blog/2016/12/19/president-obama-grants-153-commutations-and-78-pardons-individuals-deserving-second.

91. See Barkow, supra, at 802, 864–65.

92. Id.

93. Kara Brandelsky, Three Things Obama's New Clemency Initiative Doesn't Do, ProPublica (Apr. 23, 2014), http://www.propublica.org/article/three-things-obamas-new-clemency-initiative-doesnt-do.

94. Sarah Smith, Obama Picks Up the Pace on Commutations but Pardon Changes Still in Limbo, ProPublica (Jan. 5, 2017), https://www.propublica.org/article/obama-picks-up-the-pace-on-commutations-but-pardon-changes-still-in-limbo.

95. Joshua Gaines and Margaret Love, Expungement in Indiana—A Radical Experiment and How It Is Working So Far, Collateral Consequences Resource Center (Dec. 21, 2017), http://ccresourcecenter.org/2017/12/21/expungement-in-indiana-a-radical-experiment-and-how-it-is-working-so-far/#more-15476.

96. Beth Avery and Phil Hernandez, Ban the Box: U.S. Cities, Counties, and States Adopt Fair Hiring Policies, National Employment Law Project (Apr. 20, 2018), http://www.nelp.org/publication/ban-the-box-fair-chance-hiring-state-and-local-guide/ (31 states and 150 cities and counties). Such a rule does not prevent employers from "statistical discrimination"—relying on other factors to guess which applicants may have a criminal record—and hence "ban the box" may be ineffective or counterproductive. Doleac, supra (citing Amanda Y. Agan and Sonia B. Starr, Ban the Box, Criminal Records, and Statistical Discrimination: A Field Experiment, U. Mich. Law & Econ. Research Paper No. 16–012 [June 14, 2016], https://papers.ssrn.com/sol3/papers.cfm?abstract_id=2795795; and Jennifer L. Doleac and Benjamin Hansen, The Unintended Consequences of "Ban the Box": Statistical Discrimination and Employment Outcomes When Criminal Histories Are Hidden [Apr. 19, 2018], https://papers.ssrn.com/sol3/papers.cfm?abstract_id=2812811).

97. Gaines and Love, supra.

98. Id.

99. Id.

100. Barkow, supra, at 866–67.

101. Id., at 867–68.

102. News Report: Roundup of 2017 Expungement and Restoration Laws (Dec. 14, 2017), http://ccresourcecenter.org/2017/12/14/new-report-roundup-of-2017-expungement-and-restoration-laws/#more-15375.

103. Timothy Williams and Thomas Fuller, San Francisco Will Clear Thousands of Marijuana Convictions, N.Y. Times (Jan. 31, 2018), https://www.nytimes.com/2018/-1/31/us/california-marijuana-san-Francisco.html?smprod=nytcore=&smid=nytcore=ipad-share.

104. Id.

105. Id.

106. Moore, supra, at vii. Serious social commitment to second chances calls for transitional services, continuity of medical and mental health assistance, help with permanent housing, and comprehensive social integration programs. See Western, supra, at 178–86.

107. Compare Walker v. Birmingham, 388 U.S. 307 (1967), with Shuttlesworth v. City of Birmingham, 394 U.S. 147 (1969).

108. Walker v. Birmingham, supra (upholding collateral bar rule).

109. Id.

110. Martha Minow, Politics and Procedure, in David Kairys, ed., The Politics of Law: A Progressive Critique (3d ed., 1998).

111. Martin Luther King, Jr., Letter from Birmingham Jail (Aug. 1963), https://web.cn.edu/kwheeler/documents/Letter_Birmingham_Jail.pdf.

112. Margaret C. Love, The Twilight of the Pardon Power, 100 J. Crim. L. & Criminology 1169 (2010); Paul Rosenzweig, Report: The Constitution—A Federalist Conception of the Pardon Power, Heritage Foundation 1, 2

(Dec. 4, 2012), http://www.heritage.org/the-constitution-report-federalist
-conception-the-power.

113. Carrie Hagen, The First Presidential Pardon Pitted Alexander Hamilton
against George Washington, Smithsonian (Aug. 29, 2017), https://www
.smithsonianmag.com/history/first-presidential-pardon-pitted-hamilton
-against-george-washington-180964659/.

114. Assistant Attorney General Tom Perez to William R. Jones, Jr., counsel for
Maricopa County Sheriff's Office, U.S. Department of Justice (Dec. 15,
2011), https://www.justice.gov/sites/default/files/crt/legacy/2011/12/15/
mcso_findletter_12–15–11.pdf.

115. Matt Ford, President Trump Pardons Former Sheriff Joe Arpaio, Atlantic
(Aug. 25, 2017), http://www.theatlantic.com/politics/archive/2017/08/trump
-pardon-arpaio/537729/.

116. Id.

117. "No one is above the law and the individuals entrusted with the privilege of
being sworn law officers should always seek to be beyond reproach in their
commitment to fairly enforcing the laws they swore to uphold. Mr. Arpaio
was found guilty of criminal contempt for continuing to illegally profile Lati-
nos living in Arizona based on their perceived immigration status in violation
of a judge's orders. The President has the authority to make this pardon, but
doing so at this time undermines his claim for the respect of rule of law as Mr.
Arpaio has shown no remorse for his actions." Sen. John McCain, statement
on President Trump's Pardon of Joe Arpaio (Aug. 25–26, 2017), https://
www.mccain.senate.gov/public/index.cfm/2017/8/statement-by-senator
-john-mccain-on-president-trump-s-pardon-of-joe-arpaio.

118. Id.

119. Philip Allen Lacovara, How the Pardon Power Could End Trump's Presidency,
Wash. Post (Aug. 29, 2017), https://www.washingtonpost.com/opinions/how
-the-pardon-power-could-end-trumps-presidency/2017/08/29/57365dfc
-8cf7–11e7–84c0–02cc069f2c37_story.html?utm_term=.e3549c7f9563;
Laurence Tribe and Ron Fein, Trump's Pardon of Arpaio Can—and
Should—Be Overturned, Wash. Post (Sept. 18, 2017), https://www
.washingtonpost.com/opinions/the-presidential-pardon-power-is-not
-absolute/2017/09/18/09d3497c-9ca5–11e7–9083-fbfddf6804c2_story
.html?utm_term=.42eb746f63b1.

120. Tribe and Fein, supra; John W. Dean and Ron Fein, Nixon Lawyer: Donald Trump Abused Pardon Power When He Freed Joe Arpaio, Time (Oct. 3,
2017), http://time.com/4966305/trump-arpaio-pardon-abuse/.

121. Jennifer Rubin, Legal Challenge to Arpaio Pardon Begins, Wash. Post (Aug. 30,
2017), https://www.washingtonpost.com/blogs/right-turn/wp/2017/08/30/
legal-challenge-to-arpaio-pardon-begins/.

122. Lacovara asserted that an exchange of a pardon for cash would be illegal. Lacovara, supra.

123. See pages 125–126 of this book (Clinton pardon of Marc Rich).
124. Similarly, Bush's pardon of I. Lewis Libby, Jr., convicted of obstructing justice, may have been meant to signal that a pardon could be in the offing for others who protect the president. But at least one commentator concludes, "The president can't pardon his way out of his legal jam." Marcy Wheeler, Pardons Won't Save Trump, N.Y. Times (April 16, 2018), https://www.nytimes.com/2018/04/13/opinion/trump-scooter-libby-pardon.html.
125. Dean and Fein, supra; Rubin, supra (reading the pardon as a signal to others not to assist the investigations).
126. Jack Moore, It Is Impossible to Overstate How Truly Vile Joe Arpaio Is, GQ (Aug. 28, 2017), https://www.gq.com/story/joe-arpaio-history. For Phoenix New Times coverage of Arpaio's conduct, see http://www.phoenixnewtimes.com/topic/arpaio-6498482.
127. Paul Mason, Joe Arpaio's Prison Was a Circus of Cruelty; Now His Values Are Spreading, Guardian (Aug. 28, 2017), https://www.theguardian.com/commentisfree/2017/aug/28/donald-trump-far-right-joe-arpaio; and 60 Minutes Footage Shows Joe Arpaio When He Was Ruthless "Joe the Jailor," CBS (Aug. 26, 2017), https://www.cbsnews.com/news/60-minutes-footage-shows-arpaio-when-he-was-ruthless-joe-the-jailer/.
128. Michelle Mark, How Former Arizona Sheriff Joe Arpaio Became the Most Hated Lawman in America, Business Insider (Jan. 10, 2018), http://www.businessinsider.com/maricopa-county-sheriff-joe-arpaio-pardoned-by-trump-2017-8.
129. President Trump's other early pardon decisions include a surprise gift for Dinesh D'Souza, the conservative activist who pleaded guilty to violating federal campaign finance laws in 2014 after he was indicted for illegally using other people's names to hide the fact that he was exceeding federal limits to contribute to a Republican Senate candidate. The president commuted the sentence (wiping out the sentence but not the conviction) of an Iowa kosher meatpacking executive, Sholom Rubashkin, whose plant had been the target of a huge immigration raid in 2008 and who had been sentenced to twenty-seven years in prison for money laundering. He granted a full posthumous pardon to boxing legend Jack Johnson, who had been convicted under a law banning human trafficking (perhaps due to a racially motivated prosecution). At a time when his administration faced an investigation for possible obstruction of justice, he pardoned "Scooter" Libby, a former member of the Bush administration, whose sentence for perjury and obstruction of justice surrounding a leak of classified information had already been commuted by President George W. Bush. Trigging an outpouring of celebration from antigovernment extremists, President Trump pardoned and commuted the sentences for times served by Dwight Lincoln Hammond, Jr., and Steven Dwight Hammond, a father and son who were convicted of arson on federal land during their assault on public refuge land management rules. See Meg

Dalton, What Trump's Latest Pardon Means for the Future of the American West, PBS NewsHour (July 15, 2018), https://www.pbs.org/newshour/nation/hammond-pardon-bundy. Using the clemency power as a kind of entertainment activity, President Trump said he might extend clemency to former governor Rod R. Blagojevich of Illinois and to lifestyle celebrity Martha Stewart, both of whom had appeared on Trump's television show, The Apprentice; he also commuted a sentence of a cocaine trafficker (Alice Marie Johnson) at the urging of a television reality star (Kim Kardashian).

130. Veronica Stracqualursi and Ryan Struyk, President Trump's History with Judge Gonzalo Curiel, ABC News (April 20, 2017), http://abcnews.go.com/Politics/president-trumps-history-judge-gonzalo-curiel/story?id=46916250.

131. Peter Beinart, Trump Takes Aim at the Independent Judiciary, Atlantic (June 1, 2016), https://www.theatlantic.com/politics/archive/2016/06/the-gop-front-runner-takes-aim-at-the-independent-judiciary/485087/.

132. Dan Mercia, Trump Labels US Justice System "Laughingstock," CNN (Nov. 1, 2017), https://www.cnn.com/2017/11/01/politics/trump-justice-laughing-stock/index.html.

133. Matt Ford, President Trump Pardons Former Sheriff Joe Arpaio, Atlantic (Aug. 25, 2017), http://www.theatlantic.com/politics/archive/2017/08/trump-pardon-arpaio/537729/ (quoting Gupta, ACLU).

134. See Michael Edison Hayden, White Nationalists Praise Trump for "Shithole" Comment: "It's Obviously All About Race," Newsweek (Jan. 12, 2018), http://www.newsweek.com/trump-shithole-comment-white-nationalists-praise-779958.

135. Bill Chappell, Federal Judge Will Not Void Guilty Ruling on Arpaio, Despite Trump's Pardon, NPR (Oct. 20, 2017), http://www.npr.org/sections/thetwo-way/2017/10/20/558978896/federal-judge-will-not-void-guilty-ruling-on-arpiao-despite-trumps-pardon (quoting Judge Bolton).

136. See Love, supra; Barkow, supra (restoration of rights and pardons reflect at times substantive disagreement with criminal justice policies).

137. Andrew Novak, Comparative Executive Clemency (2016).

138. Id., at 64–90.

139. Id. at 17.

140. Id., at 170–94.

141. Anthony M. Kennedy, Speech at the American Bar Association Annual Meeting (Aug. 9, 2003), https://www.supremecourt.gov/publicinfo/speeches/sp_08–09–03.html. He noted that 40 percent of the prison population consists of African-American inmates.

Chapter 4: Reflections

1. Martha Minow, Between Vengeance and Forgiveness: Facing History After Genocide and Mass Violence (1998).

2. Grant Gilmore, The Ages of American Law 110–11 (1978).

3. Id.

4. For a thoughtful analysis of this idea, see Lucy Allais, Wiping the Slate Clean: The Heart of Forgiveness, 36 Philos & Public Aff. 33, 68 (2008).

5. Different considerations arise with those made to serve as sexual slaves or wives, but even for them, some process allowing them to come to grips with what they have witnessed and done could be helpful, not only in therapeutic terms but also in addressing their own sense of culpability and their community's response to them.

6. See discussion of ban the box in Chapter 3.

7. See General Requirements for Naturalization, Section 316.10, https://www.uscis.gov/ilink/docView/SLB/HTML/SLB/0–0-0–1/0–0-0–11261/0–0-0–30960/0–0-0–31086.html.

8. The case also raises the questions of whether "good moral character" should be treated as a matter of fact or of law, and whether the views of experts, public opinion surveys, or other sources would be germane to interpreting the phrase in this context.

9. Repouille v. United States, 165 F2d. 152, 153 (1947).

10. Judge Jerome Frank dissented vigorously, on the ground that judges should *not* make guesses about such important matters. Reflecting his confidence in facts, he advised the district court to ask the parties to bring to court reliable information about community attitudes—from opinion leaders, public opinion polls, or experts on ethics. 165 F2d. at 154–55. The majority did not respond publicly to Judge Frank's suggestion, but in a private letter to Supreme Court Justice Felix Frankfurter, Judge Learned Hand wrote: "I assume that he expected the district judge *sua sponte* [meaning "on his own initiative"], to call the Cardinal, Bishop Gilbert, an orthodox and a liberal Rabbi, Reinhold Niebuhr, the head of the Ethical Cultural Society, and Edmund Wilson, have them all cross-examined, ending in a 'survey.' Oh, Jesus!" Hand continued, "I don't know how we ought to deal with such cases except by the best guess we have." Quoted in Robert Burt, Death Is That Man Taking Names: Intersections of American Medicine, Law, and Culture 42 (2004).

11. "We wish to make it plain that a new petition would not be open to this objection; and that the pitiable event, now long passed, will not prevent Repouille from taking his place among us as a citizen. The assertion in his brief that he did not 'intend' the petition to be filed until 1945, unhappily is irrelevant; the statute makes crucial the actual date of filing." Repouille v. United States, 165 F2d. 152, 154 (1947).

12. Burt, supra, at 40–41.

13. Special thanks to Isabel Espinosa for her research on this issue.

14. Douglas S. Massey, Jorge Durand, and Nolan J. Malone, Beyond Smoke and Mirrors: Mexican Immigration in an Era of Economic Integration (2003).

15. Manuel García y Griego, The Importation of Mexican Contract Laborers to

the United States, 1942–1964, in David G. Gutiérrez, ed., Between Two Worlds: Mexican Immigrants in the United States 45 (1996).

16. About Bracero History Archive, braceroarchive.org.

17. The program applies only to individuals who (1) came to the United States before their sixteenth birthday; (2) lived continuously in the United States since June 15, 2007; (3) were under age thirty-one on June 15, 2012 (born on June 16, 1981, or after); (4) were physically present in the United States on June 15, 2012, and at the time of making their request for consideration of deferred action; (5) had no lawful status on June 15, 2012; (6) are currently enrolled students or completed high school or a GED or have been honorably discharged from the armed forces; and (7) have not been convicted of a felony or serious misdemeanors, or three or more other misdemeanors, and do not otherwise pose a threat to national security or public safety. U.S. Citizenship and Immigration Services, Consideration of Deferred Action for Childhood Arrivals, https://www.uscis.gov/archive/consideration-deferred-action-childhood-arrivals-daca.

18. A district court judge issued a nationwide injunction; the Supreme Court divided 4–4, leaving the injunction in place. Tal Kopan, Texas Lawsuit Brings DACA Déjà Vu, CNN (May 2, 2018), https://www.cnn.com/2018/05/02/politics/daca-lawsuit-judge-hanen-ken-paxton-deja-vu/index.html.

19. Although the court did find that the plaintiffs had standing in their complaint regarding their duties being constricted, the lawsuit did not successfully challenge the announced plan regarding treatment of the undocumented individuals who came to the United States as children. See Complaint at 4. in Crane et al. v. Napolitano, No. 3–12CV03247, 920 F.Supp.2d 724 (N.D. Texas 2013) 2013 WL 363710. For the government's plan, see Janet Napolitano, Memo: Exercising Prosecutorial Discretion with Respect to Individuals Who Came to the United States as Children (June 15, 2012), https://www.dhs.gov/xlibrary/assets/s1-exercising-prosecutorial-discretion-individuals-who-came-to-us-as-children.pdf.

20. Id.

21. Kieran McEvoy, Making Peace with the Past: Options for Truth Recovery in Northern Ireland (2006), quoted in Susan McKay, Keep in Mind These Dead 296 (2008).

22. Michael Ignatieff, The Warrior's Honor: Ethnic War and the Modern Conscience (1998).

23. Wilhelm Verwoerd, Toward Inclusive Remembrance after the Troubles: A South African Perspective, IBIS Working Paper No. 35, p. 1 (2003), http://www.ucd.ie/ibis/filestore/wp2003/35_ver.pdf.

24. Stephen Sonnenberg and James L. Cavallaro, Name, Shame, and Then Build Consensus? Bringing Dispute Resolution Skills to Human Rights, 39 Wash. U. J. L. & Policy 257 (2012).

25. Adriana Bangnulo, Maria Teresa Munoz-Sastre, and Etienne Mullet, Conceptualizations of Forgiveness: A Latin America-Western Europe Comparison, 8 Universitas Psychologica 673–82 (2009).

26. Id., at 678.

27. See Andrew Novak, Comparative Executive Clemency (2015).

28. Caution should be taken to make sure that human beings remain able to understand how computers solve what they solve. See Will Knight, The Dark Secret at the Heart of AI, Technology Rev., Apr. 11, 2017, https://www.technologyreview.com/s/604087/the-dark-secret-at-the-heart-of-ai/.

29. Julia Angwin, What Algorithms Taught Me about Forgiveness, OpenTranscripts (Oct. 19, 2017), http://opentranscripts.org/transcript/what-algorithms-taught-me-about-forgiveness/. As California replaces its cash bail system with a risk assessment tool to weigh factors relevant to the release of individuals before trial, the heightened level of policing in communities of color leading to more arrests will influence who gets released and yet seem to be an objective indicator of risk. See Sam Levin, Imprisoned by Algorithms: The Dark Side of California Ending Cash Bail, Guardian (Sept. 10, 2018), https://www.theguardian.com/us-news/2018/sep/07/imprisoned-by-algorithms-the-dark-side-of-california-ending-cash-bail?CMP=Share_iOSApp_Other. For a thoughtful treatment of forgiveness through privacy in the world of increasing uses of personal data, see Meg Leta Ambrose, Nicole Friess, and Jill Van Matre, Seeking Digital Redemption: The Future of Forgiveness in the Internet Age, 29 Santa Clara Computer & High Tech. L.J. 1 (2012).

30. See Jon Kleinberg, Himabindu Lakkaraju, Jure Leskovec, Jens Ludwig, and Sendhil Mullainathan, Human Decisions and Machine Predictions, NBER Working Paper No. 23180 (Feb. 2017), http://www.nber.org/papers/w23180.

31. Kai Schultz, Centuries of Buddhist Tradition Make Room for Bhutan's First Law School, N.Y. Times (Oct. 9, 2016), https://www.nytimes.com/2016/10/09/world/asia/centuries-of-buddhist-tradition-make-room-for-bhutans-first-law-school.html; and Julie McCarthy, The Birthplace of "Gross National Happiness" Is Growing a Bit Cynical (NPR) (Feb. 12, 2018), https://www.npr.org/sections/parallels/2018/02/12/584481047/the-birthplace-of-gross-national-happiness-is-growing-a-bit-cynical.

32. Schultz, supra.

33. Stephen Sonnenberg to author (May 17, 2018).

34. Tutu, supra; What Archbishop Tutu's ubuntu credo teaches the world about justice and harmony, Conversation (October 4, 2017), https://theconversation.com/what-archbishop-tutus-ubuntu-credo-teaches-the-world-about-justice-and-harmony-84730.

35. Pumla Gobodo-Madikizela, A Human Being Died That Night 15 (2003).

36. Esther Mujawao and Souad Balhaddad, Survantes: Rwanda, Histoire d'un Genocide 20 (2004), discussed and quoted in Thomas Brudholm and Valerie

Rosoux, The Unforgiving: Reflections on the Resistance to Forgiveness After Atrocity, 72 Law & Contemp. Probs. 33, 45–47 (2009).

37. Stephanie Zacharek, Eliana Dockterman, and Haley Sweetland Edwards, Person of the Year: The Silence Breakers, Time (Dec. 6, 2017), http://time.com/time-person-of-the-year-2017-silence-breakers/.

38. Jill Filipovic, How to Find Room for Forgiveness in the #MeToo Movement, Time (Feb. 26, 2018), http://time.com/5160427/forgiving-sexual-assault-perpetrators-metoo/.

39. Sam Barsanti, Study Says Some Viewers Are Quick to Forgive the Men of #MeToo, Newswire (May 29, 2018), https://news.avclub.com/study-says-some-viewers-are-quick-to-forgive-the-men-of-1826402499.

40. Thordis Elva and Thomas Stranger, South of Forgiveness (2017); Thordis Elva and Tom Stranger, Can I Forgive the Man Who Raped Me?, Guardian (Mar. 5, 2017), https://www.theguardian.com/books/2017/mar/05/can-i-forgive-man-who-raped-me-thordis-trust-elva-thomas-stranger-south-of-forgiveness-extract.

41. See Thordis Elva and Thomas Stranger, Our Story of Rape and Reconciliation, TEDWomen (2016), https://www.ted.com/talks/thordis_elva_tom_stranger_our_story_of_rape_and_reconciliation.

42. Katie J. M. Baker, What Do We Do with These Men?, N.Y. Times (Apr. 27, 2018), https://www.nytimes.com/2018/04/27/opinion/sunday/metoo-comebacks-charlie-rose.html.

43. Hannah Arendt, The Human Condition 238–43 (1958); Hannah Arendt, The Origins of Totalitarianism 439 (1973). More precisely, she argued that crimes against humanity cannot be forgiven because they cannot be punished, and even if all the perpetrators are punished, the crime itself cannot be forgiven. Jaco Barnarde-Naude, ThoughtLeader: Arendt, Forgiveness, Accountability, and Punishment, Mail & Guardian (Aug. 26, 2011), http://thoughtleader.co.za/jacobarnardnaude/2011/08/26/arendt-forgiveness-accountability-and-punishment/. When dealing with interpersonal forgiveness, Arendt concluded that one could forgive the person but not the act. Elisabeth Young-Bruehl, Why Arendt Matters 25, 100–1 (2006).

44. Diego Cagüeñas Rozo, Forgiving the Unforgivable: On Violence, Power, and the Possibility of Justice, M.A. Paper, University of Amsterdam (2004), http://www.banrepcultural.org/blaavirtual/tesis/colfuturo/Forgiving%20the%20Unforgivable.pdf.

45. Jacques Derrida, On Cosmopolitanism and Forgiveness 50–56 (2001).

46. Id., at 39.

47. Robert Berezin, M.D., Mourning? Yes, Forgiveness? No, Psychology Today (July 5, 2016), https://www.psychologytoday.com/us/blog/the-theater-the-brain/201607/mourning-yes-forgiveness-no ("There is nothing wrong with carrying resentment and hate toward your abuser. If it is unmourned, yes it will eat you alive. If it is mourned then you can move on with your life.")

48. Simon Wiesenthal, The Sunflower: On Possibilities and Limits of Forgive-

ness (expanded ed. 1998). In James Carroll's 2018 novel Cloisters, a character concludes, "Here is the surprise, that I have found it possible to live, precisely, as that. Unforgiven. In these months since I met you, I have begun to accept that there is no forgetting. I am who I am. I did what I did. There is no undoing" (351).

49. Linda Ross Meyer, The Justice of Mercy 89, 160–61 (2013).

50. Rozo, supra.

51. Oscar Wilde, A Florentine Tragedy (1892–94): "Always forgive your enemies; nothing annoys them so much."

52. Boese, quoted in 53 Quote: The Weekly Digest (1967).

Index